Barry Stimmel, MD

Drug Abuse and Social Policy in America: The War That Must Be Won

Pre-publication REVIEWS, COMMENTARIES, EVALUATIONS . . .

D1571085

"This is a hard-hitting, critical, yet extremely well-documented review of the failure of U. S. drug policy over the past two decades by a widely respected expert in the field of addiction medicine. Dr. Stimmel not only analyzes the reasons why approaches must change but also suggests thoughtful and workable solutions. This book contains a wealth of material useful for policymakers and health care workers as well as for the interested general reader."

Anne Geller, MD
Chief, Smithers Alcoholism Treatment and Training Center; Immediate Past President, American Society of Addiction Medicine

The Haworth Medical Press
An Imprint of The Haworth Press, Inc.

Drug Abuse
and Social Policy
in America
The War That Must Be Won

HAWORTH Therapy for the Addictive Disorders
Barry Stimmel, MD
Senior Editor

The Facts About Drug Use: Coping with Drugs and Alcohol in Your Family, at Work, in Your Community by Barry Stimmel and the Editors of Consumer Reports Books

Drug Abuse and Social Policy in America: The War That Must Be Won by Barry Stimmel

Pain and Its Relief Without Addiction: Clinical Issues in the Use of Opioids and Other Analgesics by Barry Stimmel

Drug Abuse
and Social Policy
in America
The War That Must Be Won

Barry Stimmel, MD

The Haworth Medical Press
An Imprint of The Haworth Press, Inc.
New York • London

Published by

The Haworth Medical Press, an imprint of The Haworth Press, Inc., 10 Alice Street, Binghamton, NY 13904-1580

Cover designed by Donna M. Brooks.

Library of Congress Cataloging-in-Publication Data

Stimmel, Barry, 1939-
    Drug abuse and social policy in America : the war that must be won / Barry Stimmel.
       p.   cm.
    Includes bibliographical references and index.
    ISBN 0-7890-0128-4 (alk. paper)
    1. Drug abuse–United States–Prevention. 2. Drug abuse–Government policy–United States. 3. Psychotropic drugs–United States. I. Title.
HV5825.S75 1996
362.29'17'0973–dc20
                                                    95-52541
                                                    CIP

To Matthew, Alexander, and Barbara,
whose thoughts helped shape the thrust of this book

ABOUT THE AUTHOR

Barry Stimmel, MD, is currently Dean for Graduate Medical Education at the Mount Sinai School of Medicine of The City University of New York. He is Professor in the Department of Medicine and in the Department of Medical Education and has served as Dean of Academic Affairs, Admissions, and Student Affairs at the School of Medicine for over twenty years. A practicing internist and cardiologist, Dr. Stimmel is also Executive Director of the Narcotics Rehabilitation Center at the Mount Sinai Medical Center. He is the editor of the *Journal of Addictive Diseases* and the author of over 100 articles and several books dealing with drug abuse, the effects of mood-altering drugs on the heart, and pain control. In addition, Dr. Stimmel lectures extensively on issues in medical education, substance abuse, and pain management.

CONTENTS

Preface

It has been almost four years since I wrote *The Facts About Drug Use* in an attempt to enable those with little or no background in science or health care to understand the often complex effects associated with the use of mood-altering drugs. Since that time, our government's "war" against drugs has continued unabated as has the use of both licit and illicit mood-altering substances. Although the concern expressed over such use is ubiquitous, the commitment of those expressing such concern is often less than apparent. Of course, the effects of inappropriate drug use remain obvious. Of the three leading causes of death in this country, two relate to the use of licit substances–tobacco and alcohol. Illicit drugs not only remain a tremendous drain on the economy, have devastated many lives, and are currently the leading risk factor associated with the transmission of the human immunodeficiency virus, but they continue to destroy the fabric of life in many inner-city communities.

As in the past, the solutions offered generally center around two groups: the "abolitionists," who feel that the reason for society's failure to contain drug use is because it remains "soft" on illicit drug use, and the "libertarians," who view drug use by informed adults as benign and enforcement efforts as futile. Both views have some merit. Despite the continuing seizures of impressive quantities of illicit substances, it must be realized that an extremely small proportion of illicit drugs produced throughout the world can supply this country's entire needs. It is equally true, regardless of one's feelings as to whether all mood-altering substances should be legal, that many of those charged with enforcement policies are actually far from committed to effectively diminishing the use of these substances. All too frequently, we place blame on those with whom we disagree rather than arrive at a consensus that incorporates the best of all available ideas. Until we recognize this and make an effort to change our behavior, the "war on drugs" will continue to be a metaphor or a reality of defeat.

This book attempts to emphasize the various ways we can, in fact, move toward diminishing inappropriate use of both licit and illicit mood-altering drugs. My own feelings concerning drug use remain unchanged. I believe that any substance taken primarily to produce a profound mood-altering effect—other than for a defined medical reason—is inappropriate and risky, but not criminal. Acts associated with and resulting from such use, however, may be considered criminal by the law, and those who commit such acts should be held accountable. Also, such accountability should be assigned by society to those who, though continuing to express their concern with the use of mood-altering drugs, fail in their commitment to diminish such use.

Acknowledgments

The preparation of any book requires the help of many. In dealing with social policy and the need to be current, I am especially grateful to the third estate, whose investigative reporting allowed an updating of material virtually beyond the galley stage. I am also thankful to Ms. Peg Marr at The Haworth Press, who managed to incorporate a considerable number of changes in the penultimate stage. Ms. Jacqueline Francis provided invaluable secretarial help, and Ms. Jackie Wrosch allowed the references to be verified for accuracy. My wife Barbara, as always, provided critical insight into several chapters. Finally, Ms. Mary Kennedy, as always, put the final touches in coordination and submission of the manuscript.

Chapter 1

Addressing the Use of Mood-Altering Drugs: Defining the Problem

When President Bush announced the formal initiation of our "War on Drugs," public concern over drug abuse was at an all-time high.[1] In polls conducted by *The Wall Street Journal*, NBC News, and the Gallup organization, drug abuse was listed as one of the two most important issues facing the nation.[2,3] In September 1989, 63 percent of persons surveyed by the Gallup Poll reported drug abuse as the country's most important problem, a consensus not reached on any other issue in the previous decade.[4] Almost half of those surveyed said they knew someone who had been seriously affected by illegal drug use, with 45 percent of people between the ages of 18 and 29 reporting knowledge of specific locations where drugs were sold.

The President's plan was, in general, widely accepted, with the major criticisms being an insufficient allocation of funds and a disproportionate finding for enforcement as compared to prevention and treatment. In addition to a series of initiatives to attack illicit drug use, the plan included the establishment of a new cabinet-level office–the Office of National Drug Control Policy–to oversee and coordinate all efforts pertaining to illicit drug manufacture, sales, and use. The nation was mobilized; priorities were clearly defined.

In just over one year, however, as the country's "drug czar" William Bennett resigned, it appeared that the public perception had changed considerably. In July 1990, a *Wall Street Journal*/NBC News poll found that only 25 percent of those polled identified drugs as the nation's leading threat. There was a shift toward a more "immediate" concern–the economy.[5] In February 1991, only 5 percent of those surveyed in the Gallup Poll still considered drug abuse as most important. The Gulf Crisis (37 percent) and the economy (16 percent) clearly took first and second places in the public eye, and by July 1992, only 2 percent of the population listed drug use as the nation's most important problem.[6]

Despite public perception, the war continues, as do the casualties. It is, therefore, quite appropriate to question whether we are even close to winning this war, or whether the initiatives we have undertaken have had a measurable effect on either the consumption or the availability of illicit mood-altering substances. Further, have we made any real progress in diminishing the use of nicotine, the excessive consumption of alcohol, or the inappropriate use of prescription drugs, all of which are responsible for more illnesses and societal costs than all illicit drugs combined? And finally, if indeed we are making progress in diminishing drug use, is this related to any conscious effort on our part or are we merely at a point in time in the recurring cycles of drug use seen in this country since the late nineteenth century?

TRENDS IN LICIT AND ILLICIT DRUG USE

Prior to President Bush's 1989 initiatives, which were based on population surveys, drug use had already begun to markedly decrease. The 1988 National Survey of High School Seniors and Young Adults, involving approximately 16,000 students in 130 public and private schools, revealed the use of illicit drugs to be at its lowest level since 1975 despite their increased availability.[7] Even the use of crack, the drug responsible for initiating the most recent public outcry, had diminished. Similarly, the 1990 National Household Survey on Drug Abuse found the current prevalence of illicit drug use in persons 12 years of age or older in the United States to have decreased considerably between 1985 and 1990 from 23 million (12 percent) to 13 million (6 percent), respectively.[8,9,10,11] The number of current cocaine users decreased from 2.9 million in 1988 to 1.6 million in 1990, a 72 percent decrease since 1985. In New York State, between 1983 and 1990, the percent of students using marijuana and cocaine decreased from 46 to 24 percent and 14 percent to 6 percent respectively. Among arrestees, cocaine use decreased from 69 percent in 1987 to 17 percent in 1993.[12] The 1991 National High School Senior and College Student Survey revealed the percentage of high school seniors using an illicit drug in the previous years had decreased further from 35 percent in 1990 to 29 percent in 1991. When marijuana was excluded, only 16 percent of seniors had used illicit drugs in the past year.[13]

With respect to licit drugs, many of the 1990 health objectives of the nation formulated by the Public Health Service concerning alcohol and substance abuse had already been met prior to the "kickoff" of the "War on Drugs" as had a number of the short-term objectives listed in the White House's National Drug Control Strategy.[14] In fact, perhaps in recognition of these achievements, the Surgeon General's Promoting Health/Preventing Disease: Objectives for the Nation for the Year 2000 contained a series of more challenging and appropriate objectives (Table 1.1).[15]

Other more recent indicators of success are also available. For the first time in a decade, reports from the street suggested that the price of cocaine had started to increase and its purity diminished.[16] Alcohol consumption is currently at its lowest level since 1958 and, both the mortality rates from cirrhosis of the liver and fatalities from alcohol-related motor vehicle incidents have also decreased.[17] With the exception of smoking by 18 to 25 year olds, cigarette use has decreased significantly for all other age groups surveyed. Similarly, nonmedical use of psychotherapeutic agents has also significantly diminished.

CURRENT USE OF LICIT AND ILLICIT DRUGS

Despite these observations, there is no more reason for complacency with current use of either illicit or licit drugs than there was a decade ago.[18] As documented by the 1993 National Household Survey on Drug Abuse, almost 12 million Americans had used an illicit drug within the past month and over 77 million reported illicit drug use at some time during their lives. In the 1994 National High School Senior, College Student, and Young Adult Survey, approximately 36 percent of high school seniors and 19 percent of eighth

TABLE 1.1. National Health Promotion and Disease Prevention Objectives 1995

- Reduce the proportion of persons using cocaine within the past month to 0.6% ages 12-17 and 2.3% ages 18-25.
- Increase to at least 50% estimated proportion of all injectioned drug users in treatment programs.
- Reduce drug abuse-related hospital emergency department visits by at least 25%.
- Increase to at least 75% the proportion of acting injecting drug users who use new or properly decontaminated syringes, needles, or other drug paraphernalia.
- Reduce cigarette smoking to no greater than 15% among adults aged 20 or older.
- Reduce smokeless tobacco use by males age 12-14 to no more than 4%.
- Reduce cigarette smoking during pregnancy to at least 40% of women who are smokers when they become pregnant.
- Reduce alcohol, marijuana, and cocaine consumption among people aged 12 to 25 by 50%.
- Increase social disapproval by high school seniors by 70% for heavy alcohol consumption, 85% for occasional marijuana use, 95% for occasional cocaine use, and 95% for regular cigarette use.

graders had tried some illicit drug within the past year, up by 24 and 46 percent, respectively, since 1992. Approximately 75 percent of adults had tried an illicit drug at some time by their late twenties. In fact, the American public appears more pessimistic about our ability to achieve a successful solution, with 70 percent of people surveyed thinking the problem is worse now than five years ago, and 45 percent of those surveyed in a different study knowing someone who had become addicted to a drug other than alcohol.[19]

Although the widespread use of cocaine appears to be diminishing, over 30 percent of young adults have tried cocaine by the age of 27, with 1.6 million having used cocaine in 1991, 625,000 being weekly users.[20] Because the likelihood of drug use is related to it being perceived as dangerous, the most recent finding that the proportion of high school seniors viewing illicit drugs as dangerous has decreased since 1991 is also of concern. Marijuana use, which is far from inconsequential, was perceived as being risky by only 65 percent of seniors as compared to 1991 when 79 percent felt such use was associated with risk. Among 1994 high school seniors, approximately 19 percent had smoked marijuana within 30 days of the survey, an increase of 35 percent since 1991, with annual prevalence rates of 31 percent. In contrast to the quality of marijuana used in the 1980s when over 37 million Americans acknowledged smoking this drug, potency of marijuana today is quite high and carries with it a greater dependency-producing potential. Although most marijuana use is experimental or occasional, frequent use carries with it the likelihood of progressing to other illicit substances. It has been estimated that the use of marijuana twice a week for a year is associated with a 70 percent probability of progressing to the use of cocaine.[21]

Perhaps most relevant in convincing one that complacency is folly are the findings of Johnston in his 1994 survey concerning drug use among eighth, tenth, and twelfth graders. In this population, marijuana use rose sharply by 13 to 31 percent, with use of any other illicit drug among seniors rising from 17 to 18 percent.[22] The use of licit or "gateway" drugs is even more impressive, with 15 percent of eighth graders, 24 percent of tenth graders, and 28 percent of twelfth graders having five or more drinks in a row in the two weeks preceding the survey. Cigarette smoking increased in all groups with current smoking seen in 19 percent of eighth, 25 percent of tenth, and 31 percent of twelfth graders.

In short, heroin, cocaine, and marijuana are still readily available in all major cities at a greater purity than existed a decade ago, and the number of "hard-core" users estimated at 2.7 million, threefold that of five years ago.[19] Clearly, there remains a cause for considerable concern. As observed by Johnston, despite the decline in drug use over the past decade, our high school students and young adults currently have a level of illicit drug use unmatched in any other industrialized nation in the world.[11] Equally important is the observation that among our youth, negative attitudes and beliefs about both licit and illicit drugs continue to decline.

Complications related to illicit drug use also are on the rise. Drug-related deaths increased from 2.7 per 100,000 in 1979 to 4.3 per 100,000 in 1989.[23] Between 1988 and 1994, visits to emergency rooms for adverse effects of heroin increased by more than 68 percent.[24] This was accompanied by more than a 50 percent drop in the street cost of these drugs and an increase in their potency. In fact, the potency of street heroin has increased to the extent that it is now relatively easy to achieve a high from snorting rather than injecting. This dramatic increase is illustrative of what Musto describes as the "tides" in the appeals and rejections of drugs.[25] As marijuana, heroin, and cocaine use have been declining, a new, more potent form of heroin appears on the street. Ecstasy, a stimulant type of hallucinogen (MOMA) is becoming popular at large college parties. Rohypnol, a central nervous system depressant, is being marketed on the street as the "'lude of the 90s" and methamphetamine (speed) is being illicitly synthesized in such large quantities it is replacing crack use in many cities in the West.

Licit Drugs

Tobacco

Licit drug use still remains of concern, especially among the young, with an estimated 3 million smokers consuming 1 billion packs of cigarettes a year. Smoking or chewing tobacco by our nation's youth continues unabated. In the 1992 Senior High School Survey, virtually the same proportion of seniors reported smoking (29 percent) as in 1981, with 63 percent having smoked cigarettes and 17 percent being daily smokers.[13] Of those between the ages of 14 to 15, the proportion of smokers has actually increased, with the adolescent smoking rate equal to that of adults. This has been most prominent among young women.[26] Smoking by adults remains of considerable concern, with 46 million estimated to be smokers in 1993.

It is sobering to consider that of the approximately 3,000 young people who begin smoking each day, 750 will die from a smoking-related disease. This can be compared with the estimate of only 50 dying from automobile accidents or murder.[27] Approximately 27 percent of adults remain current smokers, with 75 percent of all adults having tried cigarettes at some time in their lives. Most discouragingly, the decline in the proportion of adults smoking that has occurred over the past 25 years appears to have ended. A survey by the Princeton Survey Research Associates found that in 1992 the proportion of adults identifying themselves as current smokers increased by 5 percentage points to 30 percent over the past year.[27]

Despite all of our knowledge of the adverse effects of tobacco accompanied by an impressive decrease in the proportion of smokers over the past several decades, nonetheless in 1993 there were still 40 million smokers with the majority of those who smoke using more than a pack per day.

Of equal concern, between 1970 and 1990 the use of smokeless tobacco increased by 300 percent from 2.2 to 8.4 percent for men between 18 and 24 years of age.[29,30] The National Household Survey on Drug Abuse in 1990 reported 7 million Americans to be using smokeless tobacco, including approximately 4 percent of all boys between the ages of 12 and 17 and 6 percent of young adults. Smokeless tobacco use by all Americans increased 30 percent between 1970 and 1985, but in 17- to 19-year-olds it increased. In some surveys, smokeless tobacco has been found to be used by 34 percent of eighth grade boys, with almost 4 percent reporting daily use. In terms of quantity, the production of moist snuff in the United States increased 83 percent between 1981 and 1993, from 30 to 55 million pounds. Despite the publicity surrounding the health hazards associated with smoking, Johnston's surveys have demonstrated that of high school seniors, 39 percent perceived the risk from smoking and 55 percent the risk of smokeless tobacco use not to be "great."

Alcohol

The use of alcohol by the young also leaves much to be desired. Despite it being illegal for high school students to purchase alcoholic beverages in virtually all states, 10 percent of students reported drinking at the sixth grade level, with 4 percent getting drunk. Sixty-nine percent of eighth graders, 82 percent of tenth graders, and 90 percent of twelfth graders have all had experience with drinking.[31] Heavy drinking, defined as five or more drinks in a row at least once in a two-week period, was seen in 13, 21, and 28 percent of eighth graders, tenth graders, and twelfth graders, respectively. It has been estimated by the Inspector General that high school students account for $200 million in revenue flowing to the beer industry.[32] Heavy drinking among college students is even greater, approximating 51 percent, with a national survey documenting that 44 percent of college students remain binge drinkers. These students, who do not consider themselves problem drinkers, are more likely to experience alcohol-related problems as well as cause problems for others.[33] Alcohol-related motor vehicle accidents, although decreasing, still remain the first public health problem among young adults.

Alcohol consumption among adults remains of concern, with 100 million people or half the population being regular drinkers, and 10 million estimated to be problem drinkers. Contrary to popular belief, alcoholism among the elderly is far from infrequent. Data based on alcohol-related hospitalizations among persons 65 to 69 revealed rates to be higher than those for heart attack, with current alcohol abuse in the elderly estimated to be as high as 22 percent.[34]

Nonmedical Use of Prescription Drugs

The nonmedical use of prescription drugs is nowhere near the magnitude of illicit psychotropic agents, alcohol, or tobacco. Many people are either hesitant to take these drugs at all or only use them as prescribed for short periods.[35] Yet, in 1991, 12 percent of the population used a prescribed psychoactive drug for a nonmedical reason, with these drugs accounting for over 200 million prescriptions a year.[36] One of every three drug admissions to emergency rooms in 1990 recorded through the Drug Abuse Warning Network was for a licit manufactured substance.[37]

Ethnicity and Use of Mood-Altering Substances

It is often assumed that the devastation that illicit drug use has visited upon our inner cities is associated with a higher prevalence of drug use among minority populations. In fact, this is untrue. Even though illicit drug use does increase with decreasing income levels, drug use remains substantial in suburban and rural areas.[38] It is the income level that appears to define use rather than ethnicity. A larger proportion of white Americans use both licit and illicit drugs than do other racial or ethnic groups, with the exception of excessive alcohol use by Native Americans. In a University of Michigan study, the use of cocaine by African-American males (6 percent) was half that of white males (12 percent) and almost two-thirds that of Hispanic and Native American males. Marijuana use was significantly lower among African Americans and Hispanics as compared to white men and women.[39] In the 1992 survey, the usage rates of marijuana by white and Hispanic high school seniors were approximately equal, whereas African Americans were considerably less likely to smoke marijuana.[13]

The use of licit drugs reveals similar patterns. Cigarette use is substantially higher among white and Native American high school seniors than among African American, Hispanic, and Asian Americans. Racial differences in daily smoking have consistently become more pronounced, with only 25 percent of white male seniors decreasing daily smoking between the 1970s and 1980s as compared to 66 percent of African-American males. Daily cigarette smoking among African-American high school seniors is considerably less than whites (4 percent versus 21 percent) due to their smoking rates declining since 1983, while rates of whites and Hispanics have remained stable.[13] These differences are even more pronounced in women, where smoking rates decreased in African-American women aged 18 to 24 from 21.8 percent in 1987 to 5.9 percent in 1992 as compared to white women whose smoking rates remained relatively constant at 27 percent during these years.[26] The importance of this observation has not been lost on the tobacco companies, which have recently targeted advertising in African-American communities (Chapter 2).

Not surprising, drinking continues to be prominent among seniors, regardless of ethnicity. Yet, even in this area, frequent or heavy use of alcohol is highest among white and Native Americans as compared to other ethnic groups, with African American and Asian Americans having the lowest rates. For example, binge drinking was reported by 11 percent of African-American students as compared to white (32 percent) or Hispanic students (31 percent).[13]

Ethnicity, therefore, should not be viewed as a causative factor in either explaining the use of licit or illicit drugs or in rationalizing our inability to diminish its use in specific communities. To fall back on stereotypes is unhelpful, divisive, and ultimately offers an excuse for not effectively addressing the problem.

It is correct that, for a variety of reasons, minorities bear a disproportionate burden associated with the complications of mood-altering drug use. Complications from alcohol, such as cirrhosis and cancer of the esophagus, including mortality, are greater in African Americans and Hispanics than in whites. These groups are also more heavily represented among intravenous drug users who develop Acquired Immunodeficiency Syndrome (AIDS). Indeed, in 1990, AIDS was the leading cause of death for black men aged 35 to 44 years.[40] Similarly, underrepresented minorities are disproportionately affected through children born to mothers using cocaine or through being infected with the human immune deficiency virus (HIV).

It is also true that minorities, especially African Americans, bear a disproportionate burden with respect to enforcement of drug laws. With respect to those arrested and incarcerated for any offense in New York State prisons, both first use and regular use began an average of two years earlier among white as compared with African-American inmates.[40] Yet African Americans, disproportionately represented among prison populations, are far more likely to be arrested for drug-related offenses and receive sentences on the average of 21 months longer than whites. In Baltimore, African-American adults are five times more likely and teenagers ten times more likely to be arrested for drug offenses than are whites. In New York, of all those receiving prison sentences for drug offenses, 91 percent were African American or Hispanic.[38] In Washington, DC, 42 percent of African Americans 18 to 35 years of age are either in prison, on probation at school, or have outstanding warrants. Nationwide data provided by the U.S. Department of Justice for arrest rates in 1994 per 100,000 population for drug abuse violations reveal a greater than sixfold difference between African Americans and whites (3,000 versus 381, respectively).

Although one may argue that these figures are related to actual commissions of crimes, certain laws are geared to minority populations. For example, drunk driving, although responsible for more deaths than all illicit drug use combined, is associated with far milder punishments. In Massachusetts, only 50 percent of drunk drivers are convicted compared with an 85 percent conviction rate for offenders involving other drugs.[42] Most of those convicted of the former offenses are white, whereas those convicted of the latter are African American or Hispanic.

Several states also have much heavier penalties associated with heroin as compared to cocaine use, even though cocaine is associated with far greater antisocial behavior. Some feel that the disproportionate penalties associated with heroin are related to its predominate use by minorities as compared to a pattern of cocaine use which is more representative of the general population. Even with respect to cocaine, the possession of five or more grams of crack makes one liable to a prison term that would be imposed only if possessing 100 times the weight in cocaine powder. Simple possession of crack carries a mandatory prison term of five years. Since crack predominates in inner-city communities, African Americans are more susceptible to this penalty.[19] Data from the United States Sentencing Commission revealed that in 1993, of Federal inmates serving sentences for crack offenses, 88 percent were African American, 7 percent Hispanic, and 4 percent white. This can be compared to those convicted of powder cocaine offenses, where 32 percent were white, 27 percent African American, and 39 percent Hispanic.[43] Despite the United States Sentencing Commission voting to move toward equalizing penalties for cocaine and crack, Congress rejected this proposal.

Drugs in the Workplace

Much has been written concerning the use of licit and illicit substances for those who are gainfully employed.[44] Although the data is relatively "soft," nonetheless surveys have suggested that up to 70 percent of illicit drug users or excessive drinkers are employed. One study found that employees whose preemployment drug tests were positive and who were hired, as part of the study, were 50 percent more likely to be fired.[19] As might be expected, those with drug or alcohol problems have a greater degree of absenteeism, are considerably less effective, are more likely to injure themselves or another person in a job-related accident, and are responsible for up to 40 percent of all industrial fatalities.[19] All of this has been estimated to reduce productivity at a nationwide cost of $100 to 140 billion annually if alcohol is included.[45]

ECONOMIC COSTS OF DRUG USE

The economic and social costs of alcohol and substance abuse remain of considerable concern, yet are difficult to assess accurately. Prior to the onset of the crack/cocaine epidemic, it was estimated that, excluding costs due to alcohol and tobacco use, in 1988 illicit drugs resulted in an annual cost of $44 billion, of which 74 percent was related to crime.[46]

More recent estimates have placed the cost of illicit drug use at $67 billion.[10] The Drug Abuse and Mental Health Administration estimated that in 1990, alcohol abuse and dependence resulted in an economic cost to this country of approximately $98.6 billion, an increase of 40 percent since 1985.[47,48] The cost of smoking has been put at $72 billion and that of drug use at $67 billion.[49] With respect to health care, it has been projected that in 1994 over $140 billion of the $1 trillion to be spent on health care will be allocated for conditions related to substance abuse. Medicaid funding for inpatient care attributable to licit and illicit drug use will reach $8 billion with $3 billion spent by Medicaid on inpatient care related to tobacco use.[50]

Even the elderly are not exempt from these associated illnesses. A recent study found more elderly patients to be hospitalized for conditions related to alcohol abuse than to heart attacks.[51,52] Of the $87 billion of Medicare funds spent for inpatient care in 1993, approximately 20 percent were felt to be due to complications relating to substance abuse. Of this proportion, 80 percent was related to smoking, 17 percent to alcohol, and 3 percent to other substances.[53] In fact, medical complications due to smoking are the single largest drain on the Medicare trust fund, prospectively estimated to reach $800 billion within the next 20 years. Yet, despite these estimates, it is entirely possible that the actual costs are even greater due to the "hidden" medical and psychological complications of drug use.[54] Most of those with alcohol or drug problems who visit a physician are not so identified. In addition, the way that alcohol or drug abuse may affect family members has not been adequately considered, despite the estimate that 35 to 40 million people may be affected. These costs include those resulting in long-term care of children whose parents use drugs to partners of intravenous (IV) drug users infected with the human immune deficiency virus.

Total costs, however, must include not only the cost of the complications of substance abuse and its treatment but also such indirect costs as loss in productivity, effects of crime, and loss to the economy due to money laundering. Depending on the factors considered in calculating the indirect economic costs, figures ranging from over $200 to $500 billion have been mentioned.[55,56]

As a result of the illicit nature associated with dealing in mood-altering substances, it has been estimated that the illicit drug industry is responsible for perhaps $125 billion in U.S. currency disappearing from the economy in illegal transactions. With respect to direct purchases of these substances, in 1990, the Office of National Control Drug Policy estimated that consumers spent $18 billion for cocaine, $12 billion for heroin, $9 billion for marijuana, and $23 billion on other drugs.[57] In fact, our consumption of illicit drugs has a marked effect on the economies of several third-world countries. It has been estimated, for example, that the export of legal goods (approximately $800 million annually) in Bolivia is less than that accruing from cocaine sales. In Colombia, as many as 2 million people are felt to be employed in producing cocaine and marijuana.

It is, therefore, not surprising that to some the lure of dealing is irresistible. For every minute spent reading this text drug dealers are estimated to earn over $100,000 in profits, more money than 99 percent of Americans' annual gross income in 1991.[58] The risk/benefit ratio of dealing remains exceptionally favorable and explains the inability of enforcement to satisfactorily address this problem.

CRIME AND DRUGS

Among the most prominent social effects of both illicit and licit drug use is its relationship with crime. With respect to illicit drugs, the need to obtain money to support a habit, the actual violence associated with the drug trade, and the use of drugs to bolster one's courage prior to committing nondrug-related crimes all tear at the social fabric. A study comparing frequent and infrequent cocaine users and nonusers found over 40 percent of frequent users to have engaged in some type of property crime or violence as compared to 8 percent of nonusers. Of interest, only 11 percent of those engaging in criminal activity reported ever being arrested.[20] Yet drug use is quite prevalent in those arrested, ranging from 54 percent in Omaha to 81 percent in Chicago in 1993, based on wine tests. Nonetheless, arrests related to alcohol or other drug use have increased by 126 percent over the past decade.[53] In 1991 there were over 1,000,000 arrests due to drug violations. Of these arrests, approximately 78 percent were prosecuted and 57 percent convicted. Interestingly, the percent increase in arrests of women as compared to men was disproportionate (30 percent versus 147 percent). It is estimated that the expense of arrest, prosecution, imprisonment, and parole of those sentenced for drug use approximated $60 billion in 1991. The number of persons imprisoned as a result of drug offenses has also increased dramatically. In 1980, approximately one of every 15 court commitments to state prisons was a drug-law offender. By 1990, drug offenders represented one of every three new commitments.[59]

A report by the Bureau of Justice indicates that in state correctional facilities in 1986, over two-thirds of inmates incarcerated for violent crimes reported that either they or their victims were using alcohol and drugs at the time of the crime.[40,60] The direct costs of crime related to alcohol use is estimated at $6 billion in 1990.[47] If one eliminates those arrested for drug trafficking or possession, then 55 to 75 percent of those arrested for violent crimes had urines that tested positive for illicit drugs. The Federal Bureau of Investigation estimated that in 1991, 56 percent of all federal prisoners were incarcerated for drug offenses, up 25 percent from 1979. This percentage reached 59 percent in 1994. Of those incarcerated as youthful offenders, 19 percent reported illicit drug use before age 10, 40 percent before age 12. It is, therefore, no surprise that in many states prison populations far exceed their capacity.[61] Indeed our prison system is overflowing, and we spent $25 billion on this enterprise in 1992. The Bureau of Prisons plans to spend an additional $1.8 billion in order to accommodate its inmate populations.

It is sobering to reflect that in 1989, 2.2 percent of the U.S. population was under correctional supervision, with the District of Columbia having almost 6 percent of its population so supervised;[62] however, data pertaining to young men are even more remarkable. A 1990 study by the Sentencing Project revealed that among men aged 20 to 29, on any given day, one in four Blacks, one in ten whites, and one in sixteen Hispanics were in prison, on parole, or probation. On June 30, 1989, approximately one in every 249 men residing in the United States was incarcerated.[57,58,59] We lead the world with 455 persons incarcerated per 100,000 population. This rate is ten times higher than that of Japan or the Netherlands and four to five times greater than that of England or France.[38]

If these incarcerations resulted in the ability to rehabilitate, then the costs would be more than acceptable. Unfortunately, such is not the case. Alcohol and drugs appear to be readily available in many prisons, and recidivism after release from prisons is the rule rather than the exception.[60] Fewer than 20 percent of inmates with substance-abuse problems receive any treatment, with less than 20 percent of jails having any drug-treatment programs. Yet, studies have suggested that treatment is effective. Despite the fact that the number of persons imprisoned increased from 330,000 to almost 900,000 between 1980 and 1994, the crime rates, although diminishing somewhat, still remain unacceptably high, and with respect to youths, are increasing disproportionately.

As a result of the flourishing drug trade, handguns, including semiautomatics, have become readily available even to children, with increasing numbers of both intentional and accidental shootings reported most prominently in the inner cities. In 1988, one of every five adolescent deaths was gun related, with homicide rates due to firearms in young men aged 15 to 24 and 17 to 28, three times higher than that in other industrial nations.[61] In 1991, there was a 79 percent increase in the number of juveniles committing murder with guns compared to the last decade. The homicide arrest rate, which had remained relatively constant in adults older than 25 between 1985 and 1992, more than doubled among young men 16 to 20 years of age. In 1992, only 10 of every 100,000 33-year-olds were arrested for homicide as compared to 52 of every 100,000 17-year-olds.[61] Juvenile gang-related homicides have particularly increased by 147 percent between 1988 and 1992.

In New York City, the number of cases including loaded guns handled by juvenile court increased between 1986 and 1992 by 50 percent, with 53 percent of homicides in 1988 drug related.[63,64]

TABLE 1.2. Actual Causes of Death in the United States (1990)*

	Estimated Number of Deaths
Tobacco	400,000
Diet/Inactivity	300,000
Alcohol	100,000
Infections	90,000
Toxic agents	60,000
Firearms	35,000
Sexual behavior	30,000
Motor vehicles	20,000
Drug use	20,000

*Adapted from McGinnis, J. M., Foege, W. H. Actual causes of death in the United States. *JAMA,* 1993:2207-2212.

Much of the violence seen on our city streets is related not to the direct effects of illicit drugs but to their sales and the need to control distribution. Gang activity and violence, which have increased greatly over the past decade, have been directly associated with drug sales. A study of the effect this has had on the African-American and Hispanic communities is staggering. Homicide rates among African-American men are more than sevenfold and among Hispanic men more than threefold that of white men. Homicides are the leading killers of African-American adolescents and young men, with the association of these deaths with alcohol and drug use quite noticeable. A recent study of first and second graders in Washington, DC revealed 45 percent have witnessed muggings, 31 percent shootings, and 39 percent have seen dead bodies.[65] The results of drug use and sales remain the same: destruction of inner-city communities and, all too often, death of innocent bystanders.

MEDICAL COMPLICATIONS OF DRUG USE

Licit Drugs

The medical complications associated with licit drug use, namely alcohol and tobacco, are well known and will be only briefly discussed. The American Public Health Association has suggested that alcohol is responsible for 100,000 deaths annually. Virtually every organ system can be adversely affected by excessive consumption of alcohol. It is estimated that 40 percent of all persons hospitalized on general medical services have an alcohol-related complication. Many admissions require intensive care and are even more costly. The costs of health care for alcoholics are over 100 percent higher than those for nonalcoholics. Treatment for alcoholism is associated with a 50 percent decrease in illness and hospitalization.

Smoking is responsible for approximately 430,000 deaths a year with an estimated 36 percent of lifelong smokers dying as a result of smoking.[66] Cancer of many organs, in addition to lung cancer, has been strongly associated with smoking, as have diseases of the cardiovascular and respiratory systems. Women seem especially susceptible to continued smoking, with the Centers for Disease Control reporting that 85 percent of women smokers have symptoms of nicotine addiction. In fact, lung cancer now accounts for 27 percent of all cancer deaths in women, as compared to breast cancer which is responsible for only 18 percent of deaths.[67] In addition to the multitude of disorders found to be increased in both men and women who smoke, women smokers are especially susceptible to cervical cancer, complications during pregnancy, and osteoporosis. In any year, a smoker will use more medical care than would a nonsmoker and when hospitalized will have a longer length of stay.

Illicit Drugs

Complications associated with illicit drugs abound. In part, these are related to such direct effects of drugs on the body as the effect of cocaine on the cardiovascular system and are, in part, due to the inability of the user to know the "purity" of the drug taken, with the result often being an overdose reaction. However, most of the complications related to illicit drug use are due to the impurities with which the drugs are cut, and the contamination that occurs when the drug is taken. As a result, infections of all kinds are among the most common complications. Of these, the acquired immunodeficiency syndrome and the indemnification of new drug-resistant strains of tuberculosis are the most serious.

The Acquired Immunodeficiency Syndrome (AIDS)

From 1981 through October 1995, 501,310 cases of the Acquired Immunodeficiency Syndrome (AIDS) have been reported, with an annual new infection rate of approximately 40,000 per year. Of these, 62 percent have died. Although there are several risk factors associated with AIDS, it is prominently related to illicit drug use, whether through injection with contaminated needles (Intravenous drug use [IVDU]) or the trading of "unsafe" sex for cocaine. In the United States, approximately 34 percent of all cases of AIDS are seen in intravenous drug users or their sexual partners. As many as 60 percent of the estimated 200,000 heroin users in New York City may be already infected with the human immunodeficiency virus, with over 50 percent of AIDS-related deaths being associated with intravenous drug use. Those who inject drugs are the leading source of HIV transmission to noninjection partners. Between 1993 and 1995, AIDS cases by heterosexual contact increased by 233 percent as compared to 1981 to 1987 with most attributed to sex with an intravenous drug user.[68] The use of crack adds another risk factor for HIV positivity, with one study finding 16 percent of those who smoked crack to be HIV antibody positive compared to 5 percent of nonsmokers. Women in New York who smoke crack have an HIV antibody-positivity rate of 30 percent.[69]

AIDS has become the leading cause of death among black men between the ages of 25 and 44 and ranks second among white men in that age group.[70] In 1993, AIDS was the fourth leading cause of death in women aged 25 to 44 years. In 1988, 80 percent of children with AIDS had a parent who was an intravenous drug user. Approximately 7,000 infants are born to HIV-infected women in the United States each year. In the inner city, AIDS has virtually become a family disease.[71] The appearance of tuberculosis often caused by organisms resistant to the standard medical therapy has paralleled the increase in reported cases of HIV infections and AIDS. Other individuals are also at increased risk. These groups include alcoholics and drug abusers, especially those who live under crowded conditions or are homeless.

Infants Delivered to Women Using Drugs

Licit Drugs

The effects of licit drug use on the fetus are far from innocuous. Much publicity has been focused on the fetal alcohol syndrome associated with excessive consumption of alcohol. Although less well known but of considerable importance is the effect of nicotine on fetal development. Similar to cocaine, nicotine is a stimulant and a constrictor of blood vessels, which results in diminished blood flow to the fetus. Maternal smoking is associated with a higher risk of complications during pregnancy and delivery as well as premature delivery including spontaneous abortion, and even prenatal loss.

Illicit Drugs

Although many women may smoke or drink while pregnant, illicit drug use is also not infrequent. Indeed, illicit use is strongly associated with both smoking and heavy consumption of alcohol.[72] Surveys at numerous hospitals and clinics have found that as many as 30 percent of pregnant women use illicit drugs during their pregnancy, with marijuana being the most frequent. In 1994, over 5 percent of the women nationwide who deliver each year used illicit drugs at some time during their pregnancy.[19] Women who use any illicit drug are most likely to use multiple drugs, thus exposing the fetus to considerable risk. Their children are more likely to require intensive care, stay in the hospital longer, and, depending on the drug involved, experience developmental delays. Estimates of the number of drug-exposed infants born annually have varied considerably from a low of 48,000 to 350,000.[73] In New York City in 1989, there were 4,989 discharges of newborn infants whose mothers were known to be using illicit drugs, for a rate of 33 per 1,000.[74] In New York City crack has now exceeded marijuana as the drug most frequently noted on birth certificates.[63]

The cost of treating infants of mothers who have been addicted to cocaine/crack will continue to increase over the next decade. In the newborn period, costs are four times higher for drug-exposed infants. The social services needed for these children is considerable, and many ultimately will be placed in foster care. Between 1986 and 1990, although demand for foster care increased by 29 percent nationwide, in areas with a high prevalence of substance abuse these demands increased by 284 percent.[75,76] As these children enter schools, more intensive support will be required. The cost of preparing these children to enter elementary school is estimated at $15 billion, with even more support necessary to enable them to get through high school.[77] In New York State the number of child abuse and neglect cases has risen 650 percent in the last decade, with family violence rising 400 percent, most of this being attributed to cocaine or crack. Although it is clear that these figures are only estimates and may well be exaggerated, nonetheless, one only has to visit a neonatal intensive care unit in an inner-city hospital to realize the devastation illicit drug use visits on the newborn.

DRUG ABUSE AND THE FAMILY

The effects of both licit and illicit drug use on the family is well known. The disruption of the family unit due to excessive alcohol use is frequent and has given rise to many support groups. As many as 20 percent of men and 25 percent of women report drinking to give rise to serious family problems. Over one-third of women who are separated or divorced report marriage to men who drank excessively. Drug use and violence in the family go hand in hand. Children with parents who drink or use drugs are often permanently emotionally scarred with hyperactivity, antisocial behavior, and a high risk of drug use after they reach adulthood.

Because of the already overwhelming odds facing the youth of inner cities, given the inadequacy of housing and schooling, the stress of being a single parent, and high unemployment rates, the role that parental drug use plays on molding behavior of the child cannot be overestimated.

SELF-WORTH AND SUBSTANCE ABUSE

Finally and often less well appreciated is the relationship between substance abuse and one's sense of self. Although one usually associates the use of mood-altering drugs solely with the need or desire to become high, in fact, the continued use of these substances is extremely self-destructive. Although persistent use of these substances is believed to be related to their potential for dependency, the need to take risks associated with an unconscious desire to harm one's self is often prominent. Street terminology confirms this observation. Injecting heroin is described as a "death trip" or "shooting shit." Because one rarely knows either the concentration of street drugs or the contaminants with which they are mixed, indeed each injection poses an unknown risk.

Suicidal thoughts are also prominent among drug users and perhaps most intensely seen in adolescents. The rate of suicide among those 45 to 64 years of age decreased by almost 30 percent between 1960 and 1988; however, among persons aged 15 through 24 it more than doubled.[78] In fact, over the past four decades each cohort of adolescents has had a higher suicide rate than the preceding group.[79] Among the many factors given to explain this phenomenon, increased use of alcohol and other drugs rank among the top three.[80] A recent study of suicidal ideation and attempts among substance-dependent youths found the prevalence to be five to seven times greater than that among other groups.[79]

THE LOSS OF A WAR

Complacency is unwarranted! Our all-too-frequent attempts to accept quick solutions to enduring problems remain less than helpful. These solutions have run the gamut of extremes, from complete legalization to capital punishment, each vehemently justified through moral, legal, or pragmatic imperatives. Proposals that initially appear appealing, on closer scrutiny have serious flaws and, in most instances, fail to address the excessive use of licit substances.

However, inappropriate use of mood-altering drugs will persist regardless of whether these substances are licit or illicit. The rallying call to join a war on drugs, to eliminate drug use once and for all, allows us to forget that were there no demand for these substances, there would be no need for a war. Indeed, the 1991 survey by Johnston, O'Malley, and Bachman documented that although availability of illicit drugs was reported by 84 percent of high school seniors, drug use continued to diminish because of the decrease in demand which, in turn, was related to the increasing realization by students that these drugs are indeed dangerous.

This concept is critical in view of the findings of the most recent National Student Surveys demonstrating a statistically significant decline in perceived risk of many illicit substances, which has now been accompanied by a slight increase in illicit drug use. As observed by Johnston,

> We need to think of drug problems in society as chronic relapsing problems. . . . For the foreseeable future American youngsters are going to be aware of a smorgasbord of abusable drugs, and those drugs are going to be available to some degree . . . each new cohort of youngsters must be given the knowledge, skills, and motivation to resist using these drugs which means that adult society needs to become more effective and more committed . . . Like it or not, we are in this for the long term.[81]

Unfortunately, it is our commitment that is often lacking. Even if one were to accept the "war" paradigm, all too frequently we are confused over the enemy's identity.

As a result, some urge a "get tough approach" as the only viable solution to the problem, seeing the problem as mainly involving those at the lower socioeconomic levels of our society. As described by Musto, this need to develop ever greater punishments for drug use will be accompanied by a lack of empathy for the user, an erroneous labeling of large groups of inner-city dwellers as drug users, an erosion of support for treatment and research, and a malfunctioning of our criminal justice system.[25] We continue to focus on the more visible targets, such as illicit drug dealers, while excluding others who are "respectable" members of our society. This latter group, directly or indirectly, powerfully promotes the use of mood-altering substances. Indeed, although everyone expresses great concern with the drug problem, often the level of commitment and the nature of actions of our "generals" can be called into question. In addition, by focusing on the war against illicit drugs, we also tend to forget the societal costs of licit drug use, including alcohol, tobacco, and misuse of prescription drugs. Use of these drugs not only is actively promoted but in some cases, actually supported by the public taxes. Yet, as observed earlier, the damage inflicted by these substances exceeds that due to all illicit substances combined.

In the war against drugs, therefore, we may be the ultimate enemy. It is we who must, based on our circumstances and our values, determine the roles we should play. We can do this as individuals, as family members, as professionals, as employers, as corporate leaders of firms that directly or indirectly contribute to consumption of both licit and illicit substances, and, finally, as citizens who through the ability to exercise our right to vote can direct government policy. Only when this responsibility is accepted by each of us can we begin a comprehensive approach toward diminishing the inappropriate use of all mood-altering drugs.

It must be reemphasized, however, that mood-altering substances have been with us since antiquity and will remain regardless of any actions that we may take, no matter how draconian or enlightened. Our objectives, therefore, should be to contain such use as much as possible, prevent the excessive profits of relatively few to drive the consumption of drugs by many, clearly inform all of the adverse effects of such use, provide sufficient resources to those in need and, especially important with respect to children, provide attractive alternatives to drugs.

In the chapters that follow, the roles that all of us play in promoting the use of mood-altering substances will be discussed. This will be accompanied by suggestions as to how we may be more effective in convincing both those who profit from the use of these substances, as well as those who consume them, of the inappropriateness of their actions.

REFERENCE NOTES

1. National Drug Control Strategy. Washington, DC: Office of National Drug Control Policy, Executive Office of the President, 1989.

2. Drugs not a worry in the U.S. *San Francisco Chronicle*, August 15, 1989, p. 42.

3. Berke RL. Poll finds most in U.S. back Bush strategy on drugs. *The New York Times*, September 12, 1989, Sec. B:8.

4. *The Gallup Poll Monthly*. Princeton, NJ, 1991.

5. Barrett PM. Though the drug war isn't over, spotlight turns to other issues. *The Wall Street Journal*, November 19, 1990, Sec. A:1.

6. Treaster JB. Four years of Bush's drug war: New funds but an old strategy. *The New York Times*, July 28, 1992: Sec. A:1.

7. Johnston LD, O'Malley PM, Bachman JG. Illicit drug use, smoking and drinking by America's high school students and young adults 1975-1988. *National Institute on Drug Abuse Prevention Pipeline*. January, February, 1990.

8. National household survey on drug abuse: Highlights 1988, U.S. Department of Health and Human Services, Public Health Service. Alcohol, Drug Abuse and Mental Health Administration, Rockville, MD, 1990.

9. Summary of findings from the 1990 National Household Survey on Drug Abuse. NIDA Capsules National Institute on Drug Abuse. Rockville, MD. December, 1990.

10. National Drug Control Strategy: Executive Summary. The White House, Washington, DC, 1995.

11. Johnston LD, O'Malley PM, Bachman JG. Drug use among American high school seniors, college students and young adults 1975-1990. Vol. I. U.S. Department of Health and Human Services Alcohol, Drug Abuse, and Mental Health Administration, Rockville, MD, 1991.

12. Golub A, Johnson BD. A recent decline in cocaine use among youthful arrestees in Manhattan: 1987 through 1993. *Am J Public Health* 1994, 84:1250-1254.

13. University of Michigan press release on Johnston's 17th national survey of drug use among American high school seniors and 12th national survey of drug use among American college students. Ann Arbor, Michigan, December 12, 1994.

14. Promoting Health, Preventing Disease: Objectives for the Nation. Washington, DC: U.S. Department of Health and Human Services, Public Health Service, 1980, 67-72.

15. Healthy people 2000. Mid-course Review and 1995 Revisions Washington DC. U.S. Department of Health and Human Services, 1990. No. (PHS) 591-50212.

16. Treaster JB. Cocaine prices rise: (PHS) 91-50212 Police role is cited *The New York Times*, June 14, 1990 Sec. B:8.

17. Brooks SD, Williams GD, Stinson FS, Noble J. Apparent per capita alcohol consumption: National, state and regional trends. 1977-1987. Washington, DC: Alcohol, Drug Abuse, and Mental Health Administration, 1989. Surveillance Report 13.

18. Drug war victory not evident in NIDA surveys. *Drug Policy Action,* 2(a) January-February, 1991.

19. Keeping score: What are we getting for our federal drug control dollars? *Drug Strategies,* 1995. Carnegie Corporation, New York.

20. Gfroerer SC, Brodsky, MC. Frequent cocaine users and their use of treatment. *Am J Public Health,* 1993, 83:1149-1154.

21. Treaster JB. Study finds marijuana use is up in high schools. *The New York Times,* February 1, 1994, Sec. 1:7,14.

22. Johnston LD, O'Malley PM, Bachman JC, National Survey Results on Drug Use from the Monitoring of the Future Study, 1975-1994, Vol. 1, U.S. Department of Health and Human Services, NIDA, Rockville, MD, 1995.

23. Treaster JB. Hospital data show increase in drug abuse. *The New York Times,* July 9, 1992, Sec. B:1.

24. Purdy, M. New inmates reflect surge in use of cheap but potent heroin. *The New York Times,* December 3, 1995, p. 49.

25. Musto DF. Perception and regulation of drug use: The rise and fall of the tide. *Ann Int Med,* 1995, 123:468-469.

26. White women show rise in smoking among young. *The New York Times,* November 6, 1994, Sec. 1:43.

27. Hearn W. Unhealthy education. *Am Med News,* January 24/31, 1994, 11, 13,14.

28. Janofsky M. 25-year decline of smoking seems to be ending. *The New York Times,* December 19, 1993, Sec. 1:24.

29. Connolly GN, Orleans CT, Blum A. Snuffing tobacco out of sport. *Am J Public Health,* 1992, 82:351-353.

30. Kent C. Researchers at FDA to regulate tobacco as a drug. *Am Med News,* May 15, 1995, 15,16.

31. Klitzner M, Stewart K, Fisher D. Reducing underage drinking and its consequences. *Alcohol Health Res World,* 1993, 17:12-18.

32. Kusserow R. Youth and Alcohol–A National Survey: Drinking Habits, Access, Attitudes and Knowledge. Rockville, MD, U.S. Department of Health and Human Services, Office of the Inspector General, 1991.

33. Wechsler H, Davenport A, Dowdall G, Moeykens B, Castillo S. Health and behavioral consequences of binge drinking in college. A national survey of students at 140 campuses. *JAMA,* 1944, 272: 1672-1677.

34. Mullady SF. Aging and alcoholism. *Employee Assistance,* April 1995. pp. 6-10.

35. Impact of Prescription Drug Control Systems on Medical Practice and Patient Care: A Summary of the NIDA Technical Review. In Impact of Prescription Drug Diversion Control Systems on Medical Practice and Patient Care. Technical Review, May 30-June 1, 1991. Proceedings. Rockville, MD: National Institute on Drug Abuse. 1993. NIDA Research Monograph 131:1-17.

36. Adams EH, Kopstein AN. The nonmedical use of prescription drugs in the United States. In Cooper JR, Czechowicz DJ, Molinari SP (Eds.). *Impact of Prescription Drug Diversion Control Systems on Medical Practice and Patient Care.* Rockville, MD: National Institute on Drug Abuse, 1993. NIDA Research Monograph 131:109-119.

37. Haislip GR. Drug diversion control systems, medical practice, and patient care. In Cooper JR, Czechowicz DJ, Molinari SP (Eds.). Impact of Prescription

Drug Diversion Control Systems on Medical Practice and Patient Care. Rockville, MD: National Institute on Drug Abuse, 1993. NIDA Research Monograph 131:120-131.

38. Treaster JB. Drugs not just an urban problem study finds. *The New York Times*, October 1, 1991, Sec. B:1.

39. Black stereotype of teen alcohol, drug use shown in error. *Prevention Pipeline* 5(2) March/April 1992, p. 75-79. National Institute on Alcohol, Alcohol Abuse, Rockville, MD.

40. Drugs and crime facts, 1989. U.S. Department of Justice. Office of Justice Programs, Bureau of Justice Statistics, Rockville, MD. 1990.

41. Rothman D. The crime of punishment. *New York Review of Books*, February 17, 1994, 41(1):34-38.

42. Angell M, Kassirer JP. Alcohol and other drugs. Toward a more rational and consistent policy. *N Engl J Med,* 1994, 331:537-538.

43. Smothers R. Wave of prison uprisings provoke debate on crack. *The New York Times*, October 24, 1995, Sec. A:8.

44. Gust SW, Crouch DS, Walsh JM. Research on Drugs and the Workplace: Introduction and Summary. In Gust SW, Walsh JM, Thomas LB, Crouch SD (Eds.). *Drugs in the Workplace; Research and Evaluation Data.* Rockville, MD: National Institute on Drug Abuse. 1990. NIDA Research Monograph 100: 3-8.

45. National Survey of Worksite and Employee Assistance Programs. Chapel Hill, NC. Research Triangle Institute.

46. Rice DP, Kelman S, Miller LM. Economic costs of drug abuse. In Cartwright WS, Kaple JM (Eds.). *Economic Costs, Cost-Effectiveness, Financing, and Community-Based Drug Treatment.* Rockville, MD: National Institute on Drug Abuse, 1991.

47. Rice, DP. The economic cost of alcohol abuse and alcohol dependence: 1990. *Alcohol Health Res World,* 1993, 17:10-11.

48. Substance abuse, mental illness take toll. *American Medical News*, November 23/30, 1990, 12.

49. Substance abuse costs society billions. *The Nation's Health*, January 1994, p. 18.

50. Califano JA Jr. Revealing the link between campaign financing and deaths caused by tobacco. *JAMA*, 1994, 272:1217-1218.

51. Califano JA. America in denial. *The Washington Post*, November 14, 1993. Sec. C:7

52. Alcohol illness cited as big cost. *The New York Times*, September 12, 1993, Sec. A:22.

53. Medicare's big cigarette burn. *The New York Times*, May 18, 1994, Sec. A:22.

54. Socioeconomic Evaluations of Addictions Treatment: Executive Summary, Washington, DC: President's Commission on Model State Drug Laws. Center of Alcohol Studies, Rutgers University, 1993. Chapter 8.

55. Rice DP, Kelman S, Miller L. The economic costs of alcohol and drug abuse and mental illness: 1985. Rockville, MD: *Alcohol, Drug Abuse and Mental Health Administration* 1990. DHHS Pub. No. (ADM) 90-1694.

56. Drucker E, Arno PS. Put drug war price at $500 billion. Letter, *The New York Times*, July 1, 1992, Sec. A:22.

57. Drugs, crime, and the justice system. A National Report from the Bureau of Justice Statistics. Rockville, MD, 1992.

58. Culhane C. Drug offenders crowd federal prison cells. *U.S. Journal*, February 1990, p. 6.

59. Kline S. Jail inmates, 1989. Washington, DC. Bureau of Justice Statistics.

60. President's Commission Model State Drug Laws. Vol. 1, Economic Remedies. Washington, DC: The Commission, 1993.

61. Violent crime by youth is up 25% in ten years. *The New York Times*, August 30, 1992; Sec. 1:27.

62. Correctional populations in the United States 1989. Washington, DC: Bureau of Justice Statistics, 1991.

63. Dillon S, Hernandez R. Violence and the schools: A search for safety. *The New York Times*, December 12, 1993, Sec. 13:1.

64. Goldstein P, Brownstein HH, Ryan PJ, Bellucci PA. Crack and homicide in New York City 1988. A conceptually based event analysis. Contemporary drug problems. Winter Edition 1989, p. 651-687.

65. Prevention 93-94. Federal Programs and Progress. U.S. Department of Health and Human Services 1995. U.S. Government Printing Office, Washington, DC.

66. Mattson ME, Pollack ES, Cullen SW. What are the odds that smoking will kill you? *Am J Public Health,* 1987, 77:425-431.

67. Ernster VL. Women and Smoking, *Am J Public Health,* 1993, 33:1202-1203.

68. Heterosexually acquired AIDS: United States, 1993. *JAMA,* 1994, 271:975, 976.

69. Edlin BR, Irwin KL, Faruque S, McCoy CB, Word C, Serranoy Y, Inciardi JA, Bowser BP, Schilling RF, Holmberg SD. Multicenter Crack Cocaine and HIV Infection Study Team. Intersecting epidemics–crack cocaine use and HIV infection among inner city young adults. *N Engl J Med,* 1994, 331:1422-1427.

70. CDC tries preventing AIDS by tailoring the message. *Am Med News*, December 13, 1993, 17.

71. Des Jarlais D, Friedman S. Transmission of human immunodeficiency virus among intravenous drug users. In DeVita VT, Heilman, S, Rosenberg SA. AIDS: Etiology, diagnosis, treatment and prevention. Philadelphia: Lippincott, 1988: 385-395.

72. Johnson SF, McCarter RS, Frencz C. Changes in alcohol, cigarette and recreational drug use during pregnancy: Implications for intervention. *Am J Epidemiol,* 1987, 126:695-702.

73. Dicker M, Leighton EA. Trends in the U. S. prevalence of drug using parturient women and drug-affected newborns 1979-1980. *Am J Public Health*, 1994, 84:1433-1438.

74. New York State Department of Health. Statewide planning and research cooperative system: Neonatal drug-related discharges per 1000 births. New York State 1986-1989. Albany, NY, 1990.

75. Robbins LN, Mills JL, Krulewitch C et al. Effects of in utero exposure to street drugs. *Am J Public Health,* 1993, 83 Suppl: 1-32.

76. Kandall SR. Improving treatment for drug-exposed infants: Rockville, MD: U.S. Department Health and Human Services; 1993. DHHS Pub. No. (SMA) 93-2011.

77. Phibbs CS, Bateman DA, Schwartz RM. The national costs of maternal cocaine use. *JAMA,* 1991, 266:1521-1526.

78. Vital Statistics of the United States. Vol. II Mortality, Part A. Washington, DC: Public Health Service, 1960-1988.

79. Murphy GE, Wetzel RD. Suicide risk by brith cohort in the United States. *Arch Gen Psychiatry,* 1980, 37:519-523.

80. Deykin EY, Buka SL. Suicidal ideation and attempts among chemically dependent adolescents. *Am J Public Health,* 1994, 84:634-639.

81. Johnston LD, O'Malley PM, Bachman JA. National Survey results on drug use from monitoring the future study 1975-1992. Rockville, MD: National Institute on Drug Abuse. U.S. Department of Health and Human Services. NIII Pub. No. 93-3597.

Chapter 2

Alcohol, Tobacco, and Sports:
That's Entertainment

THE TOBACCO INDUSTRY

Profits from the sales of tobacco products are staggering. It is therefore not surprising that tobacco companies spend over $6 billion to promote smoking, a sum equal to or more than that expended for any other consumer product.[1,2,3,4] This is not surprising, since it has been estimated that the typical smoker has a 50-year, pack-a-day consumption, which for the average consumer is equivalent to $50,000.[3] With 40 million smokers in this country as of 1993, the economic potential of tobacco companies is remarkable.[5] Even though many tobacco companies have diversified, tobacco profits often far exceed those from other products. The profit margins for cigarettes are reported to be three to five times the average for most corporations, with profits from cigarette sales to have increased from 7 cents a pack in 1981 to 35 cents in 1991.[3,6] Philip Morris, the largest American tobacco company, is reported to have paid $4.5 billion in taxes on total revenues of $59 billion in 1992, which when compared with employees' and excise taxes ranks as the largest taxpayer and tax collector in the country (exclusive of the Internal Revenue Service).[7] Although television ads for cigarettes were banned in 1970 through the Public Health Cigarette Smoking Act of 1969, the money spent by tobacco companies on cigarette and smokeless tobacco advertising has increased at a rate three times that of inflation and, although the advertising may be more subtle, it is no less effective. Indeed, it is felt that the tobacco industry's proposal of this ban on television advertising was a preemptive strike to prevent the Federal Trade Commission (FTC) and the Federal Communications Commission from instituting even stronger limitations.[8]

In fact, since 1970, marketing of tobacco products has been nothing short of phenomenal. Sponsoring of sports events has allowed cigarette companies to reach television audiences without direct advertising. Tobacco companies have become the leading sponsors of automobile and motorcycle races, receiving millions of dollars of publicity without violating the technicalities of the law. If this law were applied to televised sporting events, then it would result in considerable financial pressure being placed on cigarette companies through levied fines and, understandably, result in sports organizations discontinuing tobacco-sponsored televised events. As an example, Blum has estimated that if the law were to be applied in this manner with the stated $10,000 fine for each violation, then the Marlboro Grand Prix would result in a fine of $59,330,000 based on the number of times the Marlboro logos were televised during the 1989 race.[1]

Promotional giveaways have been used quite effectively to boost sales. Furthermore, displaying cigarette brands or promotional items does not require the presence of health warning labels. In fact, a survey of adolescent smokers revealed that almost 50 percent have had access to promotional items from cigarette companies. The importance of this certainly can be assessed by the increased proportion of the industry's budget devoted to this effort. In 1980, promotional activities were responsible for 36 percent of advertising; in 1990, 78 percent of advertising was devoted to promotion.[9]

Children and Tobacco

Promoting smoking or the use of smokeless tobacco by children, a practice long denied by the industry, is pervasive. A 1991 Tobacco Institute poster claimed that "To continue its long-standing commitment that smoking is not for young people . . . [it] is supporting state legislation to make it tougher for young people to buy cigarettes."[10,11,12] In fact, youth-oriented educational materials published by the industry have been made available to schools and community groups. R. J. Reynolds' *"Right Decisions, Right Now"* and the Tobacco Institute's *"It's the Law"* discourage children from smoking as well as retailers from selling to minors.[13,14] Yet advertisements continue to be targeted toward the young and are quite effective. Studies have shown that children can become familiar with cigarette advertisements as early as age six.[9]

The industry's promotion of "old Joe camel" ranks second among the most popular print campaigns.[15] The "smooth character" clearly appeals to youth and implies the "coolness" of smoking. In fact, as documented by Di Franza et al., these advertisements are far more successful in marketing cigarettes to children than to adults with brand logo recognition being demonstrated as early as six years of age.[16] Subsequent to the appearance of these ads, the proportion of children who chose Camels rose from 0.5 percent to 32.8 percent. Because children cannot legally buy cigarettes, it has been estimated that the illegal sale of Camels to children has gone from $6 million per year prior to the appearance of the ads to $476 million in 1991, representing 25 percent of all Camel sales. In the face of the tobacco industry's professed concern with children smoking, Joe Camel has never become introduced into the anti-smoking effort, and a new campaign had been initiated to introduce Josephine Camel to the public. Advertisements for other brands have been equally effective, with the Centers for Disease Control reporting that in 1992 85 percent of adolescent smokers preferred Marlboro, Newport, or Camel, the three most heavily advertised brands.

When Harley Davidson recently attempted to break a licensing agreement with the Lorillard Tobacco Company, it quoted the report of a consultant specializing in child behavioral research which stated that the ad campaign to promote Harley cigarettes through the portrayal of a Darth Vader-like character would appeal to a "substantial minority" of children.[17] Similarly, when the industry was trying to stimulate its sales of smokeless tobacco, the ads were designed to target young men, and considered cherry-flavored products that could resemble candy.[18] These brands tend to have a low-nicotine content. With time, progression to smokeless tobacco with a much higher nicotine content occurs. One survey reported that of those who started with low-nicotine products such as Skoal Bandits (approximately 7 percent nicotine), four years later one-third had switched to brands with a nicotine content of 79 percent.[19]

In fact, the evidence clearly suggests that the tobacco industry has not only been aware of the addictive qualities of nicotine but, in addition, the advantages in marketing these drugs to the young. With the cigarette pack being considered as a storage container for a day's supply of nicotine and the cigarette as a dispenser, the goal of advertising was to have teenagers lose the visual link between advertising and point of sale. This was facilitated by producing catalogs of items that could be purchased with coupons from cigarette packs, and the identification of stores to participate in the Joe Camel campaign that were "heavily frequented" by young shoppers in close proximity to colleges and high schools.[18]

Even with this knowledge, however, it is remarkable to observe that each year 1 billion cigarettes are sold to youths under 18 years of age, with 3,000 adolescents a day estimated to become new smokers. This represents two packs of cigarettes each year for every child in this country aged 12 to 17, resulting in $1.5 billion in revenue.[13,20,21,22] In fact, estimates of teenage smokers have reached over 2 million with as many as 3,000 teenagers a day believed to begin smoking. Among the 10 million Americans using smokeless tobacco each year, 3 million are under 21 years of age.[23,24] Since 90 percent of all smokers begin smoking before age 21 and between one-third to one-half of adolescents who try smoking will become regular smokers, effective advertising guarantees a steady flow of customers as well as a prediction of hundreds of thousands of deaths due to its complications.[18,25] Yet 70 percent of young smokers regret that they had ever started.[26] Although sales and distribution of tobacco to minors is prohibited by law in over 44 states, nonetheless, the ability of adolescents to obtain cigarettes has not diminished, and prosecution of vendors is rare. The proliferation of vending machines makes cigarettes easily available to children despite the illegality of their use by minors.

Finally, the sale of single cigarettes to minors is a practice that appears to be growing. A study in California of 206 commercial stores found that 50 percent sold single cigarettes more often to minors than adults. To add insult to injury, we note the minors were charged more for fewer purchases.[27] It is easy for children who wish to smoke to obtain cigarettes, and advertising continues to entice minors to become smokers.[11,25,28] A survey of secondary and elementary school students in Chicago found 14 percent to have received free samples of tobacco at least once.[14] A recent protest by the correction officers and assistant deputy wardens in New York City revealed that the New York City Department of Corrections was selling cigarettes in New York City jails to minors on a buy-one-get-one-free basis.[29]

Women and Tobacco

Women have also been targeted as prime consumers. Recognizing the increased incidence of smoking among women who are school dropouts (33 percent versus 17 percent), several years ago the Dakota brand was introduced to appeal to the "virile female with no more than a high school education."[30] Women's magazines are frequent recipients of tobacco advertisements, as are specific events devoted to women. This, however, is not done indiscriminately. An inverse relationship has been shown between the proportion of cigarette advertisements in women's magazines and their editorial coverage of smoking and health.[31] Furthermore, a recent study has demonstrated a strong association between advertising campaigns targeted to women's brands of cigarettes in the 1960s and 1970s and a 70 to 100 percent increase in smoking rates among teenage girls.[32] That this does not represent sporadic recreational use is buttressed by the observation that 77 percent of teenage women who are smokers have tried to quit, but only 1.5 percent are successful.[33]

Ethnicity and Smoking

As noted earlier, the use of tobacco is highest among white men and women as compared to other racial groups. In attempts to increase market share, targeting of minority groups to promote smoking has also been consistently observed. This may be through direct advertising of specific brands in minority neighborhoods or through more insidious means. The term *insidious* is not used lightly. An internal memo from a major tobacco company containing the names of minority organizations that have received contributions is purported to have warned that the document was for "internal use only" due to its sensitive nature.[34] In fact, the tobacco companies target African-American organizations and African-American political leaders for considerable "largesse." Whether this "buys" silence is not known, but clearly a legislator moral conflict of interest exists.[34] It should also be emphasized that the largesse of the tobacco industries extends to all legislative groups regardless of ethnicity or gender.[34]

The Government's Approach: Concern versus Commitment

Perhaps most pernicious is that the increasing awareness of the hazards of smoking by the American public has been accompanied by a remarkable increase in the export of tobacco to foreign countries, especially those in the "third world." The United States is now reported to be the number one cigarette exporter, with 194 billion cigarettes exported in 1991, an increase of 246 percent over the past seven years, representing 25 percent of the U.S. tobacco industry's market.[35] Smoking prevalence among males has reached or exceeded 50 percent in Russia, Saudi Arabia, India, and China. In China alone, there are over 300 million smokers.[36] In 1990, *The Wall Street Journal* reported that Philip Morris would supply the Soviet Union with 20 billion cigarettes by the end of 1991, this being the largest single export order in the company's history.[37] The tendency of Soviet youths to find American habits worthy of imitation may result in exposing millions of Soviet children to the dangers of tobacco.

All of this has unfortunately been accomplished with the help of the United States government through the 1974 Trade Act. This Act threatens the imposition of sanctions on countries not permitting the sale of our tobacco products. Regrettably, the U.S. Trade Office has used this "club" to open markets in Japan, Taiwan, and South Korea. With the pressure applied to Japan, exports of tobacco increased 75 percent, with a subsequent tenfold increase in cigarette advertising. The U.S. tobacco industries, in conjunction with several multinational companies, are said to now control 85 percent of the world's tobacco production. Tobacco, similar to cocaine and opium, has become a prized cash crop for many third-world countries. Unfortunately, it has also contributed to environmental damage both by causing deforestation to provide wood to cure tobacco and administering such toxic substances as pesticides and herbicides. This has resulted in soil erosion, flooding, global warming, and pollution of the waterways.

It is tempting to draw a comparison between the cultivation and sale of tobacco in these countries and that of cocaine; however, in addition to being equally addicting, tobacco use results in considerably more deaths and illnesses. As noted by Barry, the increased consumption of tobacco in India has been estimated to raise mortality from bronchitis and emphysema sixfold.[36] Carcinoma of the lung has now become the third most frequent cancer in Bangladesh, and the most common fatal cancer in Pakistan. The frequency of bladder cancer in Egypt is greater in smokers. Perinatal mortality in Bangladesh in children of smoking mothers is more than twice the rate of those whose mothers were nonsmokers. In short, worldwide tobacco is considered responsible for 3 million deaths a year and, if current trends persist by the year 2020, may be responsible for as many as 10 million deaths a year as international sales continue to increase even as sales in this country lag.[38]

Although it is reasonable that tobacco as a legal commodity should not be unfairly restricted, neither should the U.S. Trade Office promote it.[39,40] It is possible that government support may be based on reasons other than equity in trade. Tobacco companies are avid supporters of political campaigns and often hedge their bets by donating to both parties. During the 1992 presidential and congressional campaigns it is reported that tobacco companies donated over $2 million.[41] As documented by Gerbner, tobacco companies also pay over $22 billion a year in taxes, and in 1992 contributed over $4 billion to the balance of payments. Because the employment of hundreds of thousands of people is dependent on the industry, it is not surprising that government subsidies to a large constituency of tobacco growers approximates $3 billion in loans and interest annually.[42]

The ambivalence of our legislators with respect to the hazards of smoking is most apparent in states where increased taxes on cigarettes appear on the ballot.[43] California is a prime example. In 1988, when the state passed Proposition 99 to raise cigarette taxes by 25 cents a pack and require 20 percent of revenues to be used for prevention programs, implementation of this was left to the governor and legislators. Since that time, political expenditures by the tobacco industry increased sevenfold to over $7 million in the 1991/1992 election, with only eight incumbents in the legislature failing to receive contributions.[44] Indeed, it appears that even with passage of this legislation the funds that were supposed to go toward tobacco control have instead been diverted to funding general medical services. This is alleged to be due to efforts by the tobacco industry to influence their distribution.[45] Similarly, in Michigan, the tobacco industry is reported to have spent almost $4 million in an unsuccessful attempt to defeat a proposal to increase tax on cigarettes by threefold.[46]

On a state level, although many states have laws restricting minors' access to tobacco products, adequate enforcement is absent. The 1989 Surgeon General's report on smoking noted that the number of legal restrictions on children's access to tobacco has actually decreased since 1964.[42] Even on a local level, inconsistencies abound. The mayor of a large city is quoted as saying, "We must teach children that smoking and sports don't mix." Yet, approval to hold the Marlboro Grand Prix in that city's financial district was considered.[47]

Industry Responsibility

It belabors the obvious to state that considering the huge profits realized from tobacco use, the industry has no excuse for not behaving more responsibly. Risks and hazards associated with cigarette smoking should be clearly labeled on packaging and on advertising aimed at the young. Linking cigarettes to athletic prowess should end, and bullying underdeveloped nations to accept our cigarettes should cease.

At varying times, the tobacco industry has given the impression that it is willing to shoulder this responsibility. Their actions, unfortunately, appear to be mainly proactive and induced by fear of federal or state legislation. At times, while appearing to be cooperative, they continue to promote weakening of existing controls and vigorously oppose any tobacco legislation (Chapter 5). In 1954, the Tobacco Industry Research Committee was formed to support scientific inquiry in an attempt to close the gaps in the relationship between smoking and disease. This group, renamed the Council for

Tobacco Research in 1964, currently sponsors scientific research. Yet the impartiality of this board continues to be questioned as do its actions in comparison to its words.[48] Most recently, it has been alleged that tobacco companies were well aware of the addictive nature of tobacco as early as 1964. Almost twenty years later (1983), they blocked publication of a paper by one of their scientists demonstrating conclusively that nicotine was addictive, which had already been accepted by the journal *Psychopharmacology*.[49] Even today, despite all evidence to the contrary, the industry maintains nicotine is not addictive and that it does not add nicotine to tobacco.

Subtle and not so subtle retaliation by the tobacco industry toward those perceived as being less than friendly has been observed. Tobacco companies are the single largest group of billboard advertisers, and are also among the major purchasers of magazine advertising. It is perhaps no accident that cigarette advertising in magazines is associated with a diminished coverage by these magazines of the risks of smoking.[52,53] The perceived threat of economic retaliation is demonstrated in the observation that subsequent to the advertising agency Saatchi and Saatchi publicizing Northwest Airlines' no-smoking policy, RJR/Nabisco canceled an $80 million contract with them to promote their food products.[53] More recently and much more aggressive has been the Philip Morris Company's $10 billion libel suit against Capital Cities/ABC Inc., alleging an ABC news magazine show falsely claimed their cigarettes were spiked with additional nicotine to hook smokers.[54] Of equal concern has been the efforts of the Brown and Williamson Tobacco Company to prevent their former research chief from giving evidence concerning tobacco industry practices.[51]

THE ALCOHOL INDUSTRY

Breweries and distilleries are equally culpable for inappropriate, but quite effective, advertising that approximates $1.3 billion annually. Although beer is as equally dependency producing as hard liquor, this is not always realized by the public. In fact, a 1991 survey of high school students sponsored by the Inspector General's Office revealed 80 percent to be unaware that one "shot" of whiskey had the same amount of alcohol as a 12-oz. can of beer, with one-third of students being unaware that wine coolers contain alcohol.[55]

Ignorance of alcohol content frequently extends to fortified wines as well as wine coolers. Fortified wines, which contain approximately 20 percent alcohol as compared with 8 to 12 percent in regular wines, consist of relatively expensive dessert wines and extremely inexpensive table wines. Wines in this category such as Cisco, Thunderbird, and Night Train are widely sold in a bottle containing the equivalent of six mixed drinks of 80 proof vodka.[56] Confusion about alcohol content may be one of the reasons why consumption of hard liquor (distilled spirits) diminished by 23 percent nationwide between 1980 and 1987 while consumption of beer dropped only 7 percent. Indeed, in 1990, per capita consumption of beer increased by 3 percent, with light beer sales increasing by 13 percent.[57]

Equally important is the observation that among the young, malt liquors are becoming exceptionally popular with an annual growth rate of 25 to 30 percent. These products are readily available in groceries and are being purchased by an increasing number of adolescents. Malt contains not only more alcohol by volume than beer (4.5-6 percent versus 3.5-4 percent) but is cheap (approximately $1.50 for a 40-oz bottle). The profits accruing from its sales, however, are impressive, representing $1.5 billion in 1991 or 3 percent of the total beer market.[56,57,58]

Perhaps even more pernicious is the production of alcoholic lemonades, orange drinks, and colas in England that contain 4 percent to 5.5 percent alcohol and are increasingly popular among British teenagers. These drinks, which will undoubtedly find their way across the ocean, will be exceptionally alluring to children as they are placed in beverages already acceptably and avidly consumed by the young.

Sports and Drinking

Although promotion of liquor on television has been banned, promotion of beer continues unabated. One study revealed that a single brewery, which was estimated to spend $344 million annually on advertising, recorded total annual sales of $8.5 billion.[47] Producers of alcoholic beverages sponsor every conceivable sporting event and fill the airwaves with athletes promoting their products. This advertising pays approximately 20 percent of the cost of sports programming on TV and radio. Alcohol advertising links drinking with highly desirable personal attributes, so that by age 14 such advertisements become increasingly attractive to adolescents and by age 16, alcohol commercials are listed among their most favorite.[59] Adolescents heavily exposed to such advertisements were found to be more likely to believe drinkers possessed more highly valued personal characteristics, were more likely to drink and drink heavily, and were more likely to drink in conjunction with hazardous conditions such as driving.[60]

Similar to the tobacco industry, the alcohol beverage producers claim they do not intend to promote excessive consumption to attract children to buy their products; however, the evidence suggests otherwise. The use of a dog, Spuds MacKenzie, to actually promote Budweiser beer resulted in "Spuds" becoming a household word to millions of children, obviously too young to drink, yet old enough to identify with a particular brand of beer. Similarly, the existence of the animated superhero Bud Man, the core of a $12-million advertising campaign, accompanied by the statements from Anheuser Busch that Bud Man "is not a cartoon character," stretches the limits of credibility.[61] Superbowl advertisements consisting of animated beer cans lining up to scrimmage also would hardly appeal to an adult audience but would greatly appeal to children.

The new promotional campaign for malt liquor features rap groups and the appearance of names also designed to appeal to teenagers such as Midnight Dragon and Colt 45. In one commercial, a rapper boasts he "grabbed me a 40 just to get my buzz on' cause I needed just a little more kick." Because rap is associated with violence, sex, and alcohol, it is no surprise that this advertising appeals to teenagers. The production of the malt liquor, Crazy Horse, was sold with the picture of the famous Native American chief on the bottle. It belabors the obvious to state that this product was designed to appeal to Native Americans, a group with the highest rate of alcoholism. It was not until the manufacturer was ordered to change the logo by the Bureau of Alcohol, Tobacco, and Firearms because the label contained some misleading statements that this was rectified.[62] It is, therefore, not surprising that the most active sales can be seen in the ethnic markets of our major cities.

In spite of the frequent industry claim that exposure to marketing is not followed by engaging in drinking, evidence suggests the opposite. A study of the impact of beer advertising on consumption by fifth and sixth graders found that awareness of beer commercials was related to more favorable beliefs about drinking and the intention to drink when an adult.[63] Marketing of beer is clearly targeted toward the young and is all too effective.

Industry Responsibility

Manufacturers of alcoholic beverages should present an accurate picture of the effects of excessive alcohol consumption, and the consequences of drinking even small amounts of alcohol during pregnancy and while driving. Companies that profit from the sale of alcohol should also caution against initiating consumption at an early age and reveal the adverse effects that alcohol can have on physical prowess, if used inappropriately. On the bright side, it appears that some brewers are slowly accepting this responsibility and have even enlisted help of consumer groups. Advertisements have appeared emphasizing the importance of having a designated nondrinking driver; beer companies have reportedly toned down the collegiate spring break commercials; and promotion of moderate drinking has been appearing more frequently, all accompanied by a decrease in the time allocated to advertising during some sporting events.[64,65,66] Yet the volume of these advertisements is disappointingly small. A review of alcohol advertisements during sports broadcasting revealed only 25 (4 percent) of 710 spots to address moderation and prevention.[67] Whether this effort represents a counterattack against a rising prohibitionist attitude to deter alcoholic beverages from going the way of cigarettes, or is finally an honest attempt to promote responsible drinking is unimportant. The alcohol industry is an extremely effective manipulator of the media and to the extent it uses these talents toward responsible drinking, it should be encouraged and, if not appropriately responsive, legislative remedies should be sought.

THE SPORTS COMPLEX

The position of both amateur and professional sports organizations on drug use by athletes is clear. Drug use to enhance performance is not condoned. Violators, when identified, are sanctioned, offered treatment and, if necessary, suspended or have their contracts terminated. With respect to the commonly used illicit drugs, this policy, which has been refined over the years, seems to be working relatively well. With respect to the use of anabolic steroids, however, inconsistencies in preventing their use have been the exception rather than the rule.

The use of anabolic steroids is all too frequent among high school and college athletes in sports where muscle mass is important. Fortunately, most high school, college, and professional groups have now taken unequivocal positions against such use. Most recent, the Athletic Congress has announced its intention to suspend immediately any athlete who tests positive for a banned substance or even if a male athlete shows a level of testosterone higher than that expected within a range of normal variation. Ignorance of the contents of a substance taken is not considered a valid excuse.

However, with respect to promoting use of alcohol and tobacco, athletic organizations and individual athletes still have a long way to go to fulfill their responsibilities. For each hour of professional sports programming, there are 2.4 alcohol commercials. This can be contrasted to an average of one alcohol advertisement for every four hours of prime time "fictional" programming.[59,60] We have not advanced very far since the turn of the century when baseball star Honus Wagner insisted his name and picture be removed from tins containing smokeless tobacco. Unfortunately, today's well-known athletes continue to promote smokeless tobacco and alcoholic beverages. This is of special concern because athletes serve as role models to millions of youths. Promotion of cigarettes or smokeless tobacco facilitates development of dependency on substances at a young age known to be related to more deaths than illicit drugs. In advertising alcoholic beverages, by not emphasizing the concept of responsible drinking—or the need to wait to drink until of an appropriate age—the dangers associated with excessive consumption of alcohol are minimized with especially unfortunate effects on youths whose tolerance for alcohol is less than that of adults.

Sports organizations, coaches, and promoters of events have a special responsibility not only to discourage harmful advertising during sporting events but to educate and help the players as well. On a small scale, some successes have been achieved. Professional baseball has developed tobacco-cessation programs to diminish players' public use of smokeless tobacco. The Los Angeles Dodgers have banned players from carrying or using tobacco while in uniform. The Oakland Athletics have stopped tobacco advertising in the games. Use of smokeless tobacco has been banned in several minor leagues and was banned by the NCAA for the 1991 College World Series.[19]

Although breweries still sponsor many athletic events, more controls are being placed on sales of alcoholic beverages during sporting events, with some stadiums having restricted seating for those who wish to purchase drinks. All this is encouraging, yet clearly more commitment is needed.

THE ENTERTAINMENT INDUSTRY

The role of the alcohol and tobacco companies in promoting drug use by advertising their products with athletes as spokespeople, as well as funding sporting events is clear. Less obvious is the promotion of drug use provided by some in the entertainment industry. This may produce subtle, yet effective, advertising of drug use. As emphasized by Gitlen, the comparison between compulsive television watching and drug dependence is particularly apt.[68] Television for many, especially those without sufficient economic resources, is an escape, a stimulant, a means of gratification through identification. In many households, children may spend more time with television than with their parents. In such settings television becomes dependency producing. Indeed, a forced "withdrawal" may result in anxiety, depression, and increased cigarette consumption, a symptom complex not unlike withdrawal.[69] It is, therefore, less than surprising that the ways in which drug use are depicted in the media may promote or discourage its use in real life.

Name-brand products are frequently prominently displayed in movies or on TV with their use intentionally or unintentionally glamorized by those depicted as role models to the young. Far from the appearance of these products being necessary to maintain the "reality" of the movie, payment is often accepted for the use of a particular product. Indeed, such payment is a source of revenue for many filmmakers. Agents whose specific roles are to place these products in production develop ready lines of communication with industry representatives. A recent article described the use of "product placement" by illustrating how a tobacco corporation payed $500,000 to use cigarettes in a significant way in five of a top movie star's films.[70] Rather than being solely a direct cash payment, a series of expensive gifts were delivered in addition to contributions made to a favored charity. In each case, there was no paper trail that could document specific agreements and apparently the expectations of the tobacco company were never fully realized. Nonetheless, such efforts, acceded to and perhaps sought after by Hollywood, promote smoking under the pretext of artistic license. It is of interest, as noted by the American Public Health Association, that although the Federal Communications Act initially required documentation of all products appearing on television in exchange for payment, in May of 1963 sponsorship identification was waived for all films made primarily for exhibition in theaters.[71] The reasons for this are less than clear, as many films made initially for distribution in movie theaters will find their way to television.

Less subtle than the incidental use of alcohol or cigarettes in movies or television is the prominent portrayal of drinking. Surveys have documented that approximately 55 percent of program episodes sampled have at least one person drinking alcohol with 10 percent of prime-time fictional characters being drinkers.[57] Drinking characters tend to be affluent, professional, and in other ways role models to young viewers. Underage drinking is often treated humorously, and problematic drinking oversimplified.

Unfortunately, rather than becoming more aware of the role that they could play in diminishing the attractiveness of drug use, the entertainment industry seems to be moving in the opposite direction. Many movie theaters are now overtly advertising a variety of products to the movie audiences prior to the start of the film and continue to produce a number of films where the use of alcohol is associated with attractive and desirable lifestyles, yet clearly not an integral part of the plot. The recommendation of the American Public Health Service that producers voluntarily eliminate the portrayal of alcohol and tobacco products as glamorous and desirable for films, as well as eliminate such product labels in films unless such an identification is an essential and an integral part of the script, seems more than reasonable. It must be emphasized that the goal is not to interfere with artistic endeavors but to sensitize the industry to its susceptibility to subtle intrusions upon its creativity by those seeking to promote the use of mood-altering drugs.

With respect to illicit drug use, the media is no less culpable. Although obviously unable as well as unwilling to overtly promote illicit drug use by associating such use with an exciting lifestyle and easy money, the life of the drug dealer as described in many films becomes glamorized. Just as thousands of inner-city youths emulate role models in sports, so do those with unfulfilled aspirations toward athletic prowess become stimulated by the images presented by the fast-money, glamorous lifestyle of the drug dealer depicted in movies. Although to its credit the industry also produces films that far from glamorize illicit drug use, this is the exception rather than the rule. This is not to argue that the reality of the drug dealer should be ignored but rather that, when depicted, the full picture associated with dealings in illicit drugs should be presented. In reality, for the individual drug dealer, the ending is almost always far from happy.

REFERENCE NOTES

1. Blum A. The Marlboro Grand Prix. Circumvention of the television ban on tobacco advertising. *New Engl J Med,* 1991, 324:913-917.

2. Congressional Record. Proceedings and debates of the 102nd Congress, August 12, 1992, 119.

3. Horgan CM. Substance abuse. The Nation's number one health problem. Key Indicators for Policy, NY: Robert Wood Johnson Foundation, 1993.

4. Johnson J., Ballin S. The power to regulate tobacco circulation, 1995, 92:2021-2022.

5. Warner KE. Profits of doom. *Am J Public Health*, 1993, 83:1211-1213.

6. White LC. Merchants of death: The American Tobacco Industry: NY Beech Tree Books, 1988.

7. Rosenblatt R. How do tobacco executives live with themselves? *The New York Times Magazine,* March 20, 1994, Sec. 6:36.

8. Houston TPet al. How to help patients stop smoking: Guidelines for diagnosis and treatment of nicotine dependence. Chicago IL: *American Medical Association*, 1994.

9. Elders MJ, Perry CL, Eriksen MP, Giovino GA. The report of the Surgeon General: Preventing tobacco use among young people. *Am J Public Health*, 1994, 84:543-547.

10. Davis RM. Reducing youth access to tobacco. *JAMA*, 1991, 266:3186-3188.

11. White LC. Ethical considerations of accepting financial support from the tobacco industry. New York, NY: American Council on Science Health, 1991.

12. Pierce JP, Gilpin E, Burns DM, Whalen E, Rosbrook B, Shopland D, Johnson M. Does tobacco advertising target young people to start smoking? Evidence from California. *JAMA*, 1991, 266:3154-3158.

13. Hearn W. Unhealthy education. *Am Med News*, January 24/31, 1994, 11, 13,14.

14. Di Franza JR, Brown LI. The Tobacco Institute's "It's the Law" campaign: Has it halted illegal sales of tobacco to children? *Am J Public Health*, 1992, 82:1271-1273.

15. Foltz K. Old Joe is paying off for Camel. *The New York Times*, Tuesday, August 7, 1990, Sec. D:17.

16. Di Franza JR, Richards JW, Paulman PM, Wolf-Gillespie N, Fletcher C, Jaffe RD, Murray D. RJR/Nabisco's cartoon camel promotes Camel cigarettes to children. *JAMA*, 1991, 266: 3149-3153.

17. Rose RL, Hwang SL. Marketing: Harley is suing to get its name off cigarettes. *The Wall Street Journal*, March 23, 1995, Sec. B:1.

18. Kessler DA. Remarks, Columbia University School of Law, New York, NY, March 8, 1995.

19. Kent C. Researchers ask FDA to regulate tobacco as a drug. *Am Med News*, May 15, 1995, 15-16.

20. Green M. Warning: RJR may endanger kids' health. *The New York Times*, March 13, 1990, Sec. A:29.

21. Youth access to cigarettes. Office of the Inspector General, U.S. Department of Health and Human Services, May, 1990. *Prevention Pipeline* 1991, 4:18.

22. Di Franza JR, Tye JB. Who profits from tobacco sales to children? *JAMA*, 1990; 263:2784-2787.

23. Consensus conference health applications of smokeless tobacco. *JAMA*, 1986, 255:1045-1048.

24. Connolly GN, Orleans CT, Blum A. Snuffing tobacco out of sport. *Am J Public Health*, 1992, 82:351-353.

25. State laws restricting minors' access to tobacco. MMWR, 1990, 39:349-353.

26. Teenage attitudes and behavior concerning tobacco: A report of the findings. George H. Gallup International Institute, Princeton, NJ, 1992.

27. Klonoff EA, Fritz SM, Landrine H, Riddler RW, Tully Payne L. The problem and sociocultural context of single-cigarette sales. *JAMA*, 1994, 271:618-620.

28. Jones L. Lawmakers hit tobacco ad campaign. *Am Med News*, March 16, 1990, 38.

29. City managers dispense death to minors. *The New York Times*, April 8, 1990, p. 19.

30. Ernster VL. Woman and smoking. *Am J Public Health*, 1993, 83:1202-1204.

31. Warner KE, Goldenhar LM, McLaughlin, CG. Cigarette advertising and magazine coverage of the hazards of smoking. A statistical analysis. *N Engl J Med*, 1992, 326:305-309.

32. Pierce JP, Lee L, Gilpin A. Smoking initiation by adolescent girls 1944-1988. *JAMA*, 1994, 271:608-611.

33. Kaufnan N. Smoking and young women: The physicians's role in stopping an equal opportunity killer. *JAMA*, 1994, 271:629-630.

34. Herbert B. Tobacco dollars in America. *The New York Times*, November 28, 1993, Sec. 4:11; Fisher I. On tobacco list two unlikely names. *The New York Times*, November 19, 1995.

35. Hearn W. Emptying the world's ashtrays. *Am Med News*, October 3, 1994, 13-15.

36. Barry M. The influence of the U.S. tobacco industry on the health, economy and environment of developing countries. *New Engl J Med*, 1991, 324:917-920.

37. Cockburn A. The other drug war, where tobacco firms are the pushers. *The Wall Street Journal*, September 27, 1990 Sec. A:19.

38. In the time it takes to smoke a cigarette, many will die. *Am Med News*, October 10, 1994, 17.

39. AMA assails nation's export policy on tobacco. *The New York Times*, June 27, 1990, Sec. A:12.

40. Jones L. Trade, health policies at cross purposes. *Am Med News*, June 1, 1990, 1.

41. Labaton S. With gifts from all sides, who got Clinton's ear. *The New York Times*, November 15, 1992, Sec. 1:34.

42. Gerbner. Stores that hurt: Tobacco, alcohol and other drugs in the mass media. In Resnik H, Gardner SE (Eds.), *Youth and drugs: Society's mixed messages.* Rockville, MD: Department of Health and Human Services, Public Health Service, 1990. OSAP Prevention Monograph 6.

43. Jones L. Scathing words for tobacco, but limited tax hike. *Am Med News*, September 5, 1994, 3, 12.

44. Begay ME, Traynor M, Glantz SA. The tobacco industry, state politics and tobacco education in California. *Am J Public Health*, 1993, 83:1214-1221.

45. Skolnick AA. Antitobacco advocates fight "illegal" diversion of tobacco control money. *JAMA*, 1994, 271: 1387-1388, 1390.

46. Tobacco industry's millions couldn't buy this election. *Am Med News*, May 9, 1994, 16.

47. Group hits tobacco sports sponsorship. *Am Med News*, March 23/30, 1992, 39.

48. Warner KE Tobacco industry scientific advisors: Serving society or selling cigarettes? *Am J Public Health,* 1991, 81:839-842.

49. Hilts PJ. Philip Morris blocked '83 paper showing tobacco is addictive, panel finds. *The New York Times*, April 4, 1994, Sec. A:21.

50. Hilts PJ. Tobacco company was silent on hazards. *The New York Times*, May 7, 1994, Sec. A:1.

51. Hwang SL. Wigand testifies in Mississippi lawsuit. *The Wall Street Journal*, November 30, 1995 Sec. B:10.

52. Hylton RD. An American icon's new marching orders. *The New York Times*, June 9, 1991, Sec. 3:10.

53. Warner KE, Goldenhar LM, McLaughlin CG. Cigarette advertising and magazine coverage of the hazards of smoking: A statistical analysis. *New Engl J Med*, 1992, 326:305-309.

54. Freedman AM, Stevens A. Tar wars: Philip Morris is putting TV journalism on trial in its suit against ABC. *The Wall Street Journal*, May 23, 1995, Sec. A:14.

55. Novello AC, Shosky J. From the Surgeon General; U.S. Public Health Service. *JAMA*, 1992, 268:961.

56. Deveny K. Strong brew: Malt liquor makers find lucrative market in the urban young. *The Wall Street Journal*, March 9, 1992, Sec. 9:1.

57. Charlier M. Brewers shake off a 3-year hangover. *The Wall Street Journal*, January 15, 1991, Sec. B:1.

58. Sims C. Under siege: Liquor's inner city pipeline. *The New York Times*, November 29, 1992, Sec. 3:1.

59. Grube JW. Alcohol portrayals and alcohol advertising on television. Content and effects on children and adolescents. *Alcohol Health and Res World*, 1993, 12:61-66.

60. Atkin CK, Block M. The effectiveness of celebrity endorsers. *J Advert Res*, 1993 23:57-61.

61. *The Wall Street Journal*, August 19, 1-1. Prevention pipeline, 1991, 4:23.

62. "Crazy Horse" malt liquor an insult to Native Americas. *Alcoholism and Drug Abuse Weekly*, 1992, 4(19), 4.

63. Grube JW, Wallack L. Television beer advertising and drinking knowledge, beliefs and intentions among school children. *Am J Public Health*, 1994, 84:254-259.

64. Charlier M. Big brewers will be among wallflowers at the 1991 spring break beach parties. *The Wall Street Journal*, March 13, 1991, Sec. B:1.

65. Abramson J. Alcohol industry is at the forefront of efforts to curb drunkenness. *The Wall Street Journal*, May 21, 1991, Sec. A:1.

66. *The New York Times*, November 26, 1989, Sec. 3.

67. Madden PA, Grube JW. The frequency and nature of alcohol and tobacco advertising in televised sports, 1990-1992. *Am J Public Health*, 1994, 84:297-299.

68. Gitlen T. On drugs and mass media in America's consumer society. In Resnick H. Gardner SE (Eds.), Youth and Drugs: *Society's mixed messages*, Rockville, MD: Department of Health and Human Services, ADAMHA, 1990. OSAP Prevention Monograph 6: 35-52.

69. Trost C, Grzech E. Could you kick the TV habit? *Detroit Free Press*, October 30, 1977, p. 1a, 4a.

70. Hilts PJ. Company spent $1 million to put cigarettes in movies, memos show. *The New York Times*, May 20, 1994, Sec. A:16.

71. Mosher JF. Alcohol and tobacco industry product placement in feature films. Am Public Health Association. *The Nation's Health,* September 1989, p. 21.

Chapter 3

The Pharmaceutical Companies: Profits versus Responsibility

Since consumption of mood-altering substances began in antiquity, it is only natural that an appropriate means of distribution would evolve to supply this demand. Historically, the lines between distribution of licit and illicit drugs have been somewhat blurred. When heroin was introduced in the late 1800s into medical practice, the Bayer Pharmaceutical Company actively promoted its use as a panacea for a variety of illnesses, as did the American Medical Association (AMA).[1,2] The beneficial effects of cocaine were lauded by Parke-Davis, then one of the leading producers of cocaine-containing compounds. Once controls were established for those drugs considered at high risk to produce dependency, regardless of their medical value, some companies, whether intentionally or unwittingly, became suppliers for illicit distribution by not carefully evaluating the credentials of their distributors.[3]

When the Harrison Bill was introduced to prohibit the sales of opiates, the existing pharmaceutical organizations were all opposed. Once it became clear that this legislation would be enacted, the National Wholesale Druggist Association continued to protest the inclusion of cannabis with cocaine and opiates. During the meeting of the International Opium Advisory Committee in 1923, Chinese representatives observed that smugglers were obtaining their major sources of morphine from a number of countries, including the United States.[3]

Since that time, considerable awareness has developed on the part of pharmaceutical companies concerning the social, medical, and legal dangers of inadequate drug testing prior to marketing, as well as the potential liability associated with faulty drug advertis-

49

ing. Many pharmaceutical firms have made conscientious efforts to present accurate pictures to both physicians and the public concerning risks inherent in the prescription of mood-altering drugs. Yet, some advertising continues to be indirect in addressing the dependence-producing effects of many psychotropic agents. The attempt to strike a balance between the basic corporate profit motive and social conscience remains problematic. With the introduction of the minor tranquilizers in the mid-1950s, profits accrued at times 15-fold the cost of manufacture.[4] In 1990, pharmaceutical firms sold $37.6 billion of prescription drugs, with more recent estimates reaching $58 billion annually.[4,5] As observed by Gorring,[6] both the description applied to the cartels that produce and distribute heroin, as well as the profits involved, can be equally applied to pharmaceutical firms. International organizations concerned with maximizing profits, many times greater than expenses, contain a distinct hierarchy. At the top are persons relatively free from liability, followed by midlevel employers, distributors, and, finally, the person on the street who details the drugs to the consumers.

Although much has been achieved by pharmaceutical firms to present a positive image and contribute to the public good, there still are prevailing areas of concern. These include (1) supplying the chemicals used to refine and process illicit drugs; (2) diverting both the chemicals used to synthesize mood-altering drugs and the drugs themselves; (3) minimizing the dependency potential of a drug, and broadening indications for its use to promote physician prescriptions; (4) initiating advertising campaigns that less than fairly explain the product; (5) promoting the product to physicians in a manner that creates conflicts of interest; (6) employing direct consumer advertising; and (7) engaging in direct lobbying efforts to influence the political process.

SUPPLYING CHEMICALS USED TO REFINE AND PROCESS ILLICIT DRUGS

It is discouraging but true that many of the chemicals used to produce heroin and cocaine are legally obtained from chemical or pharmaceutical firms in the United States. The Drug Enforcement Agency has estimated that 55 percent of all acetone, ether, potassium permanganate, and toluene exported to Colombia to produce cocaine came from the United States. It seems hypocritical at the least to pressure foreign governments to prevent cultivation of cocaine and opium while we are profiting from the sale of solvents to allow these drugs to be purified.

In 1988, the U.S. Government forcibly took action against suppliers through the passage of The Chemical Diversion and Traffic Act (DTA). This act requires the reporting of all transactions involved in the purchase of chemical sales to make "controlled chemicals" as well as to report to the DTA all suspicious purchases.[7] The DTA also can prevent sale of these chemicals to those who are suspected of enjoying the illicit drug trade. As a result of this act, by 1990 the percentage of chemicals originating in the United States used by drug traffickers in Colombia had considerably decreased. Unfortunately, as might be expected, this did not result in a scarcity of chemicals, but rather a change in origin with chemical firms in Europe quickly taking up the slack.

DIVERSION OF LICIT MOOD-ALTERING DRUGS

Diversion of mood-altering drugs or their precursors has always been of concern. At times, orders are unwittingly filled by pharmaceutical houses. In their desire to promote sales, the supplier may be less than critical in assessing the purchaser. Many years ago, the increased appearance of street methamphetamine (speed) was associated with several companies in California that produced chemicals involved in its synthesis and were then accused by federal and state authorities of knowingly selling these chemicals for street production.

Diversion of licit mood-altering drugs can also occur through a variety of ways. Mail orders for these drugs may be filled uncritically, especially when orders originate in foreign countries. At one time, this was a particular problem with amphetamines, which were shipped by pharmaceutical firms to Mexico and then sent back to the street drug trade. The increasing black market in anabolic steroids currently surfacing may, in part, be fueled by drugs diverted from legitimate companies in the early 1980s. Although the diversion of precursor chemicals used to manufacture amphetamines from American companies appears to have been addressed, the Middle East and Asia now have become "suppliers." As a result, a new methamphetamine epidemic has surfaced in Western cities in this country, displacing crack as the drug of choice.[8] Ephedrine and pseudo-ephedrine, the legally available precursors used to treat asthma attacks as well as colds, have been intercepted in large quantities originating in India on the way to Mexico to be converted to methamphetamine.

More pervasive and less easy to control is the time-honored practice of providing detail men with free samples with which to supply physicians in order to encourage prescription of these drugs. Although this practice does not occur for Schedule-II drugs, in the past, analgesics promoted as nonaddictive were able to be provided as trial samples. As might be imagined, the potential for abuse through diversion is enormous. In response to growing concerns about the "grey market" in drugs, the Prescription Drug Market Act of 1987 was signed into law. This legislation restricts the ability of wholesalers to send large shipments of drugs overseas as well as establishes more stringent requirements for samples to be distributed to physicians, including the need for a written request for the sample by the physician stating the quantity requested and requiring a signed receipt upon delivery. Diversion of samples through sales or trade are illegal, punishable by sentences of up to ten years imprisonment and fines as high as $250,000.[9] Ultimately, however, as with any law, enforcement can accomplish only so much; acceptance of responsibility by those who produce and distribute these substances is the only certain way to diminish diversions.

MINIMIZING DEPENDENCY-PRODUCING POTENTIAL

When a new mood-altering drug is synthesized and marketed, often the indications for its use are broadened, at times with relatively little scientific evidence to support claims of effectiveness. The Food and Drug Administration (FDA) has jurisdiction, however, over only those activities defined as promotional, as for example, labeling or advertising, not those considered for scientific exchange. In an attempt to widen its authority, the FDA incorporated in its definition of labeling any material issued or sponsored by a pharmaceutical firm, including material published in such books as the *Physician's Desk Reference* provided to the medical profession. If violators are identified, then the FDA has the authority to seize the drug and subject the manufacturer to prosecution; however, the usual response is to require the advertisement to be withdrawn, and if questions of patient safety exist, then a "Dear Doctor" letter should be sent to all physicians.[9]

Recently, the FDA has requested, but not required, that advertisements be submitted in advance for clearance as part of the drug-approval process. Not surprisingly, compliance to this request is far from complete, with some companies raising valid issues concerning violation of rights.

Because many physicians are always willing to try a new drug to relieve anxiety or pain, (especially if it is promoted as a nonnarcotic), a product may be used in the absence of appropriate evidence of effectiveness. Full-page glossy ads are placed in medical journals with eye-catching, one-line statements, and photographs of "before and after" images appear. The scientific data providing detailed, accurate information concerning the product appears in the smallest possible print. In addition to minimizing the potential for misuse, often the drug's effectiveness is overstated, and some side effects, especially behavioral, are presented in the most cursory way. Many examples can be found. Propoxyphene (Darvon) was promoted as a nonnarcotic, pain-relieving agent, although it is a derivative of methadone and was quickly accepted and injected by those well aware of its mood-altering effects. Propoxyphene was readily obtained from physicians who, based on the information received, believed that it could be prescribed without fear of dependency. The increasing abuse of Darvon resulted in its being placed in Schedule IV in 1977, with the FDA requiring a label concerning its risks placed on all products containing propoxyphene.[10] Yet, even today, most physicians are unaware of propoxyphene's pharmacological relationship to methadone or its ability to produce dependency with inappropriate use.

Pentazocine (Talwin), another analgesic agent, was developed to relieve pain without producing dependency, despite laboratory and clinical evidence that physical dependence could develop quite rapidly. Since its introduction in 1969, many cases of Talwin addiction have been reported, with the drug receiving prominence in the street as Ts and Blues, often used in lieu of heroin.[11,12]

Percodan, promoted as a pain-relieving medication "not containing codeine," resulted in many physicians prescribing this drug without realizing that, although "codeine-free," it is, in fact, a much more potent narcotic, being as powerful as morphine in relieving moderate to severe painful states. Even today, this drug is prescribed by many physicians quite freely without their realizing its dependency potential associated with continuing use. In one study, it was found to be the second most frequent drug liable to abuse.[13]

Most recently, several analgesics have been developed that, similar to pentazocine, are narcotic antagonist-analgesics (buprenorphine, Temgesic, Stadol). They are promoted by the pharmaceutical firms as being effective pain relievers associated with a low risk of dependency. These drugs can be prescribed without any of the regulations applied to narcotics; however, all of these drugs alter mood, and inappropriate use will result in dependence or withdrawal when the drug is discontinued. This is known to the companies producing these drugs and had been seen during initial trials with these agents. In addition, these drugs have been favorably compared to heroin by addicts volunteering as subjects. Not surprisingly, diversions have already been reported from pharmacies. One of these drugs, buprenorphine, has become a leading drug of abuse in New Zealand. Yet, little mention of this is made in package inserts provided to physicians.[14]

Initial claims made for the benzodiazepines were even more impressive in their promotional efforts. Valium was advertised as producing a less demanding and more compliant patient, and Vistaril was discussed as being useful for children frightened by "school, the dark, separation, dental visits, and monsters."[13] Miltown, one of the earliest marketed tranquilizers, was widely advertised as "a Penicillin for the blues." Placidyl, when first introduced, was promoted in an advertisement showing a pregnant woman with the caption, "give us her nights"–yet in small print was the caution, "not to give the drug in early pregnancy."[15]

When amitriptyline (Elavil) was first introduced to the market, it was described as a panacea for depression, with little or no potential for misuse. It soon became a common drug on the street, well known for producing a high, especially when combined with small amounts of alcohol. Almost all of the amitriptyline was physician prescribed, based on the information published by its manufacturer. More recently, the producers of Halcion and Prozac have come under public scrutiny over allegations of withholding information concerning the adverse effects associated with these drugs.[16] In fact, the hype surrounding Prozac has reached its zenith with the drug now being promoted as a "personality pill" being taken by people wanting to become more successful and better able to cope with life. It is believed that Prozac, first introduced to physicians in 1987, has been prescribed to more than 11 million people by family physicians as well as psychiatrists.[17] The extent to which the public has become enamored of this drug is at best nothing short of remarkable. It belabors the obvious to state that the physician bears responsibility for prescribing a product without critical evaluation, yet the pharmaceutical company, through misleading advertisements, must also assume its share of blame.

DIRECT PUBLIC ADVERTISING

The massive advertising campaigns directed toward consumers often emphasize the advantages of taking over-the-counter, mood-altering drugs to relieve a variety of nonspecific symptoms. Such advertising depicts the person in need of mood-altering drugs as an average everyday person. It is not at all unlikely that our current annual expenditures on the advertising of psychoactive, over-the-counter drugs may compare favorably with our annual expenditures to combat drug abuse. These advertisements, which stress the importance of relieving insomnia or increasing alertness, give lie to the appropriateness of turning to drugs to alter mood before attempting other measures of relief. The message often transmitted is that these drugs should be taken freely in order to cope with the everyday problems of living. At times, the actual sponsorship of the promotional material may not be readily apparent, giving the consumer the impression that an impartial scientific announcement has been made.

Many new products can be synthesized through subtle changes in the basic molecular structure of a class of drugs. It is, therefore, fairly safe to assume that these promotional activities will continue to expand as the competition in a relatively fixed market becomes more intense. Whereas providing direct consumer information through labeling requirements has the potential to develop a more informed public, the potential to confuse or present as fact that which is not through the use of the media is equally real.

Direct consumer advertising of over-the-counter drugs regulated by the FTC began to be accompanied by consumer prescription drug advertising in 1983. The FDA initially imposed a moratorium on this for the next two years, appropriately lifting it in 1985. At present, consumer advertising of prescription drugs is held to the same standards as that existing for physician groups and, in addition, must meet a "fair balance test" as well as provide a toll-free number that can be used to obtain additional information whenever specific products are advertised.

PROMOTION TO THE MEDICAL PROFESSION

It is in the promotion of their products to the medical profession, however, where the pharmaceutical companies excel. Advertising in journals is a massive endeavor. It is estimated that in 1994 pharmaceutical manufacturers spent $250 million just on ads for prescription drugs, a 34 percent increase in spending over 1993.[18] It is estimated that in 1987 pharmaceutical firms spent $5,000 per physician–25 percent of their sales revenue–to promote these products.[19] This has resulted in subtle and not-so-subtle conflicts of interest with physicians as well as in institutions trying to tread a fine line between using pharmaceutical companies' resources to enhance knowledge and being unduly influenced by the support provided.

Many glaring examples of "crossing the line" can be found. They include outright gifts to both physicians and (at times) to their families, the total support of conferences held in desirable areas, and allowing physicians financial interests in products being tested. Although such examples may be the exception rather than the rule, they do occur and in the past were discontinued only after being discovered. Although there is no evidence that such activities actually have directed physicians' prescribing practices, it would be naive to assume that they have not had some effect. Evidence has been presented showing a relationship between the number of prescriptions written by physicians per week and the frequency of detail representative's visits to their offices.

A similar direct relationship was observed between the number of prescriptions written and reliance predominantly on the pharmaceutical industry for information about new drugs as compared to professional resources.[20] It has been shown that not all of the information imparted to physicians is accurate. One study revealed that 11 percent of statements made by pharmaceutical representatives were inaccurate, contradicting their own readily available information. Not surprisingly, all of these statements were favorable toward the promoted drug. Unfortunately, physicians generally failed to detect these inaccuracies.[21]

Were these practices not felt to be effective, it is more than likely that drug companies would have discontinued their efforts long ago. This issue has now been addressed through the establishment of ethical guidelines by the American Medical Association, which have, in general, been accepted by both physicians and the pharmaceutical industry.

Yet, despite these guidelines, questionable marketing tactics continue. Most recently, the Office of the Inspector General of the Department of Health and Human Services issued a special "fraud alert" to make both consumers and providers aware of inappropriate and possibly illegal marketing activities by several major pharmaceutical firms. These activities have ranged from payments to physicians and pharmacists to "counsel" patients to use specific drugs to providing points toward free airline tickets to physicians for completing forms after prescribing a new drug to awarding of "research grants" for selected projects that bear little resemblance to standard research protocols (Seeding trials). Switch campaigns, whereby pharmaceutical companies provide financial incentives to pharmacists to encourage patients to switch to a similar drug, have also have been described.[15]

Pharmaceutical companies, however, can and do play an important role in supporting medical education and research. Areas of involvement that are commonly considered acceptable under defined conditions include unrestricted support of targeted scientific research. In each instance, however, the individual physician or the institution must make a decision as to whether acceptance of support will imply an obligation toward a particular company or product.

LOBBYING EFFORTS TO PREVENT RESTRICTIVE LEGISLATION

The pharmaceutical industry, not too dissimilar to the tobacco industry but on a smaller scale, has attempted to lobby against legislation designed to limit availability of psychotropic agents. In 1966, although the Federal government initiated efforts to subject benzodiazepines to control schedules due to a variety of legal maneuvers it was not able to do so until 1975, shortly before the patents expired. Presently, many manufacturers are actively opposing the increased use of multiple-copy prescriptions (MCPs), promoting the belief that patients are being denied needed medications.[19] Although it is clear that the use of these drugs in states with MCPs has dramatically decreased, it is less than certain if this has been accompanied by a decrease or an increase in quality of care.

CONCLUSION

Pharmaceutical companies have an essential role to play in diminishing the inappropriate use of mood-altering drugs. Although monitoring by the FDA and FTC is both essential and beneficial, nonetheless, it is the industry itself that must take responsibility for its actions. A number of companies have done this, and, hopefully, more will follow. Such measures that can and have been taken include voluntarily providing accurate information in simple language to patients, including the message that mood-altering drugs should be taken only when other means of relief have failed and only on a physician's advice. Journal advertising should describe scientific evidence of drug benefits and risks rather than glossy, "high-cost" marketing approaches designed to catch a physician's eye. Support of scientific endeavors without any insistence or reference to a specific product should be the rule. Finally, drug companies should markedly reduce the "gift" approach to attract physicians' prescriptions. The considerable amount of money saved through institution of this last action could, for example, be used to either decrease the cost of the product or support unrestricted scientific research. Although it is naive to assume that all pharmaceutical companies would actively embrace such approaches, it has been encouraging to note that some of these suggestions have already been adopted by more than a few.

REFERENCE NOTES

1. McCoy AW Adams LP, Read CB. *The politics of heroin in southeast Asia.* New York, Harper & Row, 1972.

2. Report of the Committee on the Narcotic Drug Situation. 1920, *JAMA*, 74:1318.

3. Musto DF, The American disease: Origins of narcotic control. New Haven, CT: Yale University Press, 1987, p. 56, 58, 216.

4. Jackson JO. The pharmaceutical industry. In Fincham JE, Wertheimer AI (Eds.). *Pharmacy and the U.S. health care system.* Binghamton, NY: Pharmaceutical Products Press, 1991, 259-287.

5. Kessler DA, Rose JL, Temple RJ, Shapiro R, Griffen JP. Therapeutic class wars–drug promotion in a competitive marketplace. *New Engl J Med*, 1994, 331: 1350-1353.

6. Goring P. Mutinationals or Mafia: Who really pushes drugs. In Wilson, PR Braithwaite J. (Eds.). *Two faces of deviance: Crimes of the powerless and the powerful.* Brisbane, Australia: University of Queensland Press, 1978.

7. Drugs, crime and the justice system. A national report from the Bureau of Justice Statistics. Washington, DC: U.S. Department of Justice, 1992.

8. Wren G. Sharp rise in use of methamphetamines generates concern. *The New York Times*, February 14, 1996.

9. Kessler DA, Pines WL. The federal regulation of prescription drug advertising and promotion. *JAMA*, 1990, 264:2409-2415.

10. Smith RJ. Federal government faces painful decision on Darvon. *Science, 1979,* 203:857-858.

11. Inciardi JA, Chambers CD. Patterns of pentazocine abuse and addiction. *NY State J Med*, 1971, 71:1727-1733.

12. Swanson DW, Weddige RL, Morse RM. Hospitalized pentazocine abusers. *Mayo Clin Proc*, 1973, 48:85-93.

13. Maruta T, Swanson DW, Finlayson RE. Drug abuse and dependency in patients with chronic pain. *Mayo Clin Proc*, 1979, 54:241-244.

14. Lavelle TL, Hammersley R, Forsyth A, Bain D. The use of buprenorphine and Temazepam by drug injectors. *J Addic Dis*, 1991, 10(3):5-14.

15. Braithwaite J. *Corporate crime in the pharmaceutical industry.* Boston, MA: Routledge and Kegan Paul, 1984, pp. 205-244.

16. Cowley G, Springen K, Larovici D, Hager M. Sweet dreams or nightmare? *Newsweek*, August 19, 1991, pp. 44-51.

17. Rothman DJ. Shiny happy people: Listening to Prozac by Peter Kramer. *New Republic*, February 14, 1994, pp. 34-38.

18. FDA debates how far drug makers can go in advertising. Associated Press *American Medical News*, December 4, 1995.

19. Haislip GR. Drug diversion control systems, medical practice, and patient care. In Cooper JR, Czechowicz D, Molinari SP (Eds.). Impact of Prescription Drug Diversion Control Systems on Medical Practice and Patient Care. Rockville, MD: National Institute on Drug Abuse, 1993. NIDA Research Monograph 131: 120-131.

20. Walker HD. *Market power and price levels in the ethical drug industry.* 1971. Indiana University Press, Bloomington, IN.

21. Ziegler, MG, Lew P, Singer DC. The accuracy of information from pharmaceutical sales representatives. *JAMA*, 1995, 273: 1290-1298.

Chapter 4

Physicians and Pharmacists: Potential Unrealized

ROLE OF THE PHYSICIAN

Whether alcoholism or other forms of drug abuse are diseases or behavioral disturbances, physicians undoubtedly play a crucial role in early identification and referral. The family physician, the pediatrician, or the general internist are all looked upon by the public to provide counseling on a variety of issues, including the effects of alcohol and mood-altering drugs. Questions concerning alcohol and drug use in both adults and children should be an integral part of a medical history and can allow identification of a problem at an early stage. It has been estimated that 70 percent of smokers see a physician at least once a year. With respect to teenagers and adolescents, visits occur with an even greater frequency due to the necessity of physical examinations for school and camp. Yet only 61 percent of smokers have reported that their physician advised them to stop smoking and 49 percent report that the health risks of smoking were never fully explained.[1] Data pertaining specifically to adolescents and young adults are even more depressing. A 1993 nationwide survey on teenage attitudes and practices revealed that only one-fourth (25 percent) of respondents said that a health care provider had said something to them about cigarette smoking and 12 percent that information concerning smokeless tobacco was provided.[2] Even among smokers, only 50 percent ever recalled receiving any communication about this habit from physicians. This is especially important not only with respect to the actual adverse effects of nicotine, but in addition, a survey of persons who used cigarettes, cocaine, alcohol, and marijuana every day for two consecutive weeks found that 91 percent of those who smoked were more likely to report a symptom of addiction than those who used these other drugs.[3] The physician can also serve as a primary source for substance abuse education as well as for referrals when problems develop. The physician is often among the first to identify depression, anxiety, and excessive stress as well as the one to decide whether these problems should be addressed through nondrug therapy or medication.

Unfortunately, more often than not, primary care physicians are reluctant to address issues of drug use, focusing instead on the medical effects of such use. The existence of a drug problem is ignored as long as possible and then managed by referring the patient to the emergency room, a clinic, or a specialist. Chart reviews of both hospitalized and ambulatory patients have found that in over 50 percent of encounters no questions were asked concerning alcohol or drug use. There are many reasons for this hesitancy to be proactive. They include (1) inadequate training; (2) a negative image of the alcoholic and addict; (3) fear of regulatory sanctions for inappropriate prescribing; (4) fear of being accused of promoting or initiating dependency on a mood-altering substance (iatrogenic addiction); (5) the lack of adequate reimbursement for the considerable time required to identify the problem and provide counseling; and (6) the inability to control some difficult patients.

INADEQUATE TRAINING

Until recently, medical education has sorely neglected educating both the medical student and the resident about alcoholism and other chemical dependencies. In medical schools these subjects are addressed in several pharmacology lectures, where the basic actions of mood-altering drugs are discussed. Little or no attention is given to early identification and management of the alcoholic or drug user. This is not surprising as medical school curricula most often reflect the composition of the faculty, and few, if any, schools have divisions or even clinical units addressing substance abuse. Such problems are addressed in publicly funded clinics that either have a loose affiliation with a medical school or, if utilized for clinical training, do not routinely receive students. As a result, a student's only exposure occurs when confronted with a patient on a medical or psychiatric service who is suffering from a complication of alcoholism or illicit drug use. Medical students are thus more likely to learn about the effects of mood-altering drugs from their own personal experiences rather than as part of their formal education. The guidance provided to residents concerning drug use also, unfortunately, leaves much to be desired. A 1988 survey revealed that only 42 percent of primary care programs provided specific training in substance abuse.[4] This training was also neglected in most specialty programs, with the exception of psychiatry. Yet, until recently, even in psychiatry, training in the diagnosis and treatment of chemical dependency has been far from adequate. The lack of such training and appropriate supervision in management of these patients leaves the resident with an understandable reluctance to become involved with such patients once entering private practice.

Licit drug use also receives short shrift in the medical curriculum. The 1990 edition of a standard textbook of pharmacology used by most medical schools devotes only five pages to nicotine and tobacco and eight to alcohol as compared to 22 pages devoted to digitalis, a drug used to treat heart failure.[5] A major textbook in medicine (2,487 pages) devotes only five pages to smoking and nine to alcoholism, as compared to 18 on hypertension.[6] It is not surprising that students often graduate medical school without sufficient knowledge to provide information to their patients as to how to successfully quit smoking or moderate their intake of alcohol. This is in no small part one reason that most physicians feel they are not qualified to or will ultimately be unsuccessful in assisting patients to quit. Their beliefs, however, fly in the face of evidence that suggests that well-designed smoking intervention programs can be successful as well as the observation that 70 percent of smokers consuming more than one pack a day said they would quit if urged by their physicians.[7]

The Image of the Alcoholic and Drug Abuser

The social history of the medical profession makes it difficult for an impartial observer to conclude other than that physicians are disinclined to trust or treat the alcoholic or substance abuser. When the physician enters residency training, persons who abuse alcohol and drugs are viewed as angry, ill-kept, disruptive individuals who impart an extremely negative image. There is reality to this as drug users, realizing that their needs concerning mood-altering drugs will in all probability not be met, develop marked adversarial relationships with physicians. The overtly antisocial behavior may be related to feelings of shame over the loss of control of their actions. Not infrequently, these relationships are accentuated by ethnic differences between physician and patient. The physiologic as well as psychologic needs of a dependent person for a specific drug, combined with the physician's hesitancy to prescribe the drug, at times results in violent outbursts. A student or resident needs only a few such encounters to form an indelible image of the alcoholic or drug user as one who should be avoided at all costs. In fact, surveys have revealed that over 50 percent of physicians have negative feelings toward treating addicts.[8]

Fear of Regulatory Sanctions

Despite the hesitancy in dealing with alcoholism and drug abuse, physicians maintain a pivotal role in prescribing mood-altering medications and, at times, may even inadvertently be the source of their inappropriate use. Historically, the medical profession was little concerned with the potential problems involved with introducing new drug therapies and more often than not enthusiastically embraced new drugs prior to their effects being fully evaluated. Opium was readily prescribed by physicians in the late 1800s; heroin, synthesized in 1874, was recommended by the American Medical Association as a substitute for morphine for various painful conditions by 1906. Not until 1920 did the hazards associated with heroin become well established, resulting in the AMA recommending its removal from medical practice. The development of the hypodermic syringe in 1865 made it possible for less morphine to be used with the same effect, resulting in the perception of a lessened danger of addiction. As described by Brecher, physicians were even suggesting that patients obtain hypodermic sets to self-inject morphine until the hazards associated with this use became known.[9]

The development of LSD was heralded by the psychiatric profession as a means of developing better insight into the origins of psychoses.[10] This drug was used in a variety of subjects as late as the 1960s at both the National Institute of Mental Health and Saint Elizabeth's Hospital. It subsequently became popular with a small number of therapists who promoted its facilitation of the analytic process. Physicians who initially personally used LSD encouraged friends and colleagues to try the drug.

Freud's enthusiasm for cocaine is perhaps one of the best known examples of uncritical drug promotion; however, lest one be too hard on Freud, in the United States cocaine was enthusiastically accepted in the late 1800s as the wonder drug, being freely available in over-the-counter medications as well as in soft drinks, notably Coca-Cola.

Although smoking is currently recognized as one of the major health hazards in our society, prior to 1950 many physicians were unaware of its harmful effects. Several physicians advocated smoking in advertisements and promoted its use in magazines, with the proportion of physicians smoking being equal to that of the general population. Even now when virtually all physicians recognize the hazards of smoking, as observed earlier, their efforts in active intervention remain inconsistent and not as effective as one would hope.

New drugs are still often used uncritically in attempts to provide relief. Propoxyphene (Darvon), introduced in 1957, has been prescribed billions of times for a multitude of painful conditions, ranking eighth in the top 200 drugs prescribed in 1987. Many physicians still consider propoxyphene a safe, nonnarcotic drug for moderately severe pain, despite the fact that it is a derivative of methadone. They remain unaware that when taken in excess propoxyphene can produce appreciable narcotic effects, including withdrawal. Physicians' prescriptions of the benzodiazepines in the form of Valium, Halcion, and Librium continue to be extensive, with Valium ranking, at one time, number 14 among the top 200 drugs prescribed. At present, the "glamour" drug is Prozac, which is being prescribed increasingly. It should be noted that primary care physicians play a pivotal role in this regard, prescribing more anxiolytic drugs than those in any other group.[11,12] In Oregon, 51 percent of physicians misprescribing medications were family physicians, whereas family physicians only comprised 18 percent of all physicians in the state.[11]

Although physicians obviously bear individual responsibility for their individual prescribing practices, nonetheless (as mentioned in Chapter 3) the pharmaceutical firms must also share some of this responsibility. Their aggressive advertising practices often accompanied by free samples and gifts are pressed upon physicians months before the results of large-scale evaluative studies appear in the medical literature. It is impressive to observe that 20 years after graduation, 85 percent of all prescriptions written by physicians will be for a drug which they did not learn about in medical school.[12,13]

Current Prescription of Controlled Substances

The casualness with which physicians prescribed mood-altering drugs ended in 1914 with the passage of the Harrison Narcotic Act, the first of many laws attempting to control inappropriate physician prescription. The definition of appropriate versus inappropriate mood-altering drug use was clearly stated in the Comprehensive Drug Abuse Prevention and Control Act of 1970, which separated mood-altering drugs by their potency, their ability to cause physical dependency, and their use medically as considered acceptable by community standards.[14] This was followed by the Psychotropic Substances Act in 1978, which specifically states that the availability of these drugs for useful and legitimate medical and scientific purposes not be unduly restricted. However, with respect to dependency-producing drugs, most specifically the narcotics, in the clinical setting this has not occurred.

Federal law requires that prescriptions for controlled substances by individual practitioners must be issued for a legitimate medical purpose and not for maintenance treatment or detoxification from addiction. An *addict* is defined by federal statute as "any individual who habitually uses any narcotic drug so as to endanger the public morals, health, safety, or welfare, or who is so far addicted to the use of narcotic drugs to have lost the power of self-control with respect to his addiction."[14]

Although the physician is primarily responsible as the initiator of the prescription, in fact, it is not solely his/her judgment that defines appropriate use. The pharmacist who fills the prescription shares an immediate responsibility in not dispensing a drug to be used in an inappropriate manner. Also overseeing this physician/patient transaction are the Food and Drug Administration, the Drug Enforcement Agency and, most important with respect to immediate consequences of inappropriate actions, the state authorities.

Virtually all states have laws monitoring the use of controlled substances, most of which are more restrictive than federal laws. These regulations were promulgated based on the Federal Controlled Substances Act as well as the Uniform Controlled Substance Act published by the National Conference on Uniform State Laws in 1970. In addition to these regulations, many states have initiated a number of monitoring systems or are participating in systems developed by other organizations.[15] These include Multicopy Prescription Programs (MCPPS) and allow a careful monitoring of designated drugs by requiring a copy of all such prescriptions to be filed with a designated state authority.

Critics of these triplicate forms have claimed they are an additional physician burden, increase the cost to patient care, and violate physician/patient confidentiality resulting in discouraging both patients and physicians from using these agents when indicated. Initially, this might have been the case as several states required that physicians report if patients were kept on these drugs for more than several months and differentiate addicts from those physically dependent. With the revision of the Uniform Controlled Substance Abuse Act, the importance of appropriately prescribing these drugs was recognized as essential to the public health. The use of opiods for intractable pain was declared appropriate, with patients (differentiated from addicts) taking these drugs. The importance of patient confidentiality was also emphasized.

The actual effect of triplicate prescriptions on physicians' prescribing practices can be best demonstrated by a review of benzodiazepine prescriptions in New York State.[16,17] In 1988, New York State added all benzodiazepines to its triplicate prescription program. The effect this had on physicians in the state was dramatic. Benzodiazepine prescriptions decreased by 44.2 percent in New York State between 1988 and 1989 as compared to 9.8 percent nationwide. Within populations in the state, more dramatic decreases were reported as, for example, a decrease of 59 percent was seen for New York Medicaid recipients. However, prescriptions for nonbenzodiazepines rose by 20 percent during this time, resulting in drugs being prescribed that were not considered as acceptable as benzodiazepines because of a greater potential for adverse side effects. However, by 1990 the number of alternate prescriptions began to make their decline.[18] When suspected areas of intentional abuse were reviewed, the changes after inclusion of benzodiaze-pines in the MCPP program were even more impressive. Forgeries, which had accounted for 12.5 percent of prescriptions, had de-creased to 0.06 percent. A group of 3,400 persons suspected of diverting benzodiazepines and who accounted for 20,000 prescrip-tions a month had their prescription claims reduced by 95 percent. Street prices for benzodiazepines increased by twofold to fivefold, indicating a scarcity on the street. Emergency room admissions for benzodiazepines decreased by 48 percent in the first year in New York State as compared to a 5 percent decrease nationwide.

A variety of computerized monitoring systems exist to keep track of prescription psychotropic agents (Table 4.1).[19] Although the goal of these monitoring systems is to identify those physicians provid-ing inadequate and harmful care, an accompanying unintentional effect may be prompting physicians to be less likely to care for patients who require these drugs. Patients with chronic pain form a group that has been consistently undertreated and is at particular risk. As demonstrated in a study of Minnesota physicians, 32 per-cent indicated a reduced willingness to prescribe opiates for chronic pain, with 25 percent of family practitioners and 32 percent of internists less willing to accept new patients who might require controlled substances.[20]

With respect to major tranquilizers, evidence suggests that ap-propriately applied regulations may both educate as well as restrict inappropriate use of these agents. Data has long been available suggesting inappropriate use of these agents. The prevalence of antipsychotic medication in nursing homes has been reported to be as high as 50 percent with little justification for such use.[21,22,23] One study found that those facilities having low staff/patient ratios had a greater proportion of their patients on major tranquilizers. In 1987, the inclusion of the Nursing Home Reform Amendments in the Omnibus Budget Reconciliation Bill had as one of its main objectives the elimination of the inappropriate prescription of mood-altering drugs in chronic care facilities. A recent study of the effect of the implementation of this act in Tennessee showed a significant decrease in the number of new prescriptions for autopsy-

TABLE 4.1. Existing Computerized Monitoring Systems

Automated Reports and Consolidated Order Systems (ARCOS)

An electronic data transfer system that records all transfers from manufacturers and distributors of Schedule-II and III drugs. Operated by the Drug Enforcement Agency, it collects all information related to wholesale drug distribution.

Prescription Abuse Data Systems (PADS)

A system developed by the American Medical Association to define drug diversion within a state. A modification of this program, PADS II, was developed to collect data from chain drugstores and insurance drug programs to identify leading prescriptions within a state. This program, however, which was voluntary, was never able to be effectively implemented.[16]

Oklahoma Schedule-II Abuse Reduction (OSTAR)

OSTAR collects data from pharmacies filling prescriptions and transmits the data to a state-supported agency to identify inappropriate use.

Medicaid System (MAOAS)

This system allows review of all Medicaid prescriptions, when Medicaid reimbursement to the pharmacist accrues. However, paying in cash for the prescription subverts the system.

chotic agents and the duration of treatment in persons receiving these drugs without any evidence of adverse effects.[13]

Iatrogenic Addiction

Iatrogenic addiction is a considerable concern to both physicians and the public. *Iatrogenic addiction* is the initiation of drug dependency through prescription of a mood-altering drug that produces such positive reinforcing effects that a person will continue to take the drug after the initial condition for which the drug was prescribed is removed. Until recently, concern over iatrogenic addiction has almost exclusively focused on narcotic dependence when narcotics are prescribed for pain relief. The fear of producing iatrogenic dependence on narcotic drugs on the part of physicians has been so great that people often suffer unnecessarily due to underprescribing. Actually, the appropriate use of narcotics for pain relief in the medical setting is associated with an exceptionally low incidence of iatrogenic addiction. Data concerning this phenomenon are not easy to develop; however, a study by Drs. Porter and Jick, as part of the Boston Collaborative Drug Surveillance Program, which monitored all drug exposures in a number of hospitals, is informative. They found that of 11,882 hospitalized patients receiving narcotics, only four showed evidence of drug use subsequent to treatment; among those without any prior history of drug addiction, only four showed evidence of drug use subsequent to treatment, with only one person described as having a continuing problem.[24] Appropriate administration of narcotics for pain from a defined cause is usually associated with minimal risk.[25]

Prescription of narcotic drugs for minor complaints or for pain of undetermined origin, however, is not infrequently associated with subsequent abuse. For example, in one survey of 144 patients referred to a pain management clinic, codeine, a very mild narcotic agent of great practical value for minor pain, was found to be the most frequent drug of abuse in those patients without a demonstrable cause of pain.[26] In many instances, those taking codeine were unaware it was a narcotic. In this particular survey, Percocet was found to be the second most frequent drug liable to abuse and dependency. Not surprisingly, patients taking Percocet reported great difficulty in discontinuing its use, with only one-third of those taking it for pain of unknown origin being able to discontinue its use successfully. In short, the appropriate use of any narcotic drug for pain of known origin results in minimal side effects and disturbance in function. Inappropriate use, regardless of perceived potency of the drug, is often associated with abuse and dependence. The conditions surrounding the use of the narcotic, not the narcotic itself, define the risk.

The possibility of dependence through use of other mood-altering drugs, however, is also quite real and, until recently, not a major concern to physicians. Many examples abound. Although now obtained outside of legal channels, amphetamines can still be obtained by abusers through physician prescription. The institution of appropriate controls resulted in a marked reduction in amphetamine prescriptions; however, the ability of amphetamines to enhance analgesia produced by narcotic drugs has resulted in some sports physicians and trainers using this combination to reduce pain in athletes. As might be expected, the use of amphetamines under such situations is associated with a high potential for iatrogenic dependence.

Dependency to barbiturates, nonbarbiturates, and minor tranquilizers can occur readily with relatively short-term consistent use. Whether used for insomnia or anxiety, the benzodiazepines can cause both psychologic and physical dependence. Not infrequently, these agents are prescribed to relieve pain in lieu of appropriate narcotic analgesics, resulting in increasing dosages in order to obtain relief. This only accentuates the potential for subsequent drug abuse and dependence. It is quite important to emphasize that all of the medically available mood-altering drugs are quite effective pharmacologic agents when utilized for the appropriate reasons in a manner consistent with their pharmacology as directed by a physician. In addition, the majority of people not only use these drugs appropriately but may be hesitant to take them even when indicated.

Inappropriate use, however, may present a problem. The 1990 National Household Survey on Drug Abuse found 8.5 million people 12 years or older to have used controlled drugs for nonmedical reasons at least once during the year preceding the survey.[27] Inappropriate use frequently carries with it a real potential for both psychological and physiological dependence. It is the physician's obligation to be aware of the benefits and risks of these drugs and prescribe them accordingly.

Lack of Time Required to Appropriately Address Excessive Drug Use

Of all the medical specialties, primary care physicians generate the least income with the smallest fee per patient visit. Unlike the surgical specialties, there is an inverse relationship between time spent and income derived. Although some third-party carriers do provide medical coverage for inpatient detoxification or treatment for substance abuse, virtually none provide specific reimbursement for the primary care physician to spend the time necessary to identify early signs of drug use or to provide the needed counseling to both the family and patient even when the need to maintain income often prevents the knowledgeable physician from spending the necessary time to address these issues. Recently, the fees paid by Medicare to physicians providing primary care have been adjusted upward in order to allow the physician to spend more time speaking with patients; however, such adjustments are minimal, and the gap between those physicians providing primary as compared to specialty care has not been meaningfully altered. Further, as managed care continues to increase its market share of health insurance, "cost efficient" medical practice will become increasingly important. The amount of time physicians may spend with individual patients will by necessity decrease.

Excessive Prescription of Mood-Altering Drugs

Despite the overall hesitancy of physicians to deal with substance abuse, in certain settings excessive mood-altering drugs may be prescribed. This may be due to a variety of reasons that include the following.

Responding to a Plea for Help

Unintentional or inappropriate prescribing may be a physician's response to a patient's plea for relief of pain or anxiety. When such a request is unaccompanied by any obvious cause of discomfort, supplying the drugs is unwarranted.

Drugs for Profit

Rarely, in a very small number of instances, a physician may intentionally prescribe a drug solely for the purpose of making a profit. Such behavior is no different from that engaged in by other drug dealers and is addressed accordingly by law enforcement agencies. Although the number of physicians involved in this activity is exceptionally small, the amount of drugs prescribed by a single physician can be quite impressive.

The Need to Provide a Quick Solution
to a Long-Standing Problem

It is often easier to prescribe a mood-altering drug to someone expressing anxiety or depressive features than to attempt to understand the reasons for concern and formulate a treatment plan. The prevalence of primary care physicians' use of anxiolytic prescriptions mentioned above is illustrative of this problem. This is of special concern in the elderly. Studies have revealed that between 5 and 21 percent of noninstitutionalized elderly had used a minor tranquilizer in the past year, with many being on these drugs for at least one year, despite evidence that these drugs are not effective when given for more than four weeks.[28]

With respect to the elderly in nursing homes, the problem is even greater. Surveys have demonstrated that up to 50 percent of nursing home residents take psychoactive drugs, with 20 percent receiving more than two drugs concurrently without an appropriate psychiatric diagnosis being made.[28] Although the suggestion has been made that such prescriptions are given mainly to sedate and allow for better behavior control, evidence suggests a more serious issue related to lack of knowledge of the indications and effects of these agents. The observation that many of these prescriptions are inappropriate is suggested by the finding of an educational program for physicians to decrease prescription of antipsychiatric drugs, benzodiazepines, and antihistamine hypnotics in nursing homes by at least twofold compared to that seen in homes where this program did not exist.[29,30] Even without intensive educational programs, however, merely stating approved indications for the use of those drugs has been shown to be effective.

Response of National Organizations

The responsibility of physicians to actively participate in diminishing inappropriate use of both licit and illicit drugs has been acknowledged by the American Medical Association, which has recently published a policy statement emphasizing the importance of the physician's role and formed a national coalition to address the use of tobacco, alcohol, and other substances felt to be harmful to adolescents; this coalition consists of over 35 national organizations and foundations and has published a policy compendium available to all interested parties.[31]

Curricular development in substance-abuse education, initiated over a decade ago through the development of the Career Teaching Program, has resulted in not only an increase in curricular time devoted to those issues but, in addition, the formation of a knowledgeable academic faculty at many medical schools. Their professional organization, the Association of Medical Educators and Researchers in Substance Abuse (AMERSA) continues to expand. The major medical professional organization addressing chemical dependency, the American Society of Addiction Medicine (ASAM), has continued to increase its membership, developed a certification examination to assess competency in this field, and provided educational programs to train Medical Review Officers to deal with drugs in the workplace.

Addiction Medicine has become recognized as a defined field by the American Medical Association, with ASAM having an official delegate in the AMA assembly. The American Psychiatry Association has recognized the importance of this field for psychiatrists through the development of the American Academy of Psychiatrists in Alcoholism and the Addictions (AAPAA). Virtually all psychiatric residencies now provide some training in the addictive behaviors. Finally, well-structured fellowships have developed at several medical centers throughout the country to provide specialty training in alcoholism and other chemical dependencies. Through these programs a cadre of physicians will hopefully be developed that will allow training in this field to be instituted at every medical center.

Defining Goals

The concern expressed by professional organizations, however, is by itself insufficient to address individual physician knowledge and behavior. This concern must be translated into a commitment by the members of these groups to make certain that defined objectives will be met. Fleming has defined a minimum series of competencies that all physicians engaging in primary care should have

(Table 4.2).[32] In order to accomplish this, change in the educational process must occur for both medical students and residents (Table 4.3). Accrediting agencies such as the Liaison Committee on Medical Education and the American Counsel in Graduate Medical Education should monitor the ability of schools to meet these objectives. Residence review committees should make certain all house staff training programs have programs to allow those competencies to develop. Certifying boards should include questions on their certifying examinations to test these competencies. Finally, professional organizations should develop continuing education programs to allow those physicians already in practice the opportunity to attain this knowledge.

Yet despite achieving the objectives, the actual physician patient interaction will remain far from optimal unless the inherent bias toward addictive behavior can be overcome. This involves developing a climate of mutual respect between physician and patient accompanied by open communication, an absence of moral indignation, and an involvement of the patient in the decision-making process.

TABLE 4.2. Minimum Competencies for Physicians Providing Primary Care*

- Ability to screen all patients for alcohol and drug use
- Assessment of problems related to alcohol and drug use
- Assist patients having alcohol or drug problems in achieving an appropriate treatment strategy
- Knowledge of pharmacotherapy for treating alcoholism and other chemical dependencies including nicotine, as well as potential of specific licit mood-altering drugs to cause dependency
- Ability to refer persons to community treatment programs when needed, including family members or close friends of affected person
- Ability to appropriately prescribe analgesics for pain management
- Knowledge of indicators for drug testing

*Adapted from reference 23.

TABLE 4.3. Enhancement of Physician's Role in Addressing Substance Abuse*

Medical School

Develop core group faculty well-versed in substance abuse.

Education to serve as role models to students.

Integrate required educational programs throughout the curriculum to allow students to become knowledgeable about substance abuse as well as overcome existing negative attitudes exhibited toward those who use drugs.

Include required on-site visits to community-based programs to address multicultural issues as well as allow students to see effects of substance-abuse firsthand.

Residency Training

Establish interdisciplinary program in substance abuse that Is offered to all residents, regardless of specialty training.

Address multicultural issues encountered in clinical practice to allow residents to have a better understanding of the relationship of ethnicity to drug-taking behavior.

Develop fellowships in substance-abuse training for those who would like to pursue an academic path in this field.

Include a core of questions pertaining to substance abuse to be part of all specialty certification examinations.

The Physician in Practice

Develop educational programs tailored to meet the need of a specific physician group.

Enhance ability of physicians to detect patterns of inappropriate use of prescriptions.

Provide specific indications for prescription of psychotropic drugs. Sensitize physicians to be aware of patient's smoking history as well as procedures to increase possibility of their quitting.

---

*Modified from Policy Report of the Physician Consortium on Substance Abuse Educators. U.S. Department of Health and Human Services. Health Resource Administration 1991, Washington, DC.[33]

ROLE OF THE PHARMACIST

Until recently, pharmacists were viewed as dispensers of pills rather than integral and critical members of the health care team. As such, they were considerably underutilized, and their ability to help consumers unappreciated by physicians. It should be observed, however, that many consumers *were* aware of their abilities, often coming to pharmacists rather than physicians to obtain medical advice.

At present, both federal and state laws recognize both the pharmacist's abilities and obligations. A pharmacist who fills a prescription that is not legitimate is subject to similar sanctions as is the prescribing physician. Several states have expanded further the pharmacist's role, requiring him/her to counsel patients about the prescriptions filled as well as develop patient profiles. In states with electronic data systems, it is the pharmacist who ultimately has the responsibility of transferring prescription information into the database.

The role of the pharmacist, however, should not just be restricted to assisting the patient. Physician feedback must be provided concerning inappropriate prescriptions, and patients with identical prescriptions from different physicians should be identified as should be persons known to accumulate over-the-counter psychotropic medications for a valid reason. This is not often easy to accomplish as criticizing a physician or restricting a patient's access to drugs may well represent a conflict of interest on the part of the pharmacist and, in addition, is associated with a real potential of a decrease in income. Nonetheless, as the pharmacist's role becomes more prominent, so does his/her responsibility. Evidence suggests that the pharmacist is willing to accept both.

Under third-party carriers and Medicaid programs, prospective drug utilization review has been initiated requiring pharmacists to assess the appropriateness and cost-effectiveness of a prescription prior to supplying the medication. Many programs encourage or even require pharmacists to provide counseling concerning alternatives to therapy as well as side effects of specific drugs. Some advocates even feel that pharmacists should have electronic access to patients' records. Reimbursement to the pharmacist for counseling patients has already been initiated by some third-party carriers.

The Health Care Financing Administration is also evaluating whether such activities will be cost-effective in diminishing inappropriate utilization.[34] Preliminary data suggest that such efforts are at the minimum cost-effective. In Maryland where all pharmacists have access to a Medicaid patient's database, drug expenditures have been reduced by over 7 percent in ten months, at a savings of $6.7 million, just from unfilled prescriptions.[25] Whether or not the medical care provided patients is actually improved, at the least the system does markedly diminish the likelihood of inappropriate use of prescription psychotropic agents.

The pharmacists have responded well to these challenges. Over 80 percent of pharmacies have instituted computer-based information systems facilitating data collection and rapid communication between pharmacists and physicians. The American Pharmaceutical Association has supported the institution of effective drug utilization review programs as well as other efforts to improve the quality of care.[35] As the relationships between physicians and pharmacists continue to develop, not only will both groups benefit, but the public will be better served as well.[26]

REFERENCE NOTES

1. Hearn W. Why don't smokers quit? *Am Med News*, December 27, 1993, 7,8.

2. Health care provider advice on tobacco use to persons aged 10-22 years–United States 1993. *Morbidity and Mortality Weekly Report*, November 10, 1995, 44:826-830.

3. Symptoms of substance dependence associated with use of cigarettes, alcohol, and illicit drugs–United States 1991-1992. *Morbidity and Mortality Weekly Report*, November 10, 1995, 44:830-832.

4. Davis AK, Cotter F, Czechowicz D. Substance abuse units taught by four specialties in medical schools and residency programs. *J Med Ed*, 1988, 63:739-746.

5. Gilman A, Rall, TW, Nies AS, Taylor P (Eds.). *Pharmacologic basis of therapeutics*, 8th edition. New York: Pergamon Press, 1990.

6. Isselbacher KJ, Braunwald E, Wilson JD, Martin JB, Fauci AS, Kasper DL. *Harrison's principles of internal medicine.* New York: McGraw Hill, 1992.

7. Fiore MC, Eps RP, Manley MW. A missed opportunity. Teaching medical students to help their patients to quit smoking. *JAMA*, 1994, 271:624-626.

8. O'Connor PG, Selwyn PA, Schottenfeld RS. Medical Care for injection drug users with human immunodeficiency virus infection. *N Engl J Med*, 1994, 331:450-459.

9. Brecher EM. Licit and illict drugs: The Consumers' Union report on narcotics, stimulants, depressants, inhalants, hallucinogens, and marijuana, including caffeine, nicotine, and alcohol. New York: Consumers' Union, 1972.

10. Freedman D. On the use and abuse of LSD. *Arch Gen Psychiatry*, 1968, 18:330-347.

11. Beardsley RS, Gardocki GJ, Larson DB, Hidalgo J. Prescribing of psychotropic medication by primary care physicians and psychiatrists. *Arch Gen Psychiatry*, 1988, 45:1117-1119.

12. Improving medical education in therapeutics, Health and Public Policy Committee, American College of Physicians. *Ann Intern Med*, 1988, 108:145-147.

13. Bloom JD, Williams MH, Kofoed L, Rhyne C. Resnick M. The malpractice claim experience of physicians investigated for inappropriate prescribing. *Western J Med*, 1989, 151:336-338.

14. Comprehensive drug abuse prevention and control act. Public Law 91-513 and 21 CFS 802(1).

15. Joranson DE. Guiding principles of international and federal laws pertaining to medical use and diversion of controlled substances. In Cooper JR, Czechowicz, DS, Molinari SP, (Eds.). *Impact of prescription, drug diversion control systems on medical practice and patient care.* Rockville, MD: Department of Health and Human Services, National Institute of Drug Abuse, 1993. NIDA Research Monograph 131:19-34.

16. Lurie P, Lee RR. Fifteen solutions to the problems of prescription drug abuse. *J Psychoactive Drugs*, 1991, 23(4):349-357.

17. Weintraub M, Singh S, Byrne L, Maharaj K, Guttmacher L. Consequences of the 1989 New York State triplicate benzodiazepine prescription regulations. *JAMA*, 1991, 266:2392-2397.

18. Eadie JC. New York State's triplicate prescription program. In Cooper JR, Czechowicz DJ, Molinari SP (Eds.). *Impact of prescription drug diversion control systems on medical practice and patient care.* Rockville, MD: Department of Health and Human Services, National Institute of Drug Abuse, 1993. NIDA Research Monograph 131:178-193.

19. Gritchel CT. Existing methods to identify retail drug diversion. In Cooper JR, Czechowicz DJ, Molinari SP (Eds.). *Impact of prescription drug diversion control systems on medical practice and patient care.* Rockville, MD: Department of Health and Human Services, National Institute of Drug Abuse, 1993. NIDA Research Monograph 131:132-140.

20. Prescribing: Legal requirements. A report of the Minnesota Medical Association Committee on Ethics and Medical-Legal Affairs. *Minn Med*, 1989, 72:359-362.

21. Ray WA, Federsiel CF, Schaffner W. A study of antipsychotic drug use in nursing homes: Epidemiologic evidence suggesting misuse. *Am J Public Health*, 1980, 70:485-491.

22. Gurqutiz JH, Soumerai SB, Avorn J. Improving medication prescribing and utilization in the nursing home. *J Am Geriatr Soc*, 1990, 38:542-552.

23. Shorr RI, Fought RL, Ray WA. Changes in antipsychotic drug use in nursing homes during implementation of the OBRA–87 regulations. *JAMA*, 1994, 271:358-362.

24. Porter J, Jick H. Addiction rare in patients treated with narcotics. Letter to the Editor. *N Engl J Med*, 1980, 302:123.

25. Stimmel B. Pain, analgesia and addiction: The pharmacologic treatment of pain. New York: Raven Press, 1983.

26. Maruta T, Swanson DW, Finlayson RE. Drug abuse and dependency in patients with chronic pain. *Mayo Clin Proc*, 1979, 54:241-244.

27. National household survey on drug abuse. Population estimates, 1990, Rockville, MD. National Institute on Drug Abuse, 1991. DHHS (ADM), 91-1732.

28. Ray WS, Federspiel DF, Schaffner W. A study of antipsychotic drug use in nursing homes. Epidemiologic evidence suggesting misuse. *Amer J Public Health*, 1980, 70:485-491.

29. Avorn J, Soumerai SB, Everitt DE, Ross-Degnan D, Beers MH, Sherman D, Salem Schatz SR, Fields D. A randomized trial of a program to reduce the use of psychoactive drugs in nursing homes. *N Engl J Med*, 1992, 327:168-173.

30. Shorr RI, Fought RL, Ray WA. Changes in autopsychotic drug use in nursing homes during implementation of the OBRA-87 regulations. *JAMA* 1994, 27:358-362.

31. Policy Compendium on Tobacco, Alcohol, and Other Harmful Substances Affecting Adolescents. American Medical Association, Chicago, Illinois, 1994.

32. Fleming M. Competences for Substance Abuse Training. In Lewis DL (Ed.). *Training about alcohol and substance abuse for all primary care physicians.* Josiah Macy Jr. Foundation, New York, NY, 1995, 213-247.

33. Policy Report of the Physician Consortium on Substance Abuse Educators. U.S. Department of Health and Human Services. Health Resource Administration, Washington, DC, 1991.

34. Borzo A. Mandated drug review expands role of pharmacists. *Amer Med News*, January 17, 1994, 1, 30.

35. Webb CE. Perspective of the American Pharmaceutical Association. In Cooper JR, Czechowicz DJ, Molinari SP (Eds.) *Impact of prescription drug diversion control systems on medical practice and patient care.* Rockville, MD: Department of Health and Human Services, National Institute on Drug Abuse, 1993. NIDA Research Monograph 131:235-239.

Chapter 5

The White-Collar Crowd

ATTORNEYS AND BANKERS

Attorneys specializing in defending major drug dealers or providing assistance in laundering drug money constitute the "white-powder" bar and receive impressive fees for their efforts. Although one cannot question that drug dealers are entitled to counsel, the additional services often performed, as well as the fees charged, suggest that equality before the law is the least of the compelling motives for mounting a defense.[1]

The appropriateness of these fees has recently been addressed by a Supreme Court ruling that assets of defendants charged with drug trafficking can be seized. This not only may prevent attorneys from being paid for their services but, in addition, due to a subsequent ruling allowing prosecutors to seize money already paid to defense attorneys, may result in their being required to return fees already received. Laundering of money is, of course, illegal, and those attorneys participating in such activities face indictment, as would others. The amount of money accruing to attorneys for direct legal services, however, is minuscule in proportion to the huge profits made in the drug trade and subsequently "laundered" through investment in legitimate enterprises.

Remarkably enough, the enormous profits obtained from illegal drug sales often present problems to those profiting from this enterprise. Although careful records may be kept of such transactions, albeit, usually in one's mind rather than in an account book, the transactions are all in cash and, unfortunately, cash is quite bulky, especially in small denominations which usually accumulate during drug transactions. It has been observed that "drug dealers no longer count their money, they weigh it."[2] As a result, the bulk of the

the money as well as the not infrequent contamination with residues of the illicit drug often makes it easy to identify and associate with drug sales in forensic analysis. In addition, all cash transactions of $10,000 or more must be reported to the Internal Revenue Service and reporting must also occur when this amount is transported across U.S. borders. It is, therefore, quite difficult for the drug traffickers to utilize cash without calling attention to themselves. In order to conceal these profits through conversion of cash into legitimate enterprises, dealers turn to those in the legal and banking professions for assistance. In the past, such cooperation (money laundering) could result in considerable financial benefits associated with little risk.

Money laundering involves the manipulation of illegally obtained funds through a variety of financial institutions to ultimately give the appearance of a legitimate disbursement of funds legally obtained. The preferable immediate conversion to acquisition of cashier's checks and money orders, which then can be transferred to other industries, is usually in transactions of less than $10,000 to avoid reporting. Some of the institutions involved in these transactions are able to provide almost complete secrecy for their investors and are located "off shore" in countries with few regulatory standards. All, however, are "legitimate," and in a global economy facilitate rapid transfer of funds, many of which flow from legitimate sources. The potential for manipulation of funds and avoidance of federal taxes through nonreported income is great. The countries where the majority of banks are located are popularly referred to as "tax havens" due to their lack of concern over depositors' evading taxes, and include Switzerland, the Netherlands entities, Montserrat, Anguilla, British Virgin Islands, Bermuda, The Isle of Mann, Luxembourg, the Bahamas, the Caymen Islands, and the Channel Islands.[3,4] To dispel the idea that tax havens are the resting place of only drug dealers, as described by Lohr, the author notes that in the Caymen Islands alone there are over 540 banks, including branches of 46 of the world's largest institutions.[3] Yet, the incentive to launder money is considerable as demonstrated by the increasing number of banks being formed across the former Soviet Union believed to be specifically developed to participate in the process.[5]

The process of money laundering is often complex and difficult to detect. Cash from drug transactions deposited in various banks in this country may be wire transferred to a single, undercover account in this country and then to foreign banks where certificates of deposits are issued. These certificates are used for collateral for loans in other countries or for a legitimate investment. The proceeds reenter the economic system through the usual channels or are wire transferred to a South American account to be accessed by the drug organizations. The total amount of money involved in these transactions has been estimated to range between $300 and $750 billion annually, of which approximately $60 to $120 billion comes from the United States.[5,6] Profits of between $40 and $100 billion are generated in this country for investment in legitimate businesses in the United States and abroad which may range from the mundane to organ transplantation and nuclear processing.[7,8] The diversion of funds from this country is but one of the detrimental effects of money laundering. Allowing the dealers to profit from their illegal activities is obviously another. A third and less commonly realized threat is the ability of dealers to take over legitimate enterprises by investing in these organizations.

However, the use of illegally obtained income can only be accomplished without attracting attention if it can be made to appear legally acquired. Because the dealers are without the skills to accomplish this by themselves, the assistance of professionals in law and finance is required. These individuals, unlike their clients, are visible and, therefore, vulnerable. Laws directed at this activity can be effective in preventing laundering and can markedly diminish its benefits accruing to the dealers.

An example of the amount of money involved in laundering was recently disclosed by the Office of the Manhattan District Attorney. Setting up a sting operation and thereby creating a fake Caribbean bank, it was able to seize within two years and in only six months of actual operations, $52 million in cash and assets. The bank had handled $39.5 million before it was even officially functioning and had established 41 corporate accounts for traffickers and handled 92 cash transactions totalling $8.9 million as well as 291 noncash transactions. By the time it closed down, it had also seized nine tons of cocaine.[9]

Prior to 1988, little or no effort was devoted to interrupting the flow of these funds; however, in 1988, the Anti-Drug Abuse Act was passed. This act contained provisions to allow monitoring by the Treasury Department of large transfers of funds out of the country as well as providing the Treasury with the ability to contact foreign countries in an attempt to coordinate such efforts. One of the regulations requires U.S. banks to record all deposits of $10,000 or more and report them to appropriate federal authorities. In an attempt to prevent illicit transport of cash from the United States to foreign countries and then back into the economy through foreign banks, foreign nations are required to sign agreements with the United States to prevent concealment of illegal drug profits. This is not too difficult to accomplish as it is more than likely that many banks already have a high index of suspicion of certain clients. In addition, unlike legitimate transactions, those from drug profits are initially virtually all in cash, usually in $100 bills.

A study by the Treasury Department found that over the past decade the percentage of $100 bills in circulation consistency increased to 50 percent of all currency in 1988. Approximately 50 percent of the $5 billion in hundreds printed annually was found to be shipped abroad.[8] A report from the Federal Reserve for the first six months in 1989 noted many banks in areas of great drug activity to record surpluses ranging from between $1.5 billion to $1.8 billion, believed in large part to be drug related. Cash sales for consumer goods have also increased markedly in these areas and are similarly believed to be related to drug trade profits.

Failure of countries to participate in this agreement may be associated with their being excluded from the United States' financial system; however, for reasons less than clear, the commitment of our own government to enforce these regulations is questionable. A confidential Treasury Report in 1990 revealed the dismal failure of the Bush Administration to meet these requirements.[10] As of December 1990, agreements had not yet been reached with Panama, Colombia, the Bahamas, Mexico, Hong Kong, and Peru, just to mention a few countries notorious for their involvement in the drug trade. Even those countries that supposedly are allies in this effort, such as Australia, Canada, Italy, and Spain, had delayed signing agreements. By failing to keep records of such transactions, prosecutors attempting to indict major drug traffickers and dealers are severely hampered.

However, even when an effort is made, at times both the efficiency and commitment can be questioned. The most famous case in point was the Bank of Credit and Commerce International (BCCI), a global operation laundering billions of dollars of drug-related money as well as financing terrorism. This bank was so well connected politically that it has been alleged even the CIA had used it to provide funds for political purposes. Indeed, the CIA was apparently aware that BCCI was involved in money laundering and financing the narcotics trade, gun runners, and terrorist groups years before the scandal broke.[11] Prior to major arrests of officials in the BCCI, millions of dollars were suddenly withdrawn by those known to be active in the drug trade.[12,13] All of this again suggests that competing political and/or profit motives amongst those in a position to seriously affect the profits accruing to illicit drug sales prevent effective action.

Because the motivating force for maintaining the illicit drug trade is money, by identifying those known to be at high risk of being involved in illicit activities, the banking community could accomplish what the drug enforcement agencies have not, a serious disruption of the financial organizations supporting the major drug cartels. This would no longer be seen as a violation of confidentiality as the process to do this has become law. Yet few banks report, and no sanctions have been levied on those who fail to do so. The individuals involved in making these decisions are all "respectable," actively engaged in the financial service, including attorneys, accountants, and stockbrokers. Most of those indicted in money-laundering schemes had not had prior criminal records.[4] In fact, it is the relative lack of prior criminal involvement that makes the "laundering" and professional status of those involved in this activity exceptionally vulnerable to intervention. Those who participate are generally responsive to deterrence and the process by its nature is always accompanied by a paper trail. It is the commitment to enforcement that needs strengthening.

LEGISLATORS

It is certainly difficult to argue that the federal government has not widely disseminated information concerning the adverse effects of smoking and, to a lesser extent, the dangers associated with excessive alcohol consumption. Similarly, although more variably, states and local municipalities have also addressed these issues, and are continuing to do so with increased vigor; however, at times the influence exacted through the industry's contributions to legislators has a not-so-subtle effect on slowing down or a not-too-active pursuit of legislation perceived as harmful.

The Coalition on Smoking on Health in its 1994 report noted that of more than the 1,000 tobacco control bills introduced in Congress over the past 30 years, most did not pass. In the last three election cycles, this group noted that congressional candidates accepted over $9.3 million in contributions from the tobacco industry. Yet, during this time, no official policy concerning regulation of tobacco products was forthcoming.[14]

During the 1991 to 1992 congressional session, the tobacco industry donated approximately $2.4 million to members of Congress with members of the House receiving an average of $2,943 and Senators an average of $11,593.[15,16,17,18] This activity was even more pronounced in California where in 1992 state legislators received $1.24 million, or $10,242 per member, with the Speaker of the House receiving $271,367.

A University of California study of the legislative behavior in promoting tobacco control legislation between 1991 and 1992 found that for every $1,000 in tobacco company contributions, a legislator's "tobacco policy score" would drop.[17] With larger contributions, greater decreases were noted. The odds of opposing tobacco control legislation were found to be directly related to the amount of money received, with House members in the top one-third of tobacco money recipients being 14.4 times more likely to oppose the legislation and being a greater factor than either party affiliation or representing a tobacco-producing state. In fact, at present California legislators are believed to receive almost twice as many campaign contributions from the tobacco industry as members of Congress.[19]

Not infrequently, California legislators' opposition to antismoking regulation often occurred despite opposition to the wishes of a representative's constituency. Proposition 99, which passed in 1988, required 5 percent of the increased state tobacco tax to be used on tobacco-related research and 20 percent directed toward antismoking educational programs. Nonetheless, as much as $200 million may have been diverted from this purpose by the governor and the legislature. This was redressed in January 1995 when a superior court judge ordered the State of California to immediately cease diverting the funds from research and education.[19] Such behavior is irresponsible and serves to call into question the commitment of legislators to act appropriately in addressing the use of all mood-altering drugs. Although this seems and is indeed a lot of money, the rationale becomes clear when one observes the results. On a national level, a proposal for a $2 per pack tax on cigarettes was killed, and in California Proposition 99, which added 25 cents to the state cigarette tax and mandated that 20 percent of the new revenue be spent on tobacco education and prevention, has never been fully implemented.

MANAGEMENT AND DRUG USE

In the past, substance abuse, mainly in the form of excessive alcohol consumption, was tolerated until it became apparent that one was not functioning on the job. The employee was then fired without any attempts at rehabilitation. As the true costs resulting from undetected, excessive alcohol consumption and use of other mood-altering drugs, namely cocaine, became known, employee assistance programs started to develop in the mid-1980s among the larger corporations, with a number of employers even providing health care insurance that included short-term treatment for alcoholism. With the establishment of these programs, the use of other illicit drugs at the workplace also became more noticeable.

The prominence that management is now required to play in addressing this issue did not appear until the late 1980s. In 1988, the Drug Free Workplace Act required all federal grant recipients and federal contractors (where contracts exceeded $25,000) to certify the existence of a drug-free workplace. This required employers to (1) develop and publish a written policy concerning substance abuse agreed upon by employees as a condition of employment; (2) initiate an awareness program to educate employees about the hazards of drug abuse and the existence of available counseling and rehabilitation; and (3) develop employee assistance programs and inform employees of the penalties that might be imposed for violation of a company's policy. In addition, all employees were required to notify their employer of any conviction for a drug offense occurring in the workplace.

A 1989 nationwide survey demonstrated the realization by employers of this issue, with 80 percent identifying weekday use of alcohol and other drugs as a major problem. As observed in Chapter 1 surveys subsequently appeared suggesting that up to two-thirds of regular drug users are employed, with up to one-fifth of workers continuing to use these substances during their workweek with a cost to industry of up to $140 billion annually.[20,21]

This Drug Free Workplace Act was followed by regulations published by the U.S. Department of Transportation (DOT) concerning mandatory random urine testing, urine testing for cause, and urine testing after accidents on all employees under DOT jurisdiction. These regulations affected over 4 million employees and 200,000 companies including natural gas and pipeline workers, motor carriers, and those in the aviation and railroad industries. Finally, the Americans with Disabilities Act of 1990, which became effective in July 1992, offered protection of job security for those persons who had been using illicit drugs who were rehabilitated or actively participating in supervisory rehabilitation programs, providing current drug use did not exist.

As a result of these regulations, at present over 68 percent of companies have instituted employee assistance programs, 55 percent reported training supervisors to spot drug abuse in the workplace, and 52 percent have drug awareness and drug education programs in existence.[18] Urine testing for job applicants exists in almost three-quarters of companies surveyed, an increase of over 246 percent between 1987 and 1992. This has resulted in approximately 30 percent of employees having access to an employee assistance program, and 20 percent being employed in firms with drug-testing programs.[22] A greater awareness of the need to provide treatment or referral services was also found. Approximately two-thirds of companies provided insurance for addiction, with 70 percent of respondents reporting referral as the initial response to a positive drug test rather than dismissal. In addition, the National Drugs Don't Work Partnership was formed by employers in 1993 and is focusing on small companies or businesses, which in the aggregate have 56 million employees, to help them provide employee assistance as well. This is quite important as until recently, of those firms employing less than 50 people, only 10 percent provided employee assistance programs, and fewer than 3 percent required drug testing. Perhaps as a result of these efforts, the number of employees reported testing positive for the presence of drugs diminished from 11 percent in 1989 to less than 4 percent in 1993.[24]

It should be noted that the response of employees to this enhanced interest on the part of management has not been routinely favorable. Although over 80 percent of employees reported drug testing to be an effective deterrent to drug use at work, many unions have protested the use of urine testing, negotiated alterations in testing regimens, and taken their concerns to court. A number of states responding to concerns expressed over violations of civil liberties have restricted workplace drug testing. These states included Connecticut, Iowa, Montana, Rhode Island, Maine, and Vermont.

Most of the controversy has centered around the institution of random urine testing of employees without cause. Although the need for management to recognize and provide rehabilitation for employees who are using mood-altering substances is recognized by all, the effectiveness, validity, and need for randomized urine testing in the absence of cause remains controversial. Further, as businesses move with ever greater speed toward curbing health care costs, benefits provided to employees now appear to be decreasing. The phenomenal rise of for-profit managed care firms to provide health care has resulted in a restriction of health services directed toward substance abuse including the number of days of treatment provided. Once again the concern over drug use in the workforce appears to be accompanied by a restrained commitment to provide appropriate care and rehabilitation.

TEACHERS

Inappropriate use of mood-altering drugs usually begins by early adolescence. Indeed, future use of most mood-altering drugs is unlikely if it has not started by age 20. As a result of this, elementary and high schools become critical sites for early identification of drug use as well as assisting students to develop the skills necessary to refrain from using these agents.

In order to achieve those objectives, teachers must be committed to identify and intervene when a student is recognized as having problems as well as informed of effective prevention techniques and adverse effects of these drugs. They must provide an environment to allow students to feel physically safe from drug dealers, secure in admitting that a personal problem exists, and confident in the knowledge of the risk associated with drugs. Unfortunately, not infrequently, teachers are afraid to intervene due to concerns of civil liability or even personal safety. These fears are not unwarranted. It is incumbent upon school administrations to allay their fears and provide professionals to assist teachers in these roles.

THE "SUBSTANCE ABUSE" PROFESSIONALS

It may seem paradoxical to discuss the role to be played by those currently engaged in rehabilitation of the drug user. One might assume that these individuals are clearly committed to rehabilitation. They often work in a tension-filled environment with minimal resources and, not surprisingly, experience a high rate of burnout and frustration. All of these observations are correct. Rehabilitative efforts are underfunded. Community resources to assist those engaging in treatment are limited and, in general, both salaries and professional respect provided to those pursuing such efforts are less than those in other health care fields. Yet, many in the field remain exceptionally parochial in their efforts to promote rehabilitation and gain funding for their efforts.

Covert and, at times, overt internecine warfare exists between those who advocate a drug-free approach and those who provide pharmacologic therapies, between those who advocate inpatient as compared to outpatient detoxification, and between those who advocate medical as compared to self-help models of treatment. Maintenance therapy for narcotic addiction utilizing methadone, although clearly demonstrated to be an effective approach in addressing narcotic dependency, continues to be roundly denounced by all others in the treatment field. Indeed, the principles behind maintenance are often little understood, even by those working in maintenance programs.

In fact, several large-scale evaluation efforts have shown that any treatment on a continuing basis, whether it be drug-free or maintenance therapy, is equally effective in promoting abstinence. These studies, however, are quite primitive with respect to carefully defining success as well as identifying those who could most benefit from a particular therapy. Such efforts are sorely needed to define which programs should be funded or expanded.

Few programs exist that provide a truly comprehensive approach to rehabilitation, having the ability to assess an individual's needs and then provide the needed services. With the exception of maintenance programs that function under specific, federally mandated admission criteria, many programs' criteria for admission consist of an individual walking through the door "admitting" drug use or, in some instances, hearing of drug use from a family member rather than the actual user. At times, the need to fill beds takes precedence over the patient. As a result, it is not uncommon to learn of persons being admitted for inpatient stays for the short period covered by insurance and then discharged with no means for further therapy. When minors are involved, allegations of involuntary commitments for reasons that are less than clear have also surfaced.

Although these instances are hopefully few and far between, what does prevail is the parochialism and, at times, blind commitment to a particular therapeutic approach. Until such barriers are broken down and the common objective of providing the best possible care is realized by all those in the field of rehabilitation, the outcome will never be optimal. The street slogan, "different strokes for different folks," is particularly apt to the rehabilitative process. Individualized assessment and treatment plans are essential, yet rarely addressed.

REFERENCE NOTES

1. Lewis NA. Drug lawyers' quandary: Lure of money vs ethics. *The New York Times*, Friday, February 9, 1990, p. A:1, B:5.

2. State Drug Laws for the 90's, Vol. 4. Alexandria, VA: American Prosecutors Research Institute, 1991.

3. Robson JE. Complex wash cycle for dirty drug money. *The Wall Street Journal*, May 29, 1991, Sec. A:11.

4. Lohr S. Offshore banking's umbrella shields more than BCCI. *The New York Times*, August 11, 1991, Sec. 4:2.

5. Cowell A. Laundering of crime cash troubles U.N. *The New York Times*, November 25, 1994, Sec. A:17.

6. Drugs crime, and the justice system. A national report: Washington, DC: The Bureau of Justice Statistics, 1992.

7. Culhane C. Feds try to clean up money laundering racket. *U.S. Journal*, 1989, 13(2).

8. Genter J. Vast flow of cash threatens country, banks, and economics. *The New York Times*, April 11, 1988, Sec. A:12.

9. Janofsky MJ. Fake bank set up by U. S. agents snares drug money launderers. *The New York Times*, December 17, 1994, Sec. 1:1.

10. Labaton S. Plan on drug cash not being pushed. *The New York Times*, December 16, 1990, Sec. A:37.

11. Morgenthau BT, Waller D, Thomas R, Waldman S. The CIA BCCI. *Newsweek*, August 12, 1991, p. 16-21.

12. Baquet D. Drug dealers fast withdrawals raise suspicion in bank inquiry. *The New York Times*, October 27, 1991, Sec. 1.1.

13. Global scandal, ragged response. *The New York Times*, July 24, 1992, Sec. A:20.

14. Marwick C. Tobacco control report card fails some Federal entities, gives all tough future assignments. *JAMA*, 1994, 271:645, 647.

15. Moore S, Wolfe SM, Lindes D, Douglas, CE. Epidemiology of failed tobacco control legislation. *JAMA*, 1994, 272: 1171-1175.

16. Glantz SA, Begay ME. Tobacco industry campaign contributions are affecting tobacco control policymaking in California. *JAMA*, 1994, 272:1176-1181.

17. Begay ME, Traynor M, Glantz SA. The tobacco industry, state politics and tobacco education in California. *Am J Public Health* 1993, 83:1214-1221.

18. Warner KE. Profits of doom. *Am J Public Health,* 1993, 83:1211-1213.

19. Skolnick AA. Judge rules diversion of antismoking money illegal. Victory for the California Tobacco Control Program. *JAMA*, 1995, 273:610-611.

20. Keeping score: What we are getting for our federal drug control dollars. New York: *Drug Strategies*, 1995. The Carnegie Corporation.

21. Langenbucher SW, McCrady BS, Brick J, Easterly R. Addictions treatment in workplace: Populations. In socio-economic evaluations of addictions treatment: Executive summary, Washington, DC: President's Commission on Model State Drug Laws, Center of Alcohol Studies, Rutgers University, 1993.

22. Hogan CM. Substance abuse: The nation's number one health problem. Princeton, NJ: Robert Wood Johnson Foundation, 1993.

23. Survey of employer anti-drug programs. Washington, DC: Department of Labor, U.S. Bureau of Labor Statistics, 1989.

24. Snapshots. *USA Today*, October 10, 1995.

Chapter 6

The Federal Strategy:
A Blueprint for Failure

We have spent an increasing amount of money over the past two decades in an attempt to curtail illicit drug use. Between 1970 and 1995, federal antidrug expenditures rose from $129.5 million to over $13.2 billion. Between 1981 and 1995 we have spent close to $100 billion in federal and almost $150 billion in state and local funds.[1] The current administration led by President Clinton initially announced a $71 million increase in spending to a total of $58 billion in four years.[2] Unfortunately, almost 65 percent of these funds remain targeted toward enforcement carried out by an impressive array of agencies, including our armed forces, with the proportion devoted to prevention remaining relatively constant since 1990. In the 1995 budget requests, this imbalance was recognized by the President, who allocated 40 percent of the budget for demand reduction, but congressional approval resulted in maintaining the federal form on law enforcement or supply control efforts. Of course, a multitude of state and local task forces are also committed to interdiction.

Despite this considerable infusion of funds, our current efforts to eliminate illicit drugs have been far from successful. The reasons for this are clear and must be addressed if we truly wish to diminish illicit drug use. Reducing the supply of/or demand for licit substances, mainly alcohol, nicotine, and prescription drugs, although not necessarily easier to achieve and certainly no less important, presents issues quite different from those involving the use of substances currently prohibited by law and will not be discussed here.

Many suggestions have been made to prevent, reduce, or even eliminate the use of illicit mood-altering drugs. All can be grouped into four categories that describe the current government initiatives: those affecting the supply, those affecting the demand, those involving the treatment and rehabilitation of individuals who are already dependent, and the support of research and evaluation (Table 6.1). The reasons for our failure to diminish illicit drug use is directly related to disproportionate emphasis on restricting supply and diminishing demand through deterrence as compared to education and treatment. Although, philosophically not unreasonable, pragmatically, effective restriction of supply is not possible to achieve. In addition, although not pleasant to confront, the commitment of our elected officials toward this goal often takes a back seat to other political priorities.

ATTACKING THE SOURCE

Diminishing Foreign Production

A formal commitment on the part of the government to eliminate the supply of illicit drugs began in the early 1970s, when countries identified by the State Department as playing major roles in the production of illicit drugs were contacted in an attempt to encourage them to use their own resources for crop reduction, including developing more active law enforcement efforts. Our own "incentives program" consisted of providing funds to allow farmers to substitute crops without experiencing severe financial loss, making available our own law enforcement expertise, and providing financial aid and equipment to local law enforcement efforts. In 1986, Congress passed a law allowing the President to impose economic sanctions on any country identified by the State Department as being a site of major drug-producing or -distributing activities.

Because the countries where illicit substances are currently being produced or packaged for distribution are well known (Table 6.2) and, our foreign aid to some of these nations not at all inconsiderable, one might think that encouraging local law enforcement efforts while providing incentives toward those who did not participate would meet with success. Unfortunately, this has not been the case. The reasons for this are all too readily apparent. Attacking the problem at its perceived source, that of the farmer whose livelihood

TABLE 6.1

Current Approaches to Control Illicit Drug Use

Reduce Supply
At source:
    Crop reduction; substitution; spraying with herbicides
    Aid to local law enforcement agencies
    Withholding aid from those countries not taking an active role in preventing
       production and distribution
Prevent drugs from entering the country
Prevent chemicals needed to manufacture other illicit drugs from leaving the
    country
Prevent distribution and sales within country
Maximize criminal penalties

Reduce Demand
Deterrence
  a) Increase penalties associated with use so as to diminish desire to take drugs:
     criminal vs. social
  b) User accountability: All users, regardless of type of drug, subject to criminal
     penalties
  c) Zero tolerance: Distributors, sellers, and users all subject to penalties
  d) Initiate widespread drug testing
Prevention: Educate as to the adverse effects of drugs

Treatment and Rehabilitation Efforts
Support of Research and Evaluation of Effective Strategies

depends on producing these crops has been, with one exception, a failure. Although a potentially successful solution, crop substitution is extremely expensive and, therefore, limited in its ability to effectively reduce the supply of drugs. As demonstrated in Turkey, a past major supplier of opium, crop substitution was successful, due to a large infusion of funds to assist farmers to switch to less profitable crops. Unfortunately, their role in opium cultivation was quickly taken over by farmers in other countries. This is not surprising, for the real problem is not the farmer but the poverty in which he or she lives. We clearly do not have sufficient resources for crop substitution to be sufficiently successful to effectively diminish the producing of illicit drugs.

Crop destruction is an equally unsuccessful policy.[2] In 1991 only 7,000 of 213,000 (3 percent) hectares of coca crops were eliminated, with 11,000 of 239,000 (5 percent) hectares of opium crops

TABLE 6.2

Sources of Production of Illicit Drugs	
Heroin	Golden Triangle: Laos, Thailand, Burma
	Golden Crescent: Iran, Afghanistan, Pakistan, Mexico, Turkey
	South America: Colombia
	Mexico
Cocaine	Bolivia, Peru, Colombia, Argentina, Brazil
Marijuana	Colombia, Jamaica, Mexico, United States

destroyed. We were much more successful in Latin America with marijuana where we were able to eliminate 12,000 of 33,000 (36 percent) hectares; however, the effects of "elimination" of Latin American marijuana crops highlights the failure of this policy even when successful. Our destruction of marijuana fields in Mexico was initially quite effective. The result of this, however, was not administered supply, but rather a "boosting" of our "home-grown" marijuana, now believed to be raised in most states, with Missouri, Oklahoma, Nebraska, Hawaii, and Kentucky among the top five. Not only has the United States taken over 18 percent of the production of marijuana consumed in this country but, in addition, we produce sinsemilla, a far more potent type of plant. Furthermore, the worldwide production of these drugs continues to increase, with the production of coca leaf rising from 294,000 metric tons in 1988 to 331,000 metric tons in 1991. Even the economy of the illicit drug trade ultimately was not affected. At present, it is believed that Mexico has now become the major site of illicit laboratories to produce methamphetamine, under the auspices of well-organized syndicates.[3] The profit margin is quite similar to that previously existing with marijuana with an investment of $3,500 for a pound of speed bought from one of those laboratories selling for over $35,000 at the street level.

The hesitancy on the part of many governments to take an active role in enforcement activities also has been well documented. Not infrequently, the profits involved are so great as to corrupt local or even national leaders. From Vietnam to current governments in Central and South America, the Far East, and the Middle East, involvement of various officials in the drug trade has been observed. The profits accruing from drug sales in these countries are truly impressive. It was estimated that trafficking in Colombian cocaine nets $20 billion annually.[4] The recent allegation that airport policy officials were charging a flat per kilogram fee to allow cocaine to pass through Colombia's security system undetected is, therefore, less than surprising.[5] In Bolivia, one dealer is alleged to have offered to pay his country's foreign debt of $3.8 billion if the narcotic laws were not enforced. In 1980, when $100 million in American aid to Bolivia was suspended due to its "indifference" to the drug trade, various government offices were estimated to be receiving approximately $1.5 billion per year from narcotic traffickers.

Indeed, the production of these drugs has been exceptionally helpful to these countries' economies. Over one million people in South America are believed to be actively engaging in growing coca, with 5 to 6 percent of Bolivia's population in some manner employed in cocaine production. Because routes of transport are needed to get the crops to shipping cartels, local communities also benefit by the construction of roads and bridges. Finally, the general economy of an area may be improved as profits from the drug trade are reinvested in economies of local communities.

Colombia: A Study in Failure

Perhaps no country illustrates the failure of our offshore drug policy more than Colombia, a country long known to be pivotal in supplying cocaine and, more recently, heroin to the United States. The magnitude of the role that cocaine plays in the Colombian economy is difficult to imagine but has been estimated to be $3.5

billion annually or 5 percent of the gross national product.* In the past, many Colombian officials have committed themselves to addressing this problem at both political and personal risk. Over the past several years, more than 20 judges dealing with narcotic offenses have been killed, and an attorney general murdered, all for their opposition to the drug cartels. Over 2,000 police were killed in action against traffickers and hundreds of civilians have been killed in periodic acts of terrorism by the drug cartels to show their power and indifference. Despite the fact that in 1990 Colombian authorities destroyed over 300 processing laboratories, confiscated over 50 metric tons of cocaine, and arrested 7,000 traffickers, the country still remains the leading supplier of cocaine.

Further, it now appears that the Colombian government has finally tired of fighting this "war." Unable to enforce the law, the president of Colombia negotiated with one of the major dealers to accept arrest, incarceration in a prison of his choice, lenient sentencing, and no extradition to the United States. The prison and guards alleged to have been "hand picked" by the drug lord resulted in little, if any, interruption of flow of cocaine through Colombia but, a "cosmetic soothing" to the United States. Nonetheless, when the president of Colombia became concerned that a trial was not forthcoming and, under a new law, the "prisoner" might be released, a "speedy trial" was ordered. The result, as predicted, was an "escape," alleged to be facilitated by a $1.5-million payment to prison guards.[6,7] In fact, it is alleged that $6 billion of profits from cocaine cut across all levels of government with the majority of government institutions recognized to have been infiltrated by the cartels.[2] This infiltration is alleged to have reached all levels of government, even that supporting the presidency.[8,9]

In Colombia, therefore, despite all of the efforts of the Colombian and U.S. governments, not only has cocaine production increased but, in addition, Colombian farmers have now made major inroads in the production of heroin as well as marijuana.[6,10] This is despite the glut of opium on the world market suggesting that the Colombian cartels are trying to develop more cost-effective ways of getting heroin to the United States.[11] And, of course, the flow of drugs is independent of which cartel controls the Colombian co-

---

The New York Times, November 24, 1995.

caine market. Despite the intensive and finally successful effort to capture Pablo Escobar Gavira, the head of the Medellin Cartel, his death and the apparent dismantling of his organization have had little or no effect on cocaine traffic. In fact, the rival Cali cartel that had been growing in strength, in no part due to the focus of the Colombian government on Escobar, has not only become dominant, but has maintained an uninterrupted flow of cocaine to the United States. This cartel will be even more difficult to stop as it appears to be pursuing less violence and appears to be better organized.[12,13] The only issue concerning the Colombian drug trade appears to be which dealer will assume prominence.

It is doubtful that anything the United States does will have a meaningful impact on the drug trade within Colombia. Indeed, the view expressed by many Colombians toward us is not at all kindly. Polls taken during the recent national elections have found Colombians to place concern with illicit drug traffic below their distress over traffic jams.[5] Extradition of drug traffickers to the United States for trial was banned by a constitutional assembly, and a plea-bargaining policy, ostensibly to encourage dealers to leave the drug trade, has been conceived as being so lenient as to amount to pardons. Not without reason, it is argued that were it not for the demand for cocaine in the United States, the destabilizing force that cocaine has produced in Colombia would not exist. Nonetheless, the United States continues to give Colombia millions annually for its law enforcement efforts despite the government's refusal to extradite many dealers and their ready acceptance of plea bargains. Even with a recent admission that, in fact, Colombia has ceased actively to try to diminish illicit drug traffic, no sanctions are being considered due to our "political interests" in maintaining the Colombian economy. The statement of Colombia's president to crack down on the cartels has been considerably softened by the increasing concern over his acceptance of campaign funds from these very cartels.[14,15]

The Political Realities

In countries that are politically unstable, illicit drug production appears to play a major economic role for each of the opposition groups. In Peru, a nation in political turmoil, cocaine is felt to be crucial to the economy, growing over half of the world's cocaine crops. Approximately one million of the country's population of 21 million are felt to be involved in some way in the production of this drug.[16] The Central Bank of Peru is alleged to take in $4 million to $5 million daily from the cocaine trade. The drug routes are believed to be controlled by the guerrilla group, Shining Path; however, allegations concerning corruption of local police and even the army have appeared.[17,18] Interception by police is estimated at less than one-half of one percent of the annual cocaine crop, which has reached 600 tons; two-thirds of the world's production now involves 300,000 Peruvians.

Another factor diminishing our efforts to limit supply is that a number of countries involved in production are our political allies. Economic sanctions against these countries have been viewed by some at the State Department as not being compatible with achieving our own overall political goals. During the Vietnam War, the Meo tribesmen, strongly supported by the United States as a bulwark against the communist forces, were a major source of opium. The Iran-Contra Hearings demonstrated our own complicity in transporting illicit drugs on government-financed flights.[19] The involvement of the government in Panama with drug dealing had been known for almost two decades, and, yet, only recently has action been taken. At the trial of General Manuel Noriega, former leader of Panama, evidence was presented to suggest that both the Reagan Administration and the Colombian Medellin Cartel were working to elect several candidates.[20] Yet, despite our invasion of this country and the arrest and conviction of its leader, it is alleged that the drug trade in Panama continues to flourish. Perhaps this is not surprising. The current president of Panama, an individual fully supported by our government, has been alleged to have been a senior official of a bank accused by the Drug Enforcement Agency of being a major link in laundering Colombia's cocaine cartel funds.[21]

Nigeria, a country increasingly involved in the drug scenario, has been only recently officially "cited" as a major drug trafficker.[22] For years it has been known that Nigerian-run drug networks have provided up to one-third of the heroin entering the United States.

The Nigerian government has steadfastly refused to crack down on traffickers or cooperate in extradition efforts.

Paraguay, Laos, and Lebanon have all been shown to be far from fully cooperating with drug enforcement efforts, yet have not been sanctioned. In fact, economic sanctions of countries not fully cooperating in preventing illicit drug production and distribution have rarely been used against a nation considered an ally. Even if action were to be taken, the loss of our financial support to that country may well be matched by the profits from the drug trade.

With respect to our oldest and closest ally, Mexico, cooperation in the drug war continues to flounder. Despite our aid to Mexican authorities in their antidrug efforts, which approximated $48 million in 1990, allegations of corruption and lack of commitment on the part of Mexican authorities persist. In fact, according to several Mexican officials who abandoned their war against drugs, the "overriding impediment to capturing major traffickers is drug-related corruption at all levels of the Mexican state."[23] This was further highlighted by a shoot-out between Mexican soldiers and Mexican drug agents, as well as the action of our Drug Enforcement Agency in abducting a Mexican physician alleged to have participated in the murder of a DEA agent. As a result, Mexico has decided to no longer accept U.S. aid to assist in antidrug efforts.[24] It has been alleged that our government was well aware of all these activities, but in an attempt to stabilize the Mexican economy failed to act aggressively.[25,26]

Evidence has appeared suggesting that an intelligence service created in Haiti with Central Intelligence Agency (CIA) support to combat cocaine distribution has actually become actively involved in the trade.[27] Despite receiving between $500,000 and $1 million annually, little information concerning the drug trade was obtained. In addition, several members of the service became involved in drug sales. It is now acknowledged that the antidrug unit actually was responsible for sending a ton of cocaine to the United States in 1990, which ultimately was sold on the streets.[28] Although no one in the unit is believed to have personally profited, this fiasco highlights not only the futility of our actions but the potential to inadvertently actually further the illicit drug trade.

Alternatively, we have had minimal or no relationships with other countries where production occurs and, therefore, competing political interests often shape our response to their involvement in the drug trade. Thus, although Syria and Afghanistan were the first two countries to be eliminated as eligible to receive foreign aid, in fact, they had been receiving neither economic nor military assistance. Remarkably enough, as politics change, so do "bedfellows." Our current approach is to establish friendship with Syria despite its support for terrorism and its involvement in Middle East heroin traffic.[29] With respect to Afghanistan, in an attempt to contain Soviet influence, the CIA gave billions to the Afghan rebels in arms as well as cash using the Bank of Credit and Commerce International, an institution also favored by the major drug dealers for laundering these funds.[30] Heroin has now become Afghanistan's major cash crop controlled by the rebel groups placed in power by the CIA. Afghanistan produces approximately one-third of the heroin reaching the United States, and also ships large quantities to Europe and Central Asia.[31]

Similarly, we have supported Pakistan where, as described by McCoy, the political and military establishments participated in transporting heroin through the country toward the United States.[32] Myanmar, formerly Burma, is still allowed to trade with the United States, despite the known complicity of its authorities in allowing the country to produce heroin believed to supply 70 percent of our country's illicit use, approximating 12 tons of heroin annually. This is only a fraction of the estimated 2,400 tons of opium grown each year, making Myanmar the world's largest producer.[33,34] This hypocrisy is not restricted to the United States. Companies in Britain, Canada, Japan, Australia, and India also promote trade with Myanmar, and India is alleged to be supplying chemicals to produce heroin not only to Myanmar but to Pakistan and Afghanistan as well.[35]

Finally, as a last and perhaps most recent example, our relationship with Russia, with respect to the drug trade, leaves much to be desired. At present, the former USSR, estimated to produce 25 times more hashish than any other country, is rapidly approaching the Golden Triangle in the production of opium, and is a transshipment point for heroin headed to Europe as well as New York. Indeed, with the destabilization of the "communist block" countries, one of the most sought-after jobs is drug dealer. Eastern Europe has become a focal point for traffic in illicit drugs.[36] More interceptions of heroin have been reported in Bulgaria and Hungary than western Europe.[37] Yet, despite the fact that the State Department knows this, Russia was not listed among either producer or transporter countries in the International Narcotics Strategy Report of 1992.[38]

In summary, despite reports from our State Department since 1986 detailing the countries involved in the drug trade whose governments did little to intervene in such activity, no ally of ours has ever received economic sanctions for failure to act. At present sanctions exist only against Afghanistan, Myanmar, Iran, Nigeria, and Syria. More important, although Bolivia, Laos, Panama, Peru, and Lebanon are also felt to be noncooperative, economic sanctions remain waived because of "vital interests."

Thus, in spite of all of our efforts and, perhaps in no small way as a result of the factors mentioned above, world production of these substances continues to increase. Between 1987 and 1991, opium production increased by 52 percent, marijuana by 72 percent, and cocaine by 15 percent. In terms of metric tons, the figures for worldwide products are quite impressive: 337,000 for cocaine, 23,000 for marijuana, and 3,400 for opium.

Preventing Illicit Drugs from Entering the United States

Once a drug has been harvested or refined in other countries, prevention of its entry to the United States to the extent that the street supply will actually decrease has proven an almost impossible task. It has been estimated that in 1991, 438 million people entered or reentered the country on 586,000 planes, 128 million vehicles, and 157,000 vessels.[39] A single cargo ship carrying cocaine can supply all of the cocaine users for this country's one-year use. Despite the best efforts by the Coast Guard, only 4 percent of the vessels boarded are found to contain drugs. Even when operating with informants, who at times may be planted by drug dealers to purposely mislead, only 12 percent of boardings result in drug seizures.

The ability to intercept aircraft is no less difficult. Unlike a ship, a plane is only susceptible to interdiction for short periods of time.

Flying drugs across the Mexican border may result in a plane being in United States' airspace for less than 30 minutes. A plane landing on a makeshift field can be unloaded and in the air again before interdiction is possible. Attempting to identify those travelers who are wittingly or unwittingly smuggling drugs from among the millions of people who cross our borders each year is equally difficult. Identification of profiles of passengers at high risk for smuggling drugs, and the use of dogs trained to "sniff out" illicit substances can result in seizures of impressive quantities of drugs, but do little to effectively reduce the supply. Yet despite all of those obstacles, the Customs Service does manage to make 19,000 seizures annually with a retail value of over $12 billion and a total weight of over 1 million pounds.[40] The flow of illicit drugs, however, continues.

Frustration with our current efforts on interdiction has resulted in the military becoming actively involved in the war on drugs. Military involvement has concerned many, not the least the commanders of our armed forces, who question both the appropriateness and effectiveness of increased military involvement.[41] This question was recently reviewed by the Rand Corporation, which, on the basis of a comprehensive analysis, concluded that a major increase in military support would be unlikely to significantly decrease drug consumption in this country.[42] Yet, despite these concerns, military involvement was initiated and 71 percent of its $1.17 billion anti-drug budget was devoted to interception of drugs entering the country. A recent assessment of the effort by the military has confirmed the Rand Corporation analysis, with the Pentagon now planning to shift its priorities away from interception efforts.[43]

In fact, there have been only two times in our history when drugs were effectively prevented from entering this country. The first was during the allied naval embargo during World War II, alleged to be successful due to support by organized crime. The second and more recent was the effect of our trade embargo against Haiti, which was alleged to have not only sharply restricted the flow of cocaine through Haiti to the United States, but also to have deprived several political and military leaders of millions of dollars;[44] however, while affecting the personal wealth of some Haitians, those in the "trade" merely opened alternate routes. In fact, short of the establishment of a totalitarian state, interception will never be effective.

THE RESULTS
OF LAW ENFORCEMENT EFFORTS

The amount of money spent on law enforcement, over 60 percent of the federal budget, is truly impressive, in no small part resulting in the United States having one of the world's highest incarceration rates. In absolute terms, this amount increased by $6.3 billion between 1981 and 1991, with the amount of funds from the federal budget allotted to state and local authorities increasing by 37-fold during this time. Of this amount, interdiction efforts were responsible for 27 percent and correctional programs for drug law violators for 19 percent. States and municipalities spent close to $5.2 billion on enforcement in 1988, with 18 percent of all law enforcement spending being for drug control activities.

Seizure of illicit drugs and arrests through federal, state, and local law enforcement efforts in this country increase each year. Between 1980 and 1988, arrests by state and local police for sales and/or manufacture of illicit drugs increased by 180 percent with 287,858 arrests made in 1988 alone.[45] In 1988, the efforts of the Drug Enforcement Agency, the U.S. Customs Service, and the U.S. Coast Guard resulted in the seizure of approximately 222,000 pounds of cocaine, 2,000 pounds of heroin, and more than 3 million pounds of marijuana. The DEA destroyed 107 million plants in this country and closed over 800 illicit laboratories.

In 1992, state and local agencies made over 1 million arrests (8 percent of all arrests) for drug abuse violations with 66 percent for posession rather than sale. The number of prosecutions for drug offenses increased by 153 percent between 1980 and 1987, with the number of convictions increased by 161 percent as compared to a 49 percent increase in all U.S. court convictions for other federal offenses. Convictions for drug offenses increased from 17 percent of all defendants convicted in 1980 to 51 percent in 1987, with over 80 percent of drug defendants tried in U.S. district court being convicted in 1990. Between 1985 and 1993, the proportion of drug offenders in federal prisons increased from 34 to 61 percent, with 25 percent of all federal prisoners being low-level offenders.[1,46]

However, despite these arrests, convictions, and the impressive recent seizures of cocaine, cocaine imports have risen by 150 percent, and the price of cocaine has decreased on the street by 10 to 40 percent due to a market glut. This drop in price has so affected distributors, that gangs have been crossing territorial lines to fight for control of the market. This is not surprising when one considers that approximately 25 times more cocaine is produced annually than that seized. With respect to heroin, of the 3,000 tons grown in 1987, no more than 70 are estimated to be needed to supply the demand in this country. The average purity of heroin, which was 5.3 percent in 1985, had increased to 37 percent in 1993 with purity of heroin from southeast Asia ranging from 54 percent to 70 percent.

In fact, our inability to meaningfully affect either the production of drugs in other countries or their transport into this country is markedly limited. This observation has been made not only by critics of our current drug policies but by supporters as well. Robert Bonner, the former head of our main drug enforcement agency agreed that the United States was ill prepared to successfully battle the cartels and that military involvement in interruption efforts was not of value.[36] Nonetheless, the focus continues to be on enforcement. It should be observed that this is not exclusively a problem of the United States. Cocaine markets have expanded in most European countries, Russia, and China, even as worldwide production of cocaine has decreased between 1992 and 1993. This decrease, however, is believed to be more related to a fungus that attacked Peruvian crops rather than enforcement efforts.

The Relationship Between Active Enforcement and the Cost of Dealing

When one considers the profit in the illicit distribution and sales of drugs, it is easy to see why our attempts to discourage trafficking have not been successful. The greatest profits, proportionally, are not made outside of the country, but occur once the drug has entered the United States and is further cut for distribution and sales (Table 6.3). It has been estimated that gross revenues from all drug sales in the United States approximate $120 billion per year, with a profit margin of up to $100 billion. After laundering in banks, a large proportion is then reinvested in legal business. The economic risk to the dealer of increased interdiction or confiscation of drugs is therefore, not great. Even if a shipment of cocaine worth $200,000 is lost

TABLE 6.3

Prices Associated with Distribution of Illicit Drugs (per kg) [1]			
	Cocaine [2]	Heroin [3]	Marijuana
Transporter	$ 40	$ 90 (opium)	
Refiner	$ 295	$ 450 (morphine base)	
Exporter	$ 3,900 [4]	$ 5,000	$ 450-2,700 $ 500-4,000 (sinsemilla)
Distributor Wholesale Midlevel Retailer	$ 16,000 $ 272,000 $ 2,720,000	$ 70,000 - $140,000 [4] $ 160,000 - $700,000 $275,000 - $1,250,000	$3,200-$4,800
Single-Unit Prices	Vial $5-$10 (Crack) Cocaine $25-$125	Hits $5-$46	Bags $25-$200

[1] Approximate values. Prices vary greatly depending on source.

[2] Coca Paste: 3 pounds produced from 345 pounds dry leaf; Cocaine base: 1 pound produced from 1 pound base; Cocaine Powder: 1 pound produced from 0.5 pound cocaine; Crack: 0.9 pounds produced from 1 pound powdered cocaine

[3] Morphine Base: 1 pound produced from 10 pounds opium; Heroin: 1 pound (70-90% pure) produced from 10 pounds opium; Heroin Binder: 10-100 pounds produced from diluting 1 pound heroin; Heroin Bags: 4,000 single dose bags produced from 1 pound heroine

[4] Prices per kg vary from $ 16,000 -$20,000.

on arrival to this country, the actual cost to the dealer is less than $5,000. Even larger seizures will have minimal effect on the cost of the drug or the dealer's economic risk. As demonstrated in the Rand Corporation study, if total seizures rise by 58 percent, there is only a 4 percent increase in cost of delivery of drug to the street. If the cost of coca leaves would triple, the street price would increase only by 2 percent. The economic resources available to the smuggler are such that major increased efforts at interdiction can be readily economically negated.

The personal risks to dealers are also not great. Although more severe sentences are currently being given, assets are being seized and, in the most recent antidrug legislation, the death penalty is permitted for murder occurring during a drug operation, most drug traffickers spend less than 40 percent of their sentence in prison. In New York City, although 34,000 were arrested for drug offenses in the last four years, only 13,466 were convicted, with only slightly more than 4,000 being imprisoned. The risk to the midlevel dealer is, therefore, slight compared to the tremendous profits that can accrue. Even with the "man on the street" at the lowest level of distribution, the risk/benefit ratio is favorable. An enterprising street dealer, usually an adolescent, can clear $800 to $900 per week from cocaine sales.[47] It has been estimated that a dealer making 1,000 transactions a year in Washington, DC faces an imprisonment risk per transaction of 1:4, 500.[48]

For someone who has nothing, at times not even a place to stay, the risk of incarceration compared to the potential profits must seem minimal. Perhaps this is the reason why 52 percent of all drug traffickers released from prison after an average sentence of five years are rearrested within three years. It is apparent that the real personal risk in drug sales comes not from law enforcement but rather from competitors who, in an attempt to maintain control over markets, will frequently resort to murder to eliminate the competition. In such situations, the public at large is also at risk. Not infrequently, the violence is diffuse and, innocent bystanders are more often victims than are the intended targets.

Finally, although hopefully rare, one of the reasons for ineffective enforcement is the corruption on the part of some public officials and police who on a daily basis confront this issue and may become tainted by it. A study by Zeese reported an average of two public officials per week linked to drug-related corruption.[49] Similarly, the opportunity on the part of police to have access to large amounts of confiscated cash, bad drugs, as well as advance information on raids may tempt some to "cross the line."[50]

It is, therefore, apparent that devoting the major part of our efforts to address the supply side of the problem has been and will remain less than successful. It was remarkable that this policy remained so actively pursued by President Bush as he, more than any other individual, through his experience as Director of the CIA and as Vice President charged with monitoring drug enforcement efforts, was aware of the limitation of this approach. It is equally discouraging that the current administration under President Clinton has allocated $2 on law enforcement for every $1 on treatment, with the requested priorities of the $13.1 billion budget almost identical to those of previous administrations. This is despite the fact that the military has realized its ineffectiveness in intercepting drugs and announced its plan to decrease the amount it now spends on drug interception.[51] Even the admission by the former head of the Drug Enforcement Agency that the United States is ill-prepared to combat the drug cartels and is wasting money on drug interception has not served to alter this emphasis on interdiction over education and treatment.[36] What has changed is the emphasis on the focus of reducing supply. Rather than focusing on tracking and seizing, now enforcement will be directed toward destruction of laboratories. This, too, will undoubtedly prove equally unsuccessful.

The decision to emphasize curtailing supply continues, despite the overwhelming evidence that it is demand that must be affected in order for drug use to decrease. The National High School Surveys clearly document that although students perceived availability of drugs more steadily since 1984, rates of drug use continued to diminish. In 1992, although eighth and tenth graders reported a significant increase in the availability of cocaine and crack, the decrease in prevalence of its use diminished by more than 66 percent. This is not to say that efficient and effective measures to diminish supply should not be reviewed and improved upon; however, it is only through diminishing demand that a timely and effective approach to illicit drug use can be developed.

AFFECTING DEMAND

Diminishing demand for mood-altering drugs may be accomplished by a variety of means which pragmatically, can be grouped as either "the carrot or the stick" approach. These include deterrence, prevention through education, and provision of viable alternatives to drug use. Unfortunately, the focus of the government remains on deterrence, suboptimally addressing prevention and treatment, and doing little to provide viable alternatives.

Deterrence

Reduction of demand through deterrence has been advocated by many and, similar to diminishing supply, is a major focus of government activities. The rationale for deterrence is that if the risk is sufficiently great, one will not use drugs regardless of the pleasure obtained or the discomfort experienced when abstinent. At its most basic level, deterrence requires that illicit drug use be associated with sanctions, civil or criminal, similar to, though perhaps not as severe as, those associated with dealing. Two of the most prominent examples of the failure of deterrence as a primary policy occurred in California and New York State.

In California, in 1968, increasing concern over marijuana use resulted in the possession of marijuana being considered a felony, carrying with it a penalty of one to ten years in prison for the first offense and life imprisonment for the third offense. This law remained on the books until 1976 when, due to the efforts of Senator George Moscone, possession of one ounce or less of marijuana was reduced to a misdemeanor, with a maximum of $100 fine. Although a number of people were convicted under the harsher law, there was no appreciable decrease in marijuana use. Since 1976, however, California has saved over $1 billion in expenses previously spent on arrest, court, prison, and parole costs. There has been no marked increase in marijuana use, with 40 percent of users surveyed reporting an actual decrease in use.

In 1973, New York State passed a law with mandatory minimum sentences without possibility of plea bargaining for possession of relatively small amounts of illicit drugs. As reviewed by Trebach, a subsequent study by the New York City Bar Association observed that, indeed, the use of heroin three years later was as widespread as it had been in 1973, with the law having had little demonstrated effect on either seller or user.[52] Similar observations could be made for marijuana, as well as cocaine use. Indeed, the widespread use of these drugs would prevent any real punitive action being taken against users without a complete paralysis of our judicial system. Yet, despite the entry of a new administration in Washington, DC, opposition continues against the use of marijuana for medical reasons.

In 1988 approximately 762,000 people were arrested for illicit drug use, although approximately 38 million were believed to be using these substances. The numbers of persons arrested for possession that year were approximately two and one-half times greater than those arrested for sales or distribution. Convictions for drug possession rose by 340 percent between 1970 and 1980, with an average sentence of 48 months given to those entering federal prisons. Nonetheless, of those serving prison time for drug possession who had been released in 1983, 63 percent had been rearrested within three years, and 30 percent of the initial cohort reincarcerated.[44] At present, our prison system is overflowing, with operating cost of $25 billion annually. The strain and cost placed on the criminal justice system by those arrests, prosecutions, and incarcerations are not able to be justified either morally or economically. This is being increasingly recognized by government officials, bar associates, and the judiciary.[53,56]

Of equal importance is the observation that incarceration in its present state does not even serve as a deterrent to drug use, even while incarcerated. Drugs are readily available in our prisons and often ignored.[57] Treatment is the exception rather than the rule with only one in six inmates receiving any treatment and less than 2 percent receiving actual rehabilitation therapy.[58] As a result, it is not surprising that upon release from prison up to 60 percent of drug offenders may be rearrested within a year.

It also belabors the obvious to observe that the cost of incarceration of an inmate for a year is far greater than the cost of the government providing the same person with a job at more than the minimal wage. Ever escalating penalties for illicit drug use, such as implementation of the death sentence, when the legal constraints associated with enforcing these penalties are such that the dealers face a far greater risk of death from their competitors, is less than helpful. Arrest and prosecution for possession of small amounts of illicit drugs cannot possibly be effectively carried out within the constraints of our existing legal system and our already severely overcrowded prisons.

Deterrents, other than incarceration, however, can be undertaken and may be more effective. Penalties associated with driving while intoxicated, when enforced in a number of countries, have been associated with moderate degrees of success. Urine testing at the workplace for cause, as well as part of a routine screening in those jobs that require constant diligence and appropriate judgment, may also be helpful. A firm approach to drug use in schools, as well as the workplace, can send an appropriate message that hopefully will be heard by all.

Unfortunately, the recent antidrug legislation approved by Congress contains additional and more severe deterrents. These include possible loss of federal student loans, living in federally supported housing, and the right to mortgage guarantors. These penalties may be accompanied by fines of up to $10,000 for possession of even small amounts of illicit drugs. The ability of the system to prosecute such cases and the constitutionality of these laws, however, remain to be determined. In addition, penalizing a user by depriving him/her of the ability to obtain loans for education or mortgage guarantees is hardly an effective approach to rehabilitation. Rehabilitation includes furthering rather than limiting one's educational possibilities as well as achieving the ability to leave an environment facilitating drug use. To illustrate the futility of this approach, a logical and consistent extension of deterrents to drug use should also include penalties to those suffering from the consequences of willful drug abuse, such as liver disease, cancer of the lungs, emphysema, and infection of the heart valves. These penalties would consist of withdrawal of federally sponsored health insurance, or even more draconian, the refusal to provide treatment. These positions are clearly not morally supportable, though logically consistent with our government's current initiatives.

Education, Treatment, and Research

The federal government continues to support many worthwhile efforts in education, treatment, and research. These efforts are not to be minimized and will be discussed in greater detail in Chapters 9 and 10; however, among federal initiatives, the funding remains skewed, with the majority still targeted for reducing the supply rather than the demand, an inequity that has even been observed by the Attorney General.[54] This figure for demand reduction is also small in absolute terms when one considers that in 1990 we spent approximately $52 billion to replace missiles and bombers that were already among the most advanced in the world.[55] Such continued expenses in view of the collapse of the Cold War cannot be justified, yet continue to be spent. Even with respect to the total health research effort, substance abuse does not fare well. As noted by Califano, although the National Institutes of Health spend over $46 billion on research targeted toward cardiovascular disease, cancer, and AIDS, less than 20 percent of that is spent on research of licit and illicit drugs, which are associative factors in producing the illness caused by these other diseases.[56]

CONCLUSION

Despite the allocation of more financial resources than ever available to diminish illicit drug use, such use continues and flourishes. In indigent communities it destroys the basic fabric of community life. This is related, in no small part, to a misdirection of priorities, with the majority of funds going to limit the supply rather than diminish the demand; however, in part, it is also due to the government's commitment taking a back seat to perceived foreign policy needs as well as a refusal to recognize the necessity to provide alternatives to illicit drug use to those whose lives are grounded in poverty and despair. Minimizing the money available for rehabilitation, and preventing treatment programs from providing other than minimal services, will only guarantee a less than satisfactory outcome and questions the extent of commitment.

Yet, drug use had been diminishing, as it has in the past, despite increasing drug availability. This is not due to effective enforcement but rather the cyclic nature of illicit drug use. As the adverse effects of cocaine and other illicit drugs become recognized, their use diminishes, except among those with no other practical alternatives. If the billions of dollars we have spent on enforcement could have been applied to education, prevention, treatment, and providing alternatives to drug use, then this process could have been accelerated. It is not too late to reverse our priorities, and such a reversal does not and should not accompany the simplistic solution of legalization of all mood-altering drugs. As will be described in Chapter 9, decriminalization for simple possession focusing on local rather than international enforcement efforts in domestic sales would save billions of dollars that could be redirected to education and treatment. Doing less does not address the role that a committed government can effectively fulfill.

REFERENCE NOTES

1. Keeping score: What we are getting for our federal drug control money. *Drug Strategies.* New York: The Carnegie Corporation, 1995.

2. Confronting the drug problems: Debate persists on enforcement and alternative approaches. Report to the Chairman's Committee on Government Operations, House of Representatives. Washington, DC: U.S. General Accounting Office, July, 1993.

3. Mexicans expand realm in drug trafficking. *The New York Times*, September 4, 1994, Sec. A:24.

4. Brooke J. In Colombia, one victory in a long war. *The New York Times*, December 13, 1993, Sec. A12.

5. Brooke J. Drug graft in Colombia is rife, giving leader a daunting task. *The New York Times*, August 14, 1994, Sec. 1:6.

6. French HW. Bogota is criticized over drug baron's prison escape. *The New York Times*, July 24, 1992, Sec. A:9.

7. Treaster JB. Jailbreak dramatizes drug-policy failures. *The New York Times*, July 26, 1992, Sec. 4:3.

8. Bennett WJ. Colombia, America's favorite "Narco democracy." *Wall Street Journal*, August 3, 1995.

9. de Cordoba J. Colombia's defense chief quits as drug money scandal widens. *The Wall Street Journal*, August 3, 1995.

10. Colombian heroin may be increasing. *The New York Times*, October 27, 1991, Sec. 1:15.

11. Treaster JB. Bush sees progress, but U.S. report sees surge in drug production. *The New York Times*, March 1, 1992. Sec. 1:12.

12. Treaster JB. Effort to curb drug flow may be more difficult, officials say. *The New York Times*, December 4, 1993, Sec. 1:7.

13. Brooke J. Drug spotlight falls on an unblinking Cali Cartel. *The New York Times*, December 17, 1993, Sec. A:8.

14. Treaster JB. U.S. and Colombia reduce army's role in drug battle. *The New York Times*, February 27, 1992, Sec. 6:16.

15. Columbia pledges crackdown on drug trade. *The New York Times*, February 8, 1995, Sec. A:10.

16. Sims C. Deaths won't halt antidrug flights in Peru. *The New York Times*, August 31, 1994, Sec. A:5.

17. Trujillo SG. Peru's Maoist drug dealers. *The New York Times*, April 8, 1992, Sec. A:25.

18. Nash NC. War on drugs in Peru shows limited gains. *The New York Times*, December 6, 1992, Sec. 1:20.

19. Tyrell RE. Let the chips fall. *The American Spectator*, October 1995, 16-18.

20. Rohter L. A cocaine baron's tales of intrigue and greed liven up Noriega's trial week. *The New York Times*, November 24, 1991, Sec. 4:3.

21. Cooper M. Same as it ever was. *The Village Voice*, May 28, 1991, p. 34.

22. Sciolino E. State Dept. report labels Nigeria major trafficker of drugs to U.S. *The New York Times*, April 5, 1993, Sec. A:1.

23. Golden T. Mexico's drug fight lagging, with graft given as cause. *The New York Times*, August 7, 1994, Sec. 1:16.

24. Golden T. Mexico says it won't accept drug aid from the U.S. *The New York Times*, July 26, 1992, Sec. A:9.

25. Golden T. To help keep Mexico stable U.S. soft-pedaled drug war. *The New York Times*, July 20, 1995, Sec. A:1, A:6.

26. Golden T. Mexican connection grows as cocaine supplier to U.S. *The New York Times*, July 20, 1995, Sec. A:1, A:6.

27. Weiner T. C.I.A. formed Haitian unit later tied to narcotics trade. *The New York Times*, November 14, 1993, Sec. 1:11.

28. Weiner T. Antidrug unit of C.I.A. sent ton of cocaine to U.S. in 1990. *The New York Times*, November 20, 1993, Sec. 1:1.

29. Twersky D. The risks of cozying up to Syria. *The New York Times*, July 28, 1992, Sec. A:19.

30. Friedman RI. Inside dope. *The Village Voice*, 1993, p. 1.

31. Weiner T. Blowback from the Afghan battlefield. *The New York Times*, March 13, 1994, Sec. 6:52-54.

32. McCoy AW. *The politics of heroin: C.I.A. complicity in the global drug trade*. Brooklyn, NY: Lawrence Hill Books, 1991.

33. Ralston SJ. Drugs, torture and Western cash. *The New York Times*, April 18, 1990, Sec. A:25.

34. Greenhouse S. Heroin from Burmese surges as U.S. debates strategy. *The New York Times*, February 12, 1995, Sec. 1:3.

35. Hazarika S. Indian heroin smugglers turn to new cargo. *The New York Times*, February 21, 1993, Sec. 1:11.

36. Treaster JB. Exiting drug chief warns of cartels. *The New York Times*, October 31, 1993, Sec. 1:27.

37. Rogers A. Reducing demand for addictive drugs. *Lancet*, 1994, 343:411-412.

38. Sterling C. Redfellas. *The New Republic*, April 11, 1994, 210(15):19-22.

39. Reuter P. Crawford G, Cave J. *Sealing the borders, the effects of increased military participation in drug interdiction*. Santa Monica, CA: Rand Corporation, 1988.

40. Source Book of Criminal Justice Statistics, 1994. In Macguire K, Pastore AL (Eds.). U.S. Department of Justice NCJ 154591. U.S. Government Printing Office, Washington, DC, 1995.

41. Meacham A. Pentagon wants out of drug war. *The U.S. Journal*, August 6, 1988.

42. Horgan CM. Substance abuse: The nation's number one health problem: Key indicators for policy. Princeton: NJ: Robert Wood Johnson Foundation, 1993.

43. Treaster JB. Pentagon plans shift in war on drug traffickers. *The New York Times*, October 29, 1993, Sec. A:6.

44. Treaster JB. Drug flow through Haiti cut sharply by embargo. *The New York Times*, November 4, 1993, Sec. A:10.

45. Drugs and crime facts 1989. Rockville, MD: Department of Justice, Office of Justice Programs, Bureau of Justice Statistics, 1990.

46. Schaenman R. Treatment, not jail, saves lives and money. *The New York Times*, February 6, 1995, Sec. A:16.

47. Treaster JB. Four years of Bush's drug war: New funds but an old strategy. *The New York Times*, July 28, 1992, Sec. A:1.

48. Dilulio JJ. Cracking down. *The New Republic*, May 10, 1993, 208(19):53-57.

49. Zeese KB. Drug related corruption of public officials. *Drug Law Report*, March/April, 1986, 20:229-237.

50. Carter DL. Drug-related corruption of police officers: A contemporary typology. *J Criminal Justice* 1990, 18:85-98.

51. Treaster JB. Pentagon shift in war on drug traffickers. *The New York Times*, October 24, 1993, Sec. A:6.

52. Trebach AS. *The great war and radical proposals that could make America safe again*. New York: Macmillan, 1987.

53. Lyall S. Without the money to supply prison beds, officials consider reducing demand. *The New York Times*, February 17, 1992, Sec. B:5.

54. Labaton V. Reno questions drug policy's stress on smuggling. *The New York Times*, May 8, 1993, Sec. 1:9.

55. $150 billion a year. *The New York Times*, March 8, 1990, Sec. A:24.

56. Califano JA Jr. America in denial. *The Washington Post*, November 14, 1993, Sec. C:7.

57. Purdy M. Bars don't stop the flow of drugs into the prisons. *The New York Times*, July 21, 1995, Sec. A:1.

58. Treaster JB. Drug therapy: Powerful tool reaching few inside prisons. *The New York Times*, July 3, 1995, Sec. A:1.

Chapter 7

Accepting Individual Responsibility

Despite the roles played by many that may actually promote drug use, and despite the inadequate and at times ineffective response of government, it is essential to realize that ultimately it is the individual who must accept responsibility for his/her actions. Inherent in an effective approach to diminishing drug use is the unequivocal statement that use of/or dependency on drugs does not relieve an individual of responsibility for his/her actions. Despite the reasons that might have led one to taking drugs, the reinforcing effects of the drug that facilitate dependence, and the need to view the drug user as one in need of assistance rather than punishment, nonetheless, any antisocial or criminal behavior on the part of the drug user should be dealt with appropriately. The use of mood-altering drugs should never be accepted, either legally or morally, as an excuse for criminal behavior. The results of driving or working while intoxicated with alcohol, cocaine, or marijuana are not dissimilar; neither should be the sanctions associated with their use.

With respect to individual drug use, most of us accept this responsibility. Regardless of the availability of mood-altering drugs, most people do not use illicit substances, do not smoke, and do not drink to excess. This includes those living in the inner cities who, despite their deprivation, try to continue their lives in a productive manner and who care greatly for their families. Those who do choose to use these substances must take responsibility for the consequences, including the medical complications associated with licit drug use, notably alcohol and tobacco.

Whereas external factors may, on an individual basis, contribute to drug use, to define these causes as primary is to relieve one of the responsibility for his/her actions. At best, this view is paternalistic, at worst racist, but, most important, it is ultimately not helpful in either prevention or rehabilitation. The "Just-say-no" media blitz, advanced during the Reagan administration, was simplistic, yet in a way emphasized the importance of free choice. However, it is interesting that adolescent illicit drug use did fall during this time. The public's responsibility to provide assistance to facilitate saying no, and the government's responsibility to make available alternatives to drug use in no way negates individual choice or individual responsibility for taking drugs or engaging in actions that promote such use.

As individuals we must also not be afraid to reflect on whether our own words are matched by our actions. Although we readily recognize the importance of attacking excessive alcohol consumption and substance abuse, nonetheless, we often overlook opportunities to confront this issue. Wambach has quite effectively questioned our commitment toward squarely facing this problem.[1] As individuals, each of us should be able to answer why, at times, we are willing to:

1. provide insufficient treatment facilities and incarcerate users, yet wonder why more prison space is needed;
2. readily agree to build more prisons rather than community centers to provide viable alternatives for youths, being content to keep many in jail who have been convicted for possession, rather than for violent acts;
3. be concerned with teenage smoking or drinking, yet allow advertising of these substances to be targeted to children;
4. know people who are using drugs, yet do little to attempt to get them help;
5. permit inadequate resources to exist for treatment of substance abuse, yet complain of the high cost of medical care due to the complications associated with using these substances;
6. ask pregnant women with drug problems to come forward, then try to take custody of their children instead of providing social support while they are in treatment;
7. advocate rehabilitation, but yet do not hire people in recovery;
8. try to establish outreach programs to get people into treatment, yet promote the development of managed care systems, the goals of which are to keep people from visiting their facilities; and

9. tell our children about the hazards of illicit drug use, yet often drink in excess and, all too frequently, make alcohol available to teenagers for parties.

It is not easy to confront these issues, yet in terms of individual action, this is essential in effecting a change in our approach to this problem.

THE COMPLICITY OF OTHERS

Individual responsibility for one's actions, however, is by no means confined to those who actually use drugs. In fact, people who consciously or unconsciously either directly promote drug use or indirectly hinder efforts at limiting demand span all walks of life, and are more numerous than those who use these substances.

At the top of the scale are the politicians who for a variety of reasons, including contributions to political campaigns, do not speak out either for legislation to restrict cigarette sales or against governments that are actively abetting the illegal drug trade. Bankers and investment counselors, by participation in laundering schemes, promote the expansion of drug cartels. Pharmaceutical firms, by supplying the chemicals needed to refine the illicit drugs into street products, contribute to a thriving industry. Athletes, actors, and others who serve as role models to youth by promoting the use of alcohol and tobacco must also accept responsibility for the continued use of these substances by our youth. It is true that most of their actions are not illegal, many are enjoyable, and all are ultimately personally financially rewarding. Nonetheless, the result is to foster the inappropriate use of both licit and illicit mood-altering substances. All of these people, by their actions, which are obvious to all, deter effective use of prevention by giving youth the message that mood-altering drugs are unavoidable.

The Schools and the Teachers

For many children and adolescents, school plays a central role in influencing behavior, as well as promoting development of healthy social constructs. This is especially true when family support is minimal or, at times, nonexistent. Because smoking and the inappropriate use of mood-altering drugs usually becomes established in early adolescence, not infrequently children at risk are able to be identified by teachers. The appearance of such behaviors as antisocial acts, boredom, poor academic performance, and inappropriate friendships, suggests that assessment and intervention efforts are warranted. Even with licit drugs, this relationship exists. Studies of adolescent smoking have shown that those students who perform below average have a threefold risk of smoking compared to above-average students.[2] The position of the school on drug use should be unequivocally clear. Use of mood-altering drugs is prohibited, with possession or distribution associated with academic sanctions, including expulsion, in addition to being subjected to any criminal actions that may ensue. This approach by itself is insufficient to address this issue as most teenagers report that both licit and illicit drugs are readily available in their schoolyards or surrounding communities. Nonetheless, the message it transmits is unequivocal.

What is needed from the education system is much more than both enforcement of antidrug policies and educational programs that merely list the risks of drug use. Teachers must be active participants in programs to enhance one's self-image, and encourage confidence and competence to allow an adolescent to feel confident of himself or herself as an individual without the need to take the path of least resistance through drug use or drug sales.

The Community

Individuals comprise communities, and it is the communities in the inner cities that are being ravaged by drug use and sale. Prevention programs should not just be limited to the schools. Neighborhood community role models should be asked to participate as well. This includes local law enforcement agencies. Although the use of police to educate students as to the risks of drug use has been criticized as being counterproductive, in fact, if an active dialogue can be developed between individual policemen, barriers traditionally existing between the police and many youths may be able to be weakened and the all-too-often image of the police as the enemy can be challenged.

Communities should adopt a zero tolerance for drug sales and bond together to identify those engaged in this activity. This is neither an easy nor safe objective to achieve. It is here that resources must be applied, and cooperation with the policy must be managed in a confidential manner to identify without fear of detection those who are engaged in sales; however, it must be understood that responsibility extends to one's children as well. All too often, parents may also be guided by the ready money that comes with the sale of drugs. They are prone to overlook the activity for the money it provides. The responsibility to provide a caring environment and its effect on the development of children cannot be overemphasized and cuts across all socioeconomic brackets.

ROLE OF THE FAMILY

Any approach to diminish drug use that does not involve the family unit can never achieve its maximum potential. This is recognized even by advocates of the biologic vulnerability to alcoholism. Preventing drug use in the young is facilitated by the presence of a warm and caring family that can diminish the chances for drug experimentation or prevent experimental use from becoming recreational use. In fact, if we can markedly diminish the initiation of drug use among the young, then "the war" will have been won without the need for unmitigated success on our other "fronts."

A cohesive family unit is not always easy to achieve. At a time when the numbers of single-parent families and families where both parents are working are increasing, much scorn has been heaped upon "traditional family values." Such derision is as misplaced as is the bias of those who hold that "traditional values" cannot be found among single parents. In the context of drug use, traditional values refer to available role models, not necessarily the presence of two parents. Most children who are raised by single parents do not turn to either inappropriate licit or illicit drug use, whereas many who are raised in a complete family unit without adequate role models or supervision, do. Unfortunately, the parent as a role model is neglected by many parents who follow the adage, "Do as I say, not as I do."

The existence of a family unit, however composed, is a minimum but not a sufficient requirement. All too often, in an attempt to be a modern parent, little guidance or supervision is offered. In an attempt not to be considered restrictive, permissiveness carries the day. Supervision is minimal, insufficient emphasis is placed on appropriate or ethical behavior, and often children are allowed a degree of decision making in advance of their years. As a result, peers rather than parents often form a nucleus to determine behavior, and peer pressure shapes how an individual develops.

Paradoxically, the lack of attention or supervision on the part of the parent is not often viewed by the child as modern parenting but rather one of disinterest. By failing to set limits or standards, the parent is perceived as not really caring about (or as tacitly approving of) the child's behavior. If inconsistencies are observed in the parents' behavior concerning ethical or moral issues, then those are readily absorbed by the child and serve to undermine the parent/child relationship. It is important to emphasize that much of a child's impression of parents is never overtly stated but rather covertly observed and incorporated into the child's value system. As parents, we should, therefore, make certain that, as much as possible, whether dealing with our children or with others, our behavior follows appropriate standards.

With specific reference to use of mood-altering substances by parents, role modeling is extremely important as is the effect that such use can have on the stability of the family unit. In fact, studies have shown that both alcohol and drug use by parents are risk factors in the dissolution of the family unit.[2] Whether such use is the cause of the division, an attempt to avoid confronting the problem is unknown; however, it seems clear that reduction in parental drug use will result in strengthening parental personality characteristics that will enhance not only parent-child attachment but also involvement.[4]

A parent's personal use of alcohol, when excessive, is quickly picked up by children. Casual use of other mood-altering drugs by parents, even when prescribed, gives the message that the use of drugs to alter mood is acceptable. Use of illicit drugs by parents destroys all credibility as to the dangers of drug abuse. Parents who drink or smoke frequently have children who behave similarly. Of teenage smokers, 75 percent have at least one parent who smokes. In one survey of ninth-grade smokers, 17 percent reportedly had obtained cigarettes from parents or other adults. Continuation of smoking, despite its risks, which are well known to children, lessens a parent's argument over the hazards of illicit drug use. Parents should support passage and inducement of all legislation restricting sales of tobacco products to children as well as actively intervene when they see their children smoking.

Similarly, the use of hard liquor by parents has been found to be a moderately good prediction of adolescent drinking. In fact, parents' behavior with respect to drug use is more important than their beliefs in predicting adolescent drug use and this emphasizes the importance of modeling.

It is ironic that many parents, appropriately concerned with the use of marijuana or other illicit drugs, show little interest in teenage drinking, which is not only inappropriate but also illegal. Many parents readily provide alcoholic beverages to their children and their friends at parties. The message this transmits is unmistakable. It is but a small step for children to move from parent-supported, underage drinking to experimenting with other drugs. It is "sobering" to reflect that alcohol is the most frequent drug preceding illicit drug use. Too often, parents try to become their childrens' best friend. Although this feeling is understandable, indeed, often it is not what the child or the adolescent wants. Laxity in parental controls has been associated with excuses for drinking. On the other hand, unfair or harsh discipline is also associated with the use of mood-altering substances. Childrens' needs are met by having the "best parent." Although those with adolescents may find this difficult to believe, the importance of setting appropriate limits and being a parent rather than a friend cannot be overemphasized.

Proving an appropriate role model, however, is only part of the parental responsibility. Development of the parent/child bond is equally important. The quality of this relationship can also exert an important deterrent effect on a child's use of mood-altering substances.[3] Being available to respond to and initiate nonconfronting discussions concerning drug use is also needed. A recent nationwide survey of over 8,000 children and 820 parents suggests that such availability is not always present.[5] Parents were found to consistently underestimate their children's use of drugs. Although 14% of parents thought their children had used marijuana, 38 percent reported trying it. Only one-third of parents thought their children might have been offered drugs, whereas 52 percent of teenagers reported they had. Most important, although 95 percent of parents reported having discussed drug use with their children, only 77 percent of children recalled such discussions.

Adolescence is a natural time for experimentation, and peer pressure becomes increasingly important in modeling behavior. Parents must recognize this and, early on, openly discuss issues pertaining to drug use. Not only should the harmful physical effects be discussed, but also the social and psychological implications. It is important to know one's children's friends, as some may be pressuring them to use drugs. Discussions as to the steps their children can take to just say no comfortably without being ostracized by the peer group are exceptionally important.

If a child acknowledges experimenting with mood-altering drugs, then rather than becoming immediately punitive and thus closing off discussion, parents should elucidate the reasons why this is inappropriate in a firm, yet nonconfronting manner. It is important to observe that in a nationwide survey, although 75 percent of parents reported that they would be upset if their children experimented with drugs and a slightly greater percentage felt that children should be forbidden to use drugs at any time, 60 percent of these parents reported using marijuana at some time during their lives.[5] When drug use in one's child is recognized, this is the time to present reasons why such behavior may be harmful and should not be continued. The child's self-esteem should be supported, rather than destroyed through immediate parental anger. The importance of expressing one's individuality by either saying no or refraining from being placed in situations associated with a high risk of drug use can be quietly, yet firmly, expressed. Neither complete permissiveness nor establishment of authoritarian control, with the child having nowhere to turn, is appropriate. Permissiveness implies noncaring; authoritativeness promotes rebellion, rather than conformity. Clear and firm limits should be set and appropriately explained. Within that framework, the child's ability to find his/her own space should be encouraged as should the development of his/her strengths and skills.

Equally important, when problems are identified and are not able to be resolved, assistance should be sought rather than ignore the problem. All too often, parents regard the need for their children to have counseling or therapy as a weakness, which, in turn, reflects on their abilities as parents. This is misplaced guilt. It is characteristic of caring and responsible parents to recognize when someone else can be of assistance to their child. Early intervention before drug-seeking or drug-taking behavior becomes established is most effective, and, unfortunately, all too frequently neglected.

DEFINING COMMITMENT

If we are truly concerned about diminishing the use of both illicit and inappropriate licit drug use, there are definite actions we as individuals can take. Although the number of people any one of us can touch may be small, this commitment by many in the aggregate can have a considerable effect and, more important, may influence others to act in a similar manner. Any comprehensive approach can be only as successful as its most basic components, and the most fundamental unit is the individual. Therefore, our potential for success is a reality enhanced if we as

- individuals, use licit mood-altering drugs appropriately, refrain from illicit drug use, fulfill our responsibility to be role models to our children and exercise our right to vote as a means of influencing current government policy;
- employers, identify those workers who are using drugs and, rather than discipline, provide assistance in addressing their problems;
- teachers, identify students with potential problems before the problem appears to allow effective intervention;
- health care providers, increase involvement with individuals at risk for or actually using illicit drugs;
- bankers, refuse to assist those obtaining funds illicitly from converting them to legitimate financial markets; and

• law enforcement officers, maintain an objective and nonjudg-
mental attitude to those who use such substances.

By accomplishing these objectives, we can take the first step in
diminishing drug use by initiating a comprehensive approach to the
inappropriate use of mood-altering substances.

CONCLUSION

All of us have something to contribute in the attempt to eliminate
drug use. This requires increasing our knowledge of the effects of
mood-altering drugs, becoming more critical in identifying those
we know who are at risk or who are currently using drugs, and,
being more compassionate in assisting those who are dependent.
All of these behaviors, however, are predicated on the ability to
address, not ignore, unpleasant situations. Whether a person who
uses drugs is a child, an adolescent, or an adult, those who are aware
of this use should attempt to intervene in a constructive manner.
Involvement as a parent, a friend, or an employer is essential in
addressing drug use on the most important level, the user. Until
everyone accepts appropriate responsibility as individuals, the war
against drugs can be, at best, only a stalemate.

REFERENCE NOTES

1. Wambach P. Statement to the President's commission on model state drug
laws. March 3, 1993, In President's Commission on Model State Drug Laws. Vol.
V: Drug-free families, schools, and workplaces. Washington, DC. The Commission, 1993.

2. Newcomb MD, Betler PM. Consequences of adolescent drug use: Impact on
the lives of young adults. Newbury Park, CA: Sage Publications, 1988.

3. Kandel DB, Andrews K. Processes of adolescent socialization by parents
and peers. *Int J of Addictions*, 1987, 22:319-342.

4. Brook JS, Whiteman M, Balka EB, Cohen P. Parent drug sue, parent personality and parenting. *J Genetic Psychol*, 1995, 156: 137-151.

5. Wren CS. Marijuana use by youths continues to rise. *The New York Times*
February 20, 1996. Sec. A:11.

Chapter 8

An Agenda for Action I: Diminishing Supply

GENERAL PRINCIPLES

Prior to recommending a specific plan of action, there are several basic tenets that must be acknowledged in order for a successful effort to be undertaken to diminish drug use (Table 8.1). First, there must be the recognition that in order for any program to be effective, it is reduction in demand, not in supply, that will ultimately determine success. It is here that most of our energy and resources must be focused. This requires the continued efforts of both private and public sectors and, most important, the individual; however, the allocation of resources must be in concert with the emphasis on demand rather than supply.

Second, there must be an unswerving commitment to diminish excessive, inappropriate, and harmful use of all mood-altering substances, be they illicit or available with minimal restriction. The irony of eliminating foreign aid to countries unable to control the growth of poppies, coca, and cannabis, while providing support for tobacco farmers in this country and actively encouraging foreign markets to be open to American tobacco companies, cannot be lost on those we try to influence. The roles that many of us, especially the government, play in tolerating or even promoting inappropriate drug use must be understood and addressed.

Third, all actions on the part of the government must be coordinated. With respect to the federal effort to limit use, the number of federal and state agencies involved in monitoring some aspect of

TABLE 8.1. Basic Tenets in Diminishing Drug Use

- Success is determined by a reduction in demand, not supply.
- A commitment must exist to diminish inappropriate use of both licit and illicit drugs.
- All efforts must be coordinated and be part of a comprehensive plan.
- Inappropriate use of mood-altering drugs will never be completely eliminated.
- Sufficient treatment facilities must be provided.
- Evaluation of all efforts must be undertaken.
- Support for basic and clinical research must be expanded.
- Viable alternatives to drug use must be provided.

alcohol and substance abuse, as described earlier, virtually precludes an effective coordinated initiative to address this problem. Unfortunately, to date, political, rather than practical, imperatives continue to prevent this objective from being achieved.[1] The most glaring examples of a lack of coordination can be seen in the relationships between the Drug Enforcement Agency and the Central Intelligence Agency. Agents from each of these organizations have clashed in a number of countries where perceptions of the need to maintain political stability have resulted in the CIA thwarting DEA efforts or even unwittingly facilitating transportation of narcotics.[2]

As an example, recent efforts to eliminate overlapping functions in the Federal Bureau of Investigation, Drug Enforcement Agency, and Bureau of Tobacco, Alcohol, and Firearms have been stymied. Instead, the government initiated yet another new agency, the National Drug Intelligence Center, which cost $50 million just to open and will duplicate the work of 19 other centers; however, as noted in a report by the General Accounting Office, even these 19 centers are not needed as many duplicate each other's activities. What is needed is a strong Administration response that will condense, rather than expand, such activity. This will allow not only effective and efficient operations, but also will enable the millions of dollars saved to be directed to diminishing demand as well as enhancing treatment opportunities. There must be a single unit charged not only with the responsibility, but also with the authority to act. Similarly, coordination must also exist at the state and local levels. Autonomy, uncoordinated efforts, and chaos must be replaced by direct leadership and cooperation.

Fourth, regardless of whether a substance is licit or illicit, there must be a recognition that one may never be able to totally eliminate its use. Responsible use and making one well aware of the social, medical, and legal risks are the minimal objectives. In presenting this message, consistency is the key to credibility and effective prevention.

Fifth, sufficient treatment facilities must be available and appropriately supported, accompanied by constant monitoring of the effectiveness of all programs. Evaluation has never been given sufficient priority. Unless we can modify approaches shown to be ineffective or support innovations that may well prove to be of value, our potential for effective prevention and rehabilitation will not be fully realized.

Sixth, high-quality research efforts into the epidemiology, psychology, pharmacology, and treatment of substance abuse must be more strongly supported. Seventh, and finally, with respect to drug use in our inner cities, there must be recognition that unless viable alternatives to drug use are provided, such use will continue. It is difficult to change behaviors of those who have "nothing to lose." To some living in the inner cities, incarceration is preferable to their daily existence. The cost of providing such alternatives, although expensive, can be somewhat offset by redirecting the billions we are currently spending in the war against drugs as well as reordering our national priorities.

With these principles in mind, this and the following chapters offer strategies to diminish supply, based on suggestions made by many, including individuals located at opposite ends of the political spectrum (Table 8.2). Until we realize the importance of evaluating all suggestions regardless of their source, our approach to addressing this issue will remain fragmented and less than effective.

TABLE 8.2. Strategies for Diminishing Drug Use: A Plan for Action Affecting Supply

ILLICIT DRUGS

Diminish Influx from Other Countries

- Consistent approach in absence of political imperatives
- Strive to obtain meaningful agreement by all nations to move against illicit drug production and those who profit from it
- Enforce existing legislation concerning efforts by other nations
- Cease direct financial and technical military support to foreign countries to eliminate drug traffickers on foreign soil
- Provide appropriate general economic assistance to countries committed to eliminating drug trafficking
- Enforce legislation attacking money laundering to prevent illegal gains from being realized

Designer Drugs

- Identify and prohibit the manufacture of all analogues of mood-altering drugs except when specifically approved for scientific research
- Allow emergency restriction of analogues shown to be hazardous and available on the street

Redirect and Increase Coordination of Law Enforcement Efforts in Preventing Illicit Sales and Distribution

- Rationalize sentencing for drug-related offenses
- Decriminalize possession and use of illicit drugs
- Focus enforcement efforts on sales rather than possession

LICIT DRUGS

Alcohol

- Enforce existing laws concerning sales to minors
- Continue liability for those who sell to one who has clearly consumed too much

Tobacco

- End financial support to tobacco farmers
- End federal facilitation of opening foreign markets to foreign sales
- Vigorously enforce state laws concerning sales to minors

Prescription Drugs

- Limit diversion of locally produced mood-altering drugs
- Establish national network to monitor prescription drug abuse
- Provide appropriate information concerning diversion to physicians, pharmacies, drug companies
- Tighten controls on prescribing substances likely to be abused
- Recognize accountability of industry to provide accurate information concerning risks associated with use of their products
- Require chemical manufacturers who deal with substances used to refine or produce illegal drugs to register with a central agency

ILLICIT DRUGS

Attacking the Influx

A great deal of effort and money has already been spent on this objective. There has been greater coordination among law enforcement agencies. Multiagency, nationwide task forces have been developed. Increased assistance has been provided for crop eradication programs in foreign countries. There has been increasing involvement from the armed forces. Whether we have been successful in these efforts depends strictly on whether one views the amount of drugs confiscated or their street availability. With respect to our ability to seize progressively larger quantities of drugs, we have been remarkably successful; however, due to the relatively small amount of drugs needed to supply "the street," our ability to influence availability at the street level has been virtually nil.

Similarly, our ability to control the actions of any foreign government is obviously limited. Nowhere is our failure in this regard more clearly seen than in South America. For the past two years, we have spent over $2 billion to diminish cultivation and distribution of cocaine in Peru, Colombia, and Bolivia; the drug trade still flourishes.[3] This is despite our providing "tactical assistance," military equipment, pilots to interdict aircraft-carrying drugs and spray insecticides to eradicate crops, support for alternative crops to be grown by farmers, and direct financial assistance to governments. The result is still a thriving drug trade, governments that negotiate with traffickers to turn themselves in so that others can take their places, and foreign economies where considerable segments of the population derive some of or all their income from the drug trade.

In fact, the only recent visible dent occurred during the embargo of Haiti when, similar to circumstances seen during World War II, the ability of smugglers to use Haiti as a shipping port for illicit drugs was seriously impaired. This, of course, ultimately had no effect on cocaine entering the United States as the cartels quickly moved to other ports of call.

Even if we objectively review our efforts in this regard, consistency in applying sanctions has not been followed. All too frequently, insufficient pressure has been placed on governments known to be tolerating or even profiting from the drug trade due to a "higher order of interest." Those who produce and transport drugs into this country are no worse than those in governments who permit the trade to flourish. Sanctions should be applied to both. A multinational agreement should be in effect not only to combat the production and sales of illicit substances but also to facilitate extradition of those who are charged with profiting from such activities. Toward this end, a United Nations' accord, signed by 43 countries to allow for extradition and confiscation or freezing of bank accounts, will, if enforced, unequivocally state international commitment to elimination of the illicit drug trade.

Economic assistance should be provided only to those countries with a demonstrated commitment toward preventing drug traffic within their borders. This assistance, however, should be to promote the economy and not to interrupt the flow of drugs. No funds should be provided to assist foreign governments in interruption of drug traffickers on foreign soil as this objective has proven impossible to achieve. Unfortunately, the current administration, while realizing the futility of some approaches, nonetheless, pursues other equally ineffective measures.[4] A prime example is the decision to proceed with our "tracking and seizure" operations, which if cut back, would save over $1 billion. Rather than using these funds productively to diminish demand, they are being directed toward an expanded effort to raid clandestine localities. This is an equally fruitless attempt that will be met by the development of high-tech mobile laboratories. The money saved from these efforts should be applied to diminishing demand and improving the quality of life in communities ravaged by drug sales.

Efforts to seize drugs at our borders should continue, but with the realization that effectively sealing these borders is impossible. Better coordination between agencies, however, must result in a more efficient operation and should be vigorously pursued.

Diminish Incentives to Prevent Those Engaged in Legitimate Enterprises from Profiting on Illegal Drug Proceeds

The illicit drug trade is ultimately only profitable if one can, in the vernacular, make "dirty" money "clean." To accomplish this requires participation of those normally engaged in legal enterprises. Although, at times, unwitting participation in laundering money may occur, more often the source of the money is purposely overlooked. This behavior should not be tolerated. Federal legislation is already in existence to address this issue and additional restrictions have been proposed. Ultimately, it should be possible to (1) penalize those knowingly dealing in the proceeds of unlawful activity or conducting transactions that conceal or disguise the source of illegally obtained funds; (2) regulate institutions that issue payments or transmit money in a manner susceptible to laundering institutions' activities; (3) revoke the licenses of businesses participating in such activities; and (4) develop a means on both state and federal levels of identifying the origins of all significant cash transactions among those who are contributors to the laundering process.[5]

Limit Diversion of Chemicals Used to Make Illicit Substances and Designer Drugs

Since 1988 with the passage of the Chemical Diversion and Trafficking Act, detailed records have been required of all companies producing chemicals that can be used to produce and purify illicit substances. As many as 37 states also have regulations controlling the sales of these substances listing them in the Controlled Substance Classification in Schedules II or III. All states should be encouraged to enact such legislation and efforts to achieve enforcement should be pursued.

Similarly existing regulations pertaining to production of designer drugs contained the 1990 Uniform Controlled Substances Act and should be more vigorously enforced. These regulations prevent the development of analogues of mood-altering drugs except those that were the focus of legitimate scientific study and allow for emergency-regulating analogues that may suddenly appear on the street.

Increase Coordination Among Law Enforcement Agencies

The myriad of agencies involved in enforcement activities once illicit drugs have arrived in this country thwarts a comprehensive law enforcement effort to halt distribution and sales. Better coordination of all federal, state, and local enforcement is needed, with rivalries among agencies put aside. Appropriate steps should be taken to ensure that any corruption of law officers, a constant threat, be detected early and appropriate action taken. Although the number of corrupt officials is quite small, the damage that can be done in allowing even a few large shipments of drugs to be delivered is enormous.

A coordinated effort at the street level to disrupt the gang activities that have turned many neighborhoods into war zones is also needed. Accompanying these arrests must also be a commitment on the part of the judiciary for rapid trials and appropriate sentencing for those convicted of sales. For those playing major roles in trafficking, plea bargain and reduction of sentencing for "good behavior" should be eliminated. Because virtually no one serves a full sentence and 60 percent of those released are incarcerated within five years, the effect that eliminating early release would have on diminishing all crime is considerable. This has been addressed in the $30 billion crime bill passed by Congress and signed into law by the President in September 1994. Under this law, over 100,000 new police officers will be hired and individuals convicted of violent crimes will be required to serve at least 85 percent of their sentence. Toward this end, $8.7 billion will be spent over six years to build more prisons. As an additional "get-tough measure," the law imposes the death penalty on about 60 capital offenses; however, this provision is more form than substance; as most of these offenses rarely occur under federal auspices, with the last federal execution being March 1983.

In addition to the threat of incarceration, an additional incentive should be the inability to profit from illegal activities. Forfeiture legislation should be adopted by all states and implemented. The resources obtained from such actions should be directed toward treatment and education programs. It is recognized that the potential for abuse with such legislation is considerable, and enforcement must be monitored carefully. Yet, it is the financial incentive that ultimately drives the illicit trade, and this must be addressed.

Sentencing of those at the lowest level of distribution, the street dealers, or those arrested only for possession, should be rational and not only punitive. Two-thirds of all drug arrests are for possession, not sales, and 20 percent of prisoners in our federal system are low-level nonviolent drug offenders.[6,7] Unfortunately, incarceration appears to be the only approach being actively pursued. While this has been criticized as resulting only in a clogging of an already crowded court system and overflow of our prisons, advocates of incarceration emphasize that unless this occurs there is no risk associated with street sales. And, it is those sales and the criminal activity associated with them that have destroyed communities and caused needless deaths of innocent bystanders. The response of the President and Congress to public concern over increasing crime has been what can be best described as a shotgun approach. Attempts have been made to federalize state crimes committed with a gun, impose more stringent mandatory minimum sentences, institute a three-strikes-and-you're-out for life provision for three-time offenders, and increase the number of violations for which the death penalty can be imposed.

These suggestions are flying in the face of the following commonly observed phenomena concerning drug-related violence. Much street violence is committed by juveniles who in many states are protected from ever receiving severe sentences, let alone being subjected to mandatory minimum sentencing or the three-strike-rule. Those arrested for simple possession have a very low recidivism rate. Repeat offenders for violent crimes already receive long sentences, and recidivism to criminal activity after the age of 60 is quite rare; however, one rarely serves a complete sentence, being paroled after one-third time is served, and plea bargaining usually results in a much shorter initial sentence.

A reasonable approach that might serve both "camps" would be to decongest our prison system, as described below, while making certain that those convicted of serious offenses regardless of age actually serve out their sentences. It does not take a mathematician to realize that if most inmates serve only one-third of their sentences before being paroled and 50 to 60 percent of all former convicts are arrested within several years of release, by merely requiring sentences to be actually served, the crime rates would immediately decrease in the absence of any other interventions. The rationale of parole is to provide an incentive for a person incarcerated to accept the penalty without causing problems for the prison staff; however, there is no reason why the concept of "time off for good behavior" cannot be adjusted to time extended for bad behavior. The motivation for behaving well can as easily be "being released on schedule," rather than decreasing one's sentence. Since it is commonly accepted by both advocates and critics of incarceration that rehabilitation resulting from incarceration is rare, and judging by recidivism rates, impossible to assess, it should not be used as an indication for early release.

The major reason advanced for not having one serve a sentence is the overcrowding of our prison system. And indeed our prison system is overflowing, with several states under court orders to relieve overcrowding. The state of California has expanded its prison system to the extent that it is predicted that by the year 2000 the number of prisoners and the number of students attending the University of California system will be equal.[6] However, as already discussed, by decongesting the prisons through imposing alternate types of punishment for minor offenses, this problem would be resolved. Far from being "soft on crime," this approach requires taking a careful look at whom we are incarcerating and why. This would maximize the chances for both rehabilitation and protection of the public.

RETHINKING THE DRUG LAWS

The frustration on the part of many, including law enforcement officers, on the failure of traditional aggressive imprisonment for violation of the drug laws has led to a great many proposals for change that range in their tolerance for use of illicit drugs. These include (1) increased use of drug courts,[8] (2) intensive supervision probation, (3) civil penalties and fines instead of incarcerations, (4) decriminalization for simple possession, (5) limitation or authorizing a regulated drug market, and (6) legislation.

Increased Use of Drug Courts

Drug courts remove low-level offenders from the usual criminal justice system and establish nonadversarial proceedings focused on treatment and rehabilitation. Agreements between prosecutors, public defenders, and judges establish criteria of eligibility for cases as well as requirements for participation. These courts function through postadjudication and deferred prosecution. Post adjudication addresses a course of treatment after guilt is determined but before sentencing. Deferred prosecution usually targets first offenders arrested for possession. Most programs involve 30 to 60 days of intensive treatment followed by supervision for one year. Minimum retention rates of 65 percent have been reported as compared to usual retention in treatment of 10 to 15 percent. Some areas have reported decreases in crime rates as well.[6] From a cost-benefit analysis, drug courts are also extremely effective, saving costs associated with bringing cases to trial as well as savings from not being incarcerated.

Intensive Supervised Probation

These programs provide intensive surveillance through electronic monitoring devices or curfews. Often they may be instituted following an early or conditional discharge when a person has agreed to complete a formal rehabilitative program. The costs of this program are less than incarceration but obviously greater than traditional parole. However, the rate at which new crimes are committed is also less than that seen with traditional paroles–but higher than those on traditional probation.[7]

Civil Penalties and Fines

Fines for first-time marijuana use ranging from $100 to $1,000 exist in nine states. These fines may be accompanied by requirements for participation in drug education or treatment programs. Civil penalties, such as loss of driver's license, or harsher federal penalties, such as loss of federal-sponsored mortgages and loans, also exist but their effectiveness has yet to be demonstrated.

Decriminalize Simple Possession of Illicit Substances

Although we have done little to stem the flow of illicit drugs into our country, we have become too efficient in arresting those who use these substances. Of the one million drug arrests each year, 250,000 (25 percent) are for simple possession of marijuana, which, incredibly, is the fourth leading cause of arrest. Drug arrests have risen considerably out of proportion to arrests for other types of crimes by a factor of 3 or 4.[9,10]

As discussed earlier, our prisons are overflowing. In fact, the increase in incarcerated drug offenders accounted for over 40 percent of the total growth in court commitments since 1977.[11] Seventeen percent of those persons in federal prisons are first-time offenders arrested for possessing small amounts of drugs.[11,12,13,14] In state prisons, 22 percent of inmates are drug offenders, one-third of whom are incarcerated only for possession. Arrest, prosecution, and incarceration for simple possession is not only remarkably expensive, clogs our criminal justice system, and overcrowds our prisons, but in addition, is completely ineffective as a deterrent. Indeed, most of those knowledgeable persons involved with law enforcement have conceded that mandatory prison sentences and incarcerations for single possession or minor drug sales saves neither the individual nor our society. The amount of money that would be saved were decriminalization to occur is considerable. It is truly sobering to consider that the basic cost of keeping one inmate in a New York City correctional facility for one year is $58,000. Associated costs such as that needed to move the person through the judicial process considerably raise this figure.[14]

Simply by decriminalizing simple possession, and having those convicted of "real" crimes actually serve out their sentences, the crime rate would of necessity decrease. Furthermore, by establishing rehabilitation programs rather than prisons for minor offenders, a further decongestion of our prisons would occur. In fact, due to mandatory minimum sentencing laws, many are spending far more time in prison for simple possession than they would have if sentenced for violent crime. Simple possession of a teaspoon of crack (cocaine) carries with it a mandatory minimum federal court sentence of five years without parole. Unlike serious drug offenders, these individuals are far less likely to commit new crimes when released.[6] In addition, in order to accommodate those serving mandatory sentences, at times, far more violent offenders are released.[15] An agreement to serve time in rehabilitation, with an automatic prison sentence for those who do not fulfill this commitment, would also decongest the judicial system. It is realized that evaluation of the effectiveness of "rehabilitation camps" as compared to prisons has not been accomplished yet, and preliminary data have not shown great differences.

Although not generally realized, we have already had considerable experience with the effects of decriminalization. In the 1970s ten states decriminalized simple possession of marijuana. Not only did those states considerably reduce their costs due to law enforcement, but in addition, the number of persons using marijuana did not increase. Neither was there any evidence of a detrimental effect on the community at large.

Decriminalization versus Legalization

It should be emphasized that decriminalization is quite different from legalization which, if implemented, would permit the sale of all formerly illicit substances. Without entering into the myriad of arguments both for and against legalization (Table 8.3), two observations are important. First, the general premise advanced by advocates of legalization is that it would reduce crime without increasing use of formerly illicit substances. Whereas one might argue the effects of legalization on crime, it is counterintuitive to consider that increased availability will not lead to increased use. Whether one cares if more people use these drugs is a different issue, but history has repeatedly demonstrated that considerable increases in use will occur.

Second, despite our failure to restrict the availability of illicit drugs, all evidence suggests that, in fact, illicit drug use by our nation's youth has considerably declined. The driving force behind this decline appears to be student realization of the harm caused by these drugs. Even with respect to marijuana, the drug consistently having the most advocates for legalization, the overwhelming majority of students feel that this drug should not be legalized. Students have increasingly viewed the use of illicit substances as dangerous, in no small part due to their illicit status. This feeling can be contrasted to students' use of licit substances, such as alcohol and tobacco, which are currently responsible for more adverse effects

TABLE 8.3. Arguments For and Against Legalization of Illicit Drugs

Advocates	Opponents
People have and will continue to use illicit drugs.	Continued illicit drug use does not justify legalizing a harmful activity.
People have the right to pursue behavior that may harm them as long as it does not affect others.	Use of illicit drugs does affect others in a multitude of ways unrelated to their legal status, including child neglect and antisocial behavior. The majority has the right to create laws reflecting values. Most of society will regard legalization as morally wrong.
Funds currently used for enhancement could be better used in prevention, education, and treatment.	There is no reason to believe any financial savings would go where they are needed.
Current enforcement has little impact on criminal activities and slight deterrent effect.	Enforcement has not been effective due to the manner in which it has been pursued.
The failure of Prohibition should serve as a lesson with legalization of illicit drugs carrying the same benefits and risks.	Prohibition had reduced many complications related to alcohol. Many illicit drugs have far greater potential for antisocial behavior than alcohol as well as a much smaller likelihood of their consumption being controlled.
Crime would decrease as the cost of drugs would plummet.	If drugs were more readily available, use would increase, productivity would decrease, and crime might well increase to provide users with money for other needs. At present, more than 50% of violent crime is committed under the influence of drugs.

Advocates	**Opponents**
Workable models of legalization exist in other countries.	Cultural differences prevent these models from being pursued here. Those countries with the most lenient laws are rethinking their approach to drug use.
Legalization would not be accompanied by an inordinate increase in drug use.	There are currently 50 million smokers, 18 million alcoholics, yet only 2 million cocaine users. The potential for increase in use is enormous.
Legalization would still not permit access to drugs by children.	At present, children's access to alcohol and tobacco is rampant. Access to other drugs would be similarly difficult to control. Low cost would facilitate purchases.
Education would prevent individuals from unknowingly using substances with adverse effects.	The mere act of legalization implies a certain approval by society. Similar to children's perceptions concerning alcohol, the complications associated with use of these drugs would be trivialized.

than all of the illicit drugs combined. In fact, despite the widespread publication of the adverse effects of tobacco, the 1993 University of Michigan study found only 50 percent of eighth graders felt that a risk existed with smoking a pack of cigarettes a day. Since the time of greatest risk for mood-altering drugs is during adolescence, legalizing illicit substances would provide exactly the wrong message at a time when demand continues to decrease.

Decriminalization for use or simple possession, however, would have the effect of recognizing the user as one in need of assistance, not punishment. In addition to being more socially productive, decriminalization is also exceptionally cost-effective and would allow impressive savings that could be better applied to prevention and rehabilitation. This would also have the effect of clarifying the issue when one is arrested for a crime and is obviously under the influence of a mood-altering substance. The actual offense can be appropriately addressed without focusing on whether the drug use should be a mitigating factor.

Although there are many benefits associated with decriminalization, the distinction between possession for personal use or for use by others is often less than easy to define. In addition, it might well send a mixed message concerning the appropriateness of refraining from use of these substances. At the least, such a policy directed at "simple possession" would decongest our courts and overcrowded prison system, and result in a considerable savings that can be well directed toward prevention and treatment. Decriminalization need not eliminate sanctions or supervision, but rather confinement.

Limitation: Authorizing a Regulated Drug Market

Limitation would make certain drugs available, but only under certain circumstances and to certain people. Further, there would be a clear definition as to those who would be permitted to distribute those substances, with the options being a medical or a nonmedical model. Limitation under the medical model has existed for many years in England specifically restricting prescription of drugs to physicians who may provide them to persons felt to be physically dependent.

Authorization of a regulated drug market would convert a specific drug to the status of sales of alcohol or tobacco, but this, in reality, is limited legislation. Proponents of this approach argue that the use of the drug would not substantially increase, crime would diminish as would drug dealing, and due to the low costs involved, the profit margin would be greatly decreased; however there is no good evidence that this would occur. In fact, it is difficult to believe that use would not increase, especially among the young, despite their purchases of these drugs remaining against the law.

Although decriminalization remains controversial, and legalization, even when restricted to marijuana, is not considered a possibility by the majority, the other alternatives to traditional imprisonment for simple possession or street sales offer real possibilities for decongesting our prisons and encourage minor offenders to enter treatment. They also place a greater burden on the individual for determining his/her future and as such should be seriously considered.

LICIT DRUGS

Enforce Existing Laws

Existing laws with respect to sales of licit substances must be enforced. This is especially important since delaying the age of regular alcohol use is associated with a decreased risk of excessive consumption of alcohol as an adult.[16] Similarly, prevention of smoking by children and teenagers can markedly decrease the prevalence of adult smokers, as virtually no one begins to smoke after 20 years of age. Although all 50 states are now in compliance with the National Minimum Drinking Age Act of 1984, requiring a person to be 21 years of age before buying or consuming alcoholic beverages, more often than not this is honored in the breach. Sales of alcohol to those under 21 should be carefully monitored, and sanctions should be applied to those in violation of the law. Driving while intoxicated is too often handled lightly by our judicial system and then only after considerable delays between arrest and sentencing, during which time licenses may be retained.

Cigarette sales to youths under 18 are prohibited in 48 states. Yet surveys have shown that minors have been successful 70 to 100 percent of the time in purchasing cigarettes. Although vending machines placed in nonmonitored locations have been viewed as the "culprit," in fact, this is not the case. A national survey revealed that 85 percent of minors purchased cigarettes directly from a salesperson, with only 15 percent using a vending machine. The message this transmits to youth concerning our commitment, as well as the dangers of smoking, is only too clear. State and local laws should be vigorously enforced, with penalties for store owners strictly applied.

End Federal Support for Tobacco: Provide Alternatives to Tobacco Farmers

It is often ironic to consider our attempts to influence farmers in Asia or South America to cease growing opium or cocaine when we actively subsidize the growth of tobacco despite our recognition of its adverse effects on a far greater number of persons than for those that use illicit drugs. While the tobacco industry should be free to export its products, the not-so-gentle pressure that our government has placed on several countries to be hospitable to the industry should cease. Support should be offered to develop viable alternatives for our farmers who may wish to grow alternate crops rather than provide assistance to supply a substance that is not only extremely harmful but also extremely profitable to those engaged in its sale. Although the tobacco industry has consistently argued that it plays a critical role in the economic health of the country, and insists any further attempt to restrict sales will result in unemployment and federal deficits, their arguments are not compelling.[17] A recent economic analogy as to the economic effects of diminishing or even eliminating tobacco sales in the state of Michigan demonstrated that, in fact, with the elimination of tobacco sales employment would actually increase.[18] The U.S. Department of Agriculture has also shown that tobacco control can be successful without a devastating effect on tobacco growers. A study has revealed that a 30 percent drop in tobacco production would reduce the economy of that area by less than 3 percent.[19]

In fact, this is still an ideal time to assist those who grow tobacco to find alternate means of support. The tobacco farmers were in considerable financial difficulty unrelated to antismoking campaigns. Similar to cultivation of illicit drugs, tobacco is fast becoming an important crop in many foreign countries in both Asia and Latin America, and is selling at one-half to two-thirds that of American tobacco.[20] This resulted in a 10 percent decline in American tobacco prices as well as the need of the industry-financed Flue-Cured Tobacco Cooperative Stabilization Agency to buy 23 percent of flue-cured harvest in 1994 in an attempt to stabilize prices with a prediction that production of American tobacco would decrease by 20 to 40 percent in 1995. These events led many to feel that far from harming tobacco farmers, beginning to provide them with viable alternatives would prevent the total collapse of their livelihood in the not-so-distant future. Yet, once again, at a time when decisive action on the part of the government would be critical in assisting tobacco farmers to make "the change," the lack of commitment became evident. The U.S. Department of Agriculture announced its intention to increase the quota for growing tobacco by 16 to 19 percent, as manufacturers anticipated an increase in purchases of flue-cured tobacco by 98 percent from 288 to 570 million pounds. Tobacco exports began to increase and may have exceeded $200 billion for 1994.

Regulate Nicotine Content of Cigarettes

Because development of dependence is a dose/frequency phenomenon, it has been suggested that by limiting the content of nicotine in cigarettes, dependence will be less likely.[21] Others have suggested that in an attempt to obtain a greater nicotine level, individuals will consume more cigarettes. In addition, such cigarettes might be perceived by adolescents to be safe and, therefore, more of them would smoke.[22]

Public Action

Despite the inconsistencies and ambivalence on the part of those ostensibly concerned with diminishing smoking, much can be done. Removing children's access to cigarettes can be accomplished by developing a licensing system similar to that of alcohol sales, with revocation of this license if cigarettes are sold to minors.[23] Advertising in any form targeted toward children, such as free-posters coupon ads allowing people to write away for free packs of cigarettes, should be eliminated. Existing laws prohibiting all promotion, direct or indirect, of cigarettes on television, including sponsoring of sports telecasts, can be enforced. Most recently, several bills have been introduced requiring tobacco companies to release one negative ad about smoking for every three positive ads published.

In an attempt to involve the federal government in the regulation of the tobacco industry, President Clinton introduced through the Food and Drug Administration a series of regulations including requiring the industry to spend $150 million annually to support an antismoking educational campaign directed at children; prohibit cigarette sales to those under 18 years of age, with vendors being required to check photo identification; prohibit vending machine sales, mail order sales, and packs containing fewer than 20 cigarettes; prohibit promotional items with brand-name sponsorship at sporting or entertainment events; prohibit outdoor advertising within 1,000 feet of schools and playgrounds, and permit only black and white advertising for outdoor ads.[24,25] Not surprisingly, the tobacco industry has vigorously protested those resolutions on a variety of grounds and is attempting to gain legislative support to soften the final regulations, submitting over 47,000 pages of rebuttal with supporting documents to the FDA.

Active enforcement at a community level also can be quite effective. In Woodridge, Illinois, passage and monitoring of community antismoking legislation resulted in a decrease in merchants selling to adolescents from 70 percent before the legislation to less than 5 percent in less than two years. Cigarette experimentation and regular use by adolescents were diminished by 50 percent.[26]

Also, pressure can be applied to organizations dealing directly or indirectly with health care issues to divest their investment portfolios of tobacco company stocks. This action is supported by a formal recommendation of the American Public Health Association and spearheaded by the actions of the Tobacco Divestment Project, which has specifically targeted several universities and insurance companies to be pressured to divest.[27] Institutions that have taken such action include Harvard, Johns Hopkins, the Rockefeller Family Fund, and the Robert Wood Johnson Foundation.[28] The American Medical Association and the Robert Wood Johnson Foundation have recently announced a $10 million antismoking campaign in 19 states to allow tobacco tax revenues to be directed toward antismoking educational efforts. Finally, an unambiguous statement by the U.S. Trade Office not to pressure countries to accept tobacco exports would go a long way toward promoting the health of these nations as well as maintaining consistency with respect to our own demands concerning the production of illicit drugs by foreign nations.

Independent Initiation of Legal Action

With the change in control of Congress to the Republican Party, hopes of tobacco control advocates for a national legislative solution have considerably diminished. As a result, a number of independent legal challenges to the tobacco industry have arisen in an attempt to increase corporate responsibility (Table 8.4).[29] Several massive class action suits have been initiated against the tobacco industry contending that the companies, while aware of the addicting qualities of nicotine, spent millions of dollars on research to refute reports that smoking was hazardous, often disregarding or stopping research when findings were contrary to their objectives.[30,31] Several states have also initiated legal action in an attempt to reclaim from the tobacco industry the billions of Medicaid dollars spent on health care due to smoking, charging the industry of "willfully" misleading the public. Finally, individual smokers have filed suits on the adverse effects they claim smoking has caused.

Whether those will prevail remains to be seen. It is quite impressive, however, that for the first time one of the tobacco companies–the Liggett group–has offered to settle perhaps the most financially damaging suit against the industry brought by states to force tobacco companies to pay for tobacco-related injuries. Although it is alleged that the cost of the settlement is actually less than Liggett would pay for defending the suit, this action nonetheless is the first time the tobacco industry has not acted "as one" or has ever agreed to settle a smoking-related lawsuit. [34,35] Their suits signal a persistent commitment to hold the tobacco industry responsible for their action and, at the least appear to be making companies that do business with the tobacco industry increasingly anxious over being named as codefendants in liability suits. Two examples of this are the actions of the Manville Corporation to stop RJR/Nabisco Holdings Corporation from using their fiberglass in cigarettes and the Harley Davidson

TABLE 8.4. Recently Instituted Lawsuits Against the Tobacco Industry

State Level

Medicaid lawsuits to recoup costs of treating smoking-related problems

Class action suit to hold tobacco industry liable for knowingly addicting smokers

Nonsmokers claiming respiratory ailments caused by tobacco smoke

Challenge to Food and Drug Administration to reclassify tobacco as an addictive substance

Corporation attempts to dissociate itself from an agreement with the Lorillard Tobacco Company to market the Harley brand.[32] More recently, the Kimberly Clark Corporation announced its divestment of $404 million of tobacco-related business allegedly over liability concerns.[33]

Institute Appropriate Monitoring of Prescription Drug Use

Because misuse of prescription drugs is greater than use of all illegal drugs combined, the importance of preventing their diversion is obvious. A number of reasonable suggestions proposed to diminish prescription drug abuse have been discussed earlier (Chapter 4).[36,37,38]

These systems should continue to be implemented without restricting the availability of mood-altering drugs to those who are in legitimate need. For this reason, data banks based solely on patient identification will not only violate the long-standing principle of physician/patient confidentiality, but, in addition, will inhibit the physician from appropriately treating patients in genuine medical need of a drug.

Tighter controls on prescribing drugs susceptible to abuse on a federal level are also worth considering. Ongoing reviews by the FDA of existing Drug Control Schedules should continue, with drugs being placed in schedules appropriate to their abuse potential, as well as proven effectiveness. This information should be quickly transmitted to the practicing physicians to allow for a change in prescribing practices. Continued monitoring with respect to phase-II and -III trials should continue. Accelerated approval processes should be considered only for those drugs developed to meet an acute, hither unmet, medical condition–situations rarely occurring with respect to mood-altering drugs. The FDA should become more involved in monitoring compliancy with respect to postmarketing or phase-IV studies. Adverse reactions reported by physicians should be quickly acted upon, and side effects evaluated. Assuring compliancy with respect to "truth in advertising" by both the FDA and FTC should continue, with appropriate sanctions where violations knowingly occur. Triplicate prescription or multiple prescription forms should be expanded, with appropriate safeguards provided to assure patient confidentiality and no limitation in appropriate access.

Federal guidelines for state implementation of drug utilization review by pharmacists should be evaluated as to their effectiveness. If successful, guidelines should be established for Medicare patients as well. In the process pharmacists should become an integral member of the health care team, providing information not only to patients but physicians as well.

Develop Educational Programs for Physicians and Other Health Care Providers

Appropriate education as to the effects of mood-altering drugs and indications for use should be an integral part of their professional education, with information updated on a regular basis for all those participating. With respect to physicians, a group that bears a special burden in limiting supply of prescription drugs and ensuring appropriate use, educational programs describing appropriate prescribing practices, drug effects and actions, the nonpharmacologic means of relieving anxiety, effective ways of relieving pain, and the enhancement of skills in physician/patient communication should be provided at undergraduate, graduate, and postgraduate levels. Such progress should not be "purely" educational, but should also attempt to overcome the negative attitudes often encountered by all who deal with persons with substance-abuse problems as well as address the multicultural issues that constantly arise in addressing those problems.

The importance of appropriate physician/patient interactions in prescribing mood-altering drugs cannot be overemphasized. Only by spending sufficient time with a patient can the physician be assured that drug therapy is appropriate and the patient well informed as to the risks and benefits of taking the drug. Once the drug is prescribed, continued contact is even more important, to not only assure compliance, but also identify any side effects that may develop, as well as diminish the chances of dependency or misuse.

In order to assist the physician, objective sources of information concerning specific products should be available, without having to rely solely on pharmaceutically produced material, such as the *Physician's Desk Reference* (*PDR*). Hospital formularies should actively restrict availability of drug products shown to be more expensive, and associated with greater adverse reactions without additional benefits than other available agents. Information concerning these decisions should be transmitted to all physicians.

REFERENCE NOTES

1. deCourcy Hinds M. Center for drug intelligence opens, but some ask if it is really needed. *The New York Times*, November 17, 1993, Sec. A:16.

2. Werner T. Suit by drug agent says U.S. subverted his Burmese efforts. *The New York Times*, October 27, 1994, Sec. A:9.

3. Brooke J. U.S. aid hasn't stopped drug flow from South America, experts say. *The New York Times,* November 21, 1993, Sec. 1:10.

4. Fratello DH, Trebach AS, Zeese KS. What's new in Clinton's new drug strategy. *Drug Policy Letter*, November-December 1993 (21), pp. 15-23.

5. Socioeconomic evaluations of addictions treatment: Executive summary. Washington, DC: President's Commission on Model State Drug Laws, Rutgers Center of Alcohol Studies, 1993.

6. Keeping score: What we are getting for our federal drug control dollars. *Drug Strategies*, 1995. Carnegie Commission, New York, NY.

7. 21% of U.S. inmates are called nonviolent. *The New York Times*, February 5, 1994, Sec. 1:9.

8. Drug courts focus on treatment. *Prevention Pipeline*. July/August 1995, 29-32. Center for Substance Abuse Prevention.

9. Confronting the drug problem, debate persists on enforcement and alternative approaches: A report to the Chairman, Committee on Government Operations, House of Representatives. Washington, DC: U.S. General Accounting Office, 1993.

10. Grinspoon L, Bakalar JB. The war on drugs–a peace proposal. *New Engl J Med*, 1994, 330:357-360.

11. Prisoners in 1992. Bureau of Justice Statistics Bulletin, U.S. Department of Justice, Office of Justice Programs, Bureau of Justice Statistics, Washington, DC.

12. Rosen J. Crime bill follies. *The New Republic*, March 21, 1994; 210(12):22-25.

13. Mandatory minimum sentences in the federal criminal justice system: A special report to the Congress. Washington, DC: United States Sentencing Commission, 1991.

14. Rotham DJ. The crime of punishment. *The New York Review of Books*, February 17, 1994, pp. 34-38.

15. Kopel DB. Prison blues: How America's foolish sentencing policies endangered public safety. Washington, DC, Cato Institute, 1994.

16. O'Malley M, Wagenaar AC. Effects of minimum drinking age laws on alcohol use, related behaviors, and traffic crash involvement among American youth. 1976–1987. *J Stud Alcohol*, 1991, 52:478-491.

17. Warner KE. Health and economic implications of a tobacco-free society. *JAMA*, 1987, 258:2080-2086.

18. Warner KE, Fulton GA. The economic implications of tobacco product sales in a nontobacco state. *JAMA*, 1994, 271:771-776.

19. Gale F. Tobacco economies: What's ahead? *Agricultural Outlook*, September, 1993, pp. 27-31.

20. Kilborn T. Along tobacco road, a way of life withers. *The New York Times*, August 28, 1994; Sec. 1:1.

21. Benowitz NL, Henningfield JE. Establishing a nicotine threshhold for addiction. The implications for tobacco regulation. *N Engl J Med*, 1994, 331:123-125.

22. Hughes JR. Regulation on the nicotene contents of cigarettes. *N Engl J Med*, 1994, 331:1530-1531.

23. Di Franza JR, Brown LJ. The Tobacco Institute's "It's the Law" campaign: Has it halted illegal sales of tobacco to children? *Am J Public Health*, 1992, 82:1271-1274.

24. Purdham TS. Clinton urges sweeping plan to curb teenage smoking. *The New York Times*, August 11, 1995, Sec. A:1.

25. Hilts PJ. President to give FDA a big role to fight smoking. *The New York Times*, August 10, 1995, Sec. A:1.

26. Jason LA, Ji-PY, Anes MD, Birkhead SH. Active enforcement of cigarette control laws in the prevention of cigarette sales to minors. *JAMA*, 1991, 266:3159-3161.

27. Group urges divestment of tobacco stock. *The New York Times*, May 27, 1990, Sec. 1:35.

28. APHA and others call on institutions to divest tobacco stocks. *The Nation's Health*, April 1991, p. 11.

29. McCormick B. Antitobacco lawsuits. *Am Med News*, February 27, 1995, pp. 3,23.

30. Geylen M. Plaintiff lawyers subpoena data of tobacco industry law firms. *The Wall Street Journal*, August 8, 1995, Sec. B:8.

31. Geylen M. Smokers' suit tries new approach: The industry made them do it. *The Wall Street Journal*, March 21, 1995, Sec. B:1.

32. Rose RL, Hwang SL. Marketing: Harley is suing to get its name off cigarettes. *The Wall Street Journal*, March 23, 1995, Sec. B:1.

33. Collins G. Paper maker to spin off tobacco units. *The New York Times*, May 10, 1995, Sec. D:1.

34. Freedman AM, Hwang SL, Lipiy S, Geylen M. Liggett group offers first ever settlement of cigarette law suits. *The Wall Street Journal*, March 13, 1996, Sec. A:6.

35. Hwang SL. Will Liggett deal split big and small rivals? *The Wall Street Journal*, March 14, 1996, Sec. B:17.

36. Chappel JN. Educational approaches to prescribing practices and substance abuse. *J Psychoactive Drugs*, 1991, 23:359-363.

37. Drug abuse in the United States. Strategies for Prevention. *JAMA*, 1991, 265:2102-2107.

38. Lurie P, Lee PR. Fifteen solutions to the problems of prescription drug abuse. *J Psychoactive Drugs*, 1991, 23:349-357.

Chapter 9

An Agenda for Action II: Diminishing Demand

A variety of approaches can be effective in diminishing the demand for both licit and illicit drugs (Table 9.1). Because decreasing demand is the only long-lasting solution, all should be evaluated and, if effective, strongly supported.

REORDER FUNDING PRIORITIES

As discussed earlier, the proportion of funding targeted toward affecting demand, as compared to limiting supply, should be markedly increased. In addition, the considerable savings accruing through pursuing a policy of decriminalization of personal use, rather than incarceration, should also be applied to these efforts.

Deterrents and Demand

Advocates of a predominant enforcement approach to diminish the supply of illicit drugs are often equally supportive of deterrents to effectively alter demand. Deterrents link civil or criminal sanctions with drug use. Those associated with civil sanctions may have been quite effective in diminishing excessive alcohol consumption. This is especially true for enforcement of driving while intoxicated (DWI) laws resulting in loss of a driver's license. In order to circumvent the often time-consuming legal process before action is taken, 31 states have enacted administrative license suspension and revocation laws that allow the police to suspend or revoke the license of any driver with blood alcohol levels of 0.1 percent. Mandated jail sentences or

TABLE 9.1. Strategies for Decreasing Demand

- Increase proportion of federal funding for prevention and treatment
- Value-added tax on alcohol and tobacco products
- Pursue deterrents to drug use only to the extent that they have been proven effective
- Increase regulation of advertising alcohol and tobacco products
- Enhance role of office for substance abuse prevention
- Enhance effective prevention strategies

    Increase educational efforts to allow others to recognize inappropriate drug use:

    Enhance available employee assistance programs

    Deglamorize use of all mood-altering substances

- Provide viable alternatives to drug use
- Emphasize individual responsibility for actions
- Increase liability of advertising agencies for providing misleading or inaccurate information

community service legislation exist for first offenders in 12 states and for repeat offenders in 25 states. Similarly, assigning liability to bars that serve drinks to those obviously impaired has also been deemed helpful in diminishing alcohol consumption.

Assessment of fees above any specific penalties involved has also been suggested, with those unable to pay such fines required to participate in community service. The money accumulated from such fines would then be directed toward treatment and education programs. Such a system was established in New Jersey in 1987, with fees imposed ranging from $500 to $3,000, depending on severity of the offense.

Whether these strategies have been effective for the observed decrease in alcohol-related fatalities between 1982 and 1992 is difficult to determine. Other factors such as increased efforts at education and diminishing per capita alcohol consumption may have also played a role; however, little evidence has consistently been found documenting school programs to decrease drinking behavior. The decrease in per capital alcohol consumption of 9 percent between 1980 and 1990 is also considerably less than the broad decrease in the proportion of legally intoxicated drivers involved in fatal accidents.[1]

In contrast to civil penalties, the effects of criminal sanctions on diminishing illicit drug use remain unproven. As described earlier, in California, no increase in marijuana use was observed when the law making marijuana use a felony with a one to ten-year imprisonment for first offenders was repealed in 1976. An evaluation of New York State's mandatory sentencing for drug-related offenses by the New York City Bar Association found the use of heroin, marijuana, and cocaine in 1976, three years after this law was passed, to be unchanged.

Other more recent punitive actions passed by Congress involving the ability to revoke federally supported student loans, occupy federally financed housing, and possess federal mortgage guarantees have also not been demonstrated to be effective. Indeed, they may even be unconstitutional. Deterrence, especially for personal use of drugs without any associated untoward efforts for others, does not seem to be a logical approach to pursue to effectively decrease demand. In addition, for one to successfully complete a rehabilitative process after discontinuing drug use, it would seem that the more recent sanctions denying the availability of federally supported loans and mortgage programs are, in fact, counterproductive.

VALUE-ADDED TAX ON ALCOHOL AND TOBACCO PRODUCTS

It has been clearly demonstrated that to a certain extent the consumption of a drug is directly proportional to its price. Increasing cigarette taxes in this country will exert a powerful effect on diminishing demand as well as raising revenues that could be directed toward education and treatment. In Canada, recent tax increases are estimated to have reduced the number of adult smokers by 32 percent, and adolescent smokers by 62 percent.[2] In 1988, after voters in California passed Proposition 99, which increased the state cigarette tax by 25 cents a pack, smoking prevalence had decreased threefold faster than elsewhere in the country, with the number of smokers decreasing by one million and the number of packs smoked by over 1.1 billion with an average savings in direct health care costs of $211 million.[3]

A $2 increase in the federal tax on cigarettes would not only raise approximately $35 billion dollars annually but would also discourage 7 million smokers from smoking.[4] Lest one feels this tax increase is excessive, it should be observed that between 1972 and 1992 both federal and state cigarette taxes did not keep pace with inflation. In 1992, taxes were only 25 percent of the retail price of a pack of cigarettes as compared to representing almost 50 percent of the price in 1972. In addition, on a comparative basis our cigarette tax, which is 30 percent of the retail price of a pack of cigarettes, lags far behind other countries where we rank 22. Among the top ten countries on the list, the tax ranges from 73 to 85 percent per pack of cigarettes.[5]

Similarly, with respect to alcohol, taxes have been raised so infrequently that the real price of alcoholic beverages (accounting for inflation) has actually decreased between 1974 and 1990 by 32 percent for distilled spirits, 28 percent for wine, and 20 percent for beer.[4,6] Although taxes were increased on beer and wine in 1981, the increase was still not proportional to offset the effects of inflation. Such an increase has been estimated to diminish the number of youths who drink beer by 7 percent, and heavy drinkers by almost 20 percent. If the beer tax were equalized–to that of wine and distilled spirits–the decrease in drinkers would be even greater (32 percent). Based on alcohol-related motor vehicle accidents, loss in productivity, and industrial injuries, such a tax would have a marked beneficial social value as well.

The magnitude of a value-added tax on cigarettes and alcohol, however, should be carefully considered. Too great a tax may result in an active black market. This would be especially likely if the inequities between prices of alcohol or cigarettes among states became too great. With respect to alcohol, this might lead not only to a black market, but also to increased motor vehicle accidents as drivers cross state lines to drink. The difficulties that can be associated with too great a tax on tobacco products have already been observed in Canada. The marked increase in a pack of cigarettes imported by the Canadian government has resulted in an active black market estimated at $500 million annually as accompanied by the entry of organized crime into several towns in Ontario that border the United States. This response has resulted in provincial and federal governments rescinding a significant portion of the added tax.[7]

In this country the profit margin for cigarette products is so great that in order to prevent a decrease in consumption, cigarette companies may lower the base price of a pack of cigarettes should the value-added tax be increased. In fact, perhaps in response to the President's suggested $2 per pack federal excise tax, Philip Morris announced it was lowering the price of Marlboro by 40 cents.[4,8] Although this is an obvious scenario that may be followed, it does have its limits and should not deter uniform tax increases across state lines. In addition, due to the active lobbying efforts of the tobacco industry, the likelihood of a tax of this magnitude ever being passed is quite small. In fact, in the recent House Ways and Means Committee bill on health system reform, the committee recommended an increase in the tax of only 45 cents.[5]

INCREASE REGULATION OF ADVERTISING ALCOHOL AND TOBACCO PRODUCTS

The roles to be played by industries concerned with the production of mood-altering substances have been discussed earlier. Most effective in diminishing demand is voluntary self-monitoring with respect to advertising and the establishment of clear "informed consent" regarding the adverse effect of mood-altering drugs. Because most patterns of tobacco and alcohol consumption begin to form during preadolescence or adolescence, both the alcohol and tobacco industries can voluntarily do much to limit the exposure to the young of their products. Brewers, unlike tobacco companies, being free to advertise on television, have a special responsibility. Such advertising should be restricted to non-prime-time hours. Advertisements should be designed to reduce their appeal to children and adolescents and should contain direct warnings against excessive drinking. Advertisements targeted to certain groups such as those seen with malt liquors and certain beer commercials designed to sell in minority communities should be discontinued. Warning labels should be placed on all alcoholic beverages sold and should be strengthened. Similarly, warnings concerning tobacco should be correctly placed on cigarette packages. All advertisements on billboards should display this information in a place where it can be readily seen. Although the effectiveness of these warnings remains controversial, research has demonstrated that they have a high degree of public acceptance as well as the belief by the public that they are effective.[9]

As this is against the industry's self-interest, as discussed in the preceding chapter, the President has already initiated action to allow the FDA to regulate the industry. The tobacco industry would greatly prefer existing state ordinances to remain rather than allow local governments to be able to enact legislation to further restrict tobacco availability, counting on their ability to be more effective at diluting antitobacco legislation at the national and state level. They are understandably unalterably opposed to FDA regulations that have been proposed.

HOLD PHARMACEUTICAL FIRMS ACCOUNTABLE FOR ADVERTISEMENTS

Pharmaceutical companies should be held accountable for the information they provide to both physicians and patients. The former group needs specific, detailed, written information, rather than glossy brochures provided by the myriad of detail persons who regularly visit physicians' offices. Such information should also give the cost of the drug compared to others prescribed for similar reasons. Any inadvertent misrepresentation should be quickly corrected and sent in a "Dear Doctor" letter to all physicians. Appropriate sanctions should be provided for deliberate omissions or publication of incomplete information.

Interactions of pharmaceutical firms with physicians should be informational rather than directly or indirectly financially rewarding, unless the physician provides a specific service. The guidelines adopted by the American Medical Association should be adhered to by both physician and the pharmaceutical industry.[10] These guidelines should not result in diminished financial support for either research or scientific meetings, but will make available considerable funds previously spent to advertise products in a less rigorous scientific manner.

Product advertising to consumers should be clearly written in easily understandable, nonmedical terms and accompany all drug purchases.

The FDA should become more involved in this process to ensure compliance.

ENHANCE ROLE OF OFFICE
FOR SUBSTANCE ABUSE PREVENTION

The Office for Substance Abuse Prevention, elevated to Institute status in the Anti-Drug Abuse Act of 1988, should continue to be supported to explore effective community-based strategies to diminish use. The office should also take a greater role in identifying the effect of state initiatives as, for the past decade, block grants for prevention and treatment have been awarded directly to the states. While this has given state authorities more latitude and flexibility, it has also been accompanied by less accountability. All efforts should be vigorously evaluated and those shown to be effective strongly supported.

ENHANCE PREVENTION EFFORTS

Although considerable efforts have been spent on development of programs in an attempt to prevent alcohol and drug abuse, evidence to date on the effectiveness of these programs has been conflicting. In part, this has been related to a failure to clarify goals and objectives of many programs. Thought must be given to the variety of objectives that can exist within prevention programs and determine which approach for which group will be most successful.[11] It is equally important, however, to realize that the group toward which most efforts will be directed is the young and, it has been demonstrated that by the age of 20, the risks for initiating the use of alcohol, cigarettes, and marijuana are basically over.[12] In fact, use of marijuana and excessive alcohol consumption starts to decrease in the mid-twenties, accelerating by the mid-thirties.[12] This pattern of diminishing use is not seen with cigarettes.

Classification of Prevention Programs

Primary Prevention

Primary prevention attempts to prevent or deter initiating the use of mood-altering drugs. Many advocate that a primary prevention program should be all-inclusive, preventing the use of any mood-altering drug, including alcohol and cigarettes. However, the ability for success of a program advocating total abstinence from all mood-altering drugs is limited. Furthermore, a credibility gap is created by attempting to equate responsible alcohol use with the harmful use of cigarettes or illicit substances that may prevent participants from taking seriously the information presented.

A discussion of alcohol use in general prevention programs, therefore, should focus on delaying such use until an appropriate age, the importance of responsible use, the risks of attempting to engage in activities requiring judgment and motor skills even with minimal alcohol consumption, and the hazards of regular or escalating alcohol consumption. This approach clearly recognizes society's approval of social use of alcohol while warning the potential user or abuser of its hazards. It is also quite pragmatic as legal drugs are used before illicit drugs—at a time when their use may be illegal due to the user's age.

A primary prevention program that focuses on the use of only illicit drugs may also run into difficulty as it is well realized that inappropriate alcohol use and nicotine are associated with more severe health consequences. This observation is not lost on adolescents who are at a time in their lives when inconsistencies in logic are quickly detected. Prevention programs must, therefore, address both licit and illicit drugs. The personal risks involved in the use of an illicit substance by virtue of its being illegal should also be emphasized.

Development of prevention programs must also consider the population to be served. Ages at which individuals are at particular risk for initiating drug abuse vary considerably. Smoking begins most frequently at around age 12, peaking at age 16, then declining. Marijuana use begins around age 13, peaking at age 18 before slowly diminishing. Cocaine use, however, follows a completely different pattern. Initiation increases with age, with a peak at age 18 when the rates for the initiation of alcohol and cigarettes appear to be declining. Alcohol use begins at a much earlier age, with almost 20 percent of children ever using alcohol having done so by age ten, with over 50 percent having done so by age 14. Therefore, to be most effective, information concerning alcohol use should be initiated earlier, even prior to the onset of junior high school.

Secondary Prevention

The goal of secondary prevention is to identify those who have used mood-altering drugs in an attempt to convince them to discontinue such use. It must be emphasized that adolescence is a period of experimentation and confrontation. The great majority of adolescents who engage in increased risk-taking behavior may indulge in alcohol and illicit drug taking once or, at the most, a few times without ever becoming either regular users or drug dependent; however, certain factors are associated with continuing drug use and, when identified, suggest a need for intervention. These include antisocial behavior, poor school performance, inappropriate peer groups, adverse family relationships, and antisocial values and beliefs.

Tertiary Prevention

Tertiary prevention involves treatment of those already dependent on mood-altering substances as well as ways to maintain abstinence once treatment has been completed. This will be discussed more fully in Chapter 11.

Principles of Effective Prevention

Regardless of the type of prevention effort, there are several general principles in health to be considered in the design of any program (Table 9.2).[11,13,14] Unless these are followed, not only will the success of the program be placed in jeopardy, but at times the effort may be actually associated with a tendency toward drug use.

Identify Populations at Special Risk

Although there is no one cause of drug use, there are a number of known associated risk factors. Groups particularly vulnerable include youths, especially those with few alternatives for recreational activities or who are from single-parent families, and those who live with severe and unrelenting stress. Depending on the target group, the program should be modified to specifically appeal to the group served as well as address specific risk factors that are incurred. People often in

TABLE 9.2. Principles to Be Followed in Designing Effective Prevention Programs

- Identify the specific population at risk for whom the program is intended
- Identify appropriate objectives of the program
- Provide consistent, easily understandable interactive programs
- Address reasons why one uses mood-altering drugs as well as appropriate responses to prevent individual use
- Incorporate information on the Acquired Immunodeficiency Syndrome
- Deglamorize the use of mood-altering drugs
- Promote acceptance of responsibility
- Provide healthy alternatives to drug use
- Include a mechanism for assessing effectiveness

contact with those at risk, such as teachers, social workers, physicians, and even employers, should be educated as to early identification and should be active participants in secondary prevention. As an example, programs to prevent smoking must focus on young children. All available data indicate that if adolescents do not smoke, they never will. Surveys have shown that almost 90 percent of persons who had ever smoked did so by age 18. The average age of beginning smokers was 14.5 years, with 17.7 years being the average age of daily smokers. Prevention programs concerning tobacco, therefore, should begin in elementary school and continue through high school. Such programs, if effective, will also diminish use of illicit substances, as one of these agents is most often preceded by smoking.

Identify Appropriate Objectives

This becomes quite important especially when addressing specific mood-altering drugs. Because alcohol use is the precedent to the use of other drugs, both licit and illicit, all prevention programs should also target drinking patterns. Several of the main risk factors, such as family history of alcohol abuse and low economic status, really cannot be addressed in prevention programs; other factors can and will apply to all mood-altering substances and must be also kept in mind when designing prevention programs. These include the influence of peer pressure, misconceptions about safety of certain drugs, the ability to develop effective interpersonal relationships, and the ability to tolerate and manage stress.[9]

Provide Easily Understandable Programs

Educating the public as to the risks of drug abuse has the potential to be one of the most effective ways of diminishing the demand for mood-altering drugs. Unfortunately, in the past, even once objectives have been defined, a program may not be effective for a variety of reasons. First, scare tactics have been used often in an attempt to portray the evils of illicit drug abuse. Not only has this been ineffective, but due to the association between drug abuse and risk-taking behavior, such approaches may have even stimulated some to initiate use.

Second, at times the information presented may not have been accurate. This is especially true regarding alcohol or tranquilizers. Because those participating in these programs may have either used the drug in question on occasion or have known people who have been users, presenting information inconsistent with their own experience may result in the entire program becoming suspect. Drugs make people feel good. This is obvious, yet often denied in many programs. It is the transient nature of the "good feeling," accompanied by the adverse effects that surround drug use, that must be explored.

Merely presenting correct factual information will also not guarantee an effective prevention approach. The manner of presentation is equally important. Utilizing a strict lecture format may be less effective than a program that actively solicits student participation. An evaluation of Project DARE (Drug Abuse Resistance Education), the most widely used school-based drug prevention program, found its short-term effectiveness for reducing or preventing drug use to be quite small and considerably less than interactive programs.[15]

When information is presented in a confronting manner by individuals considered not only authority figures but even authoritarian, drug use may become glamorized in an attempt to rebel against that authority. Information concerning the adverse effects of drugs is best presented by those who are respected and who can serve as role models to the participants. The drug user should not be presented as a criminal but as one with a problem in need of assistance. Because risk-taking behavior is one of the more frequent factors associated with illicit drug use, presenting the adverse effects of drugs in a light so as to make such behavior appear daring and/or risky glamorizes drug use and may stimulate youths to initiate or continue such activities.

An understanding of the actual harm associated with the use of a drug may be an effective deterrent. This is best illustrated by adolescent marijuana and cigarette consumption, which has markedly diminished. As described by Johnston and his colleagues, the use of marijuana on a daily basis increased between 1975 and 1978 from 6 to 11 percent among high school seniors;[16] however, this use significantly decreased again between 1978 and 1987, despite the absence of any decrease in the perceived availability of marijuana during this time. It is not by chance that the perceived risk associated with daily marijuana use also doubled from 35 to 74 percent during this period. With respect to cocaine use, it is encouraging that the percentage of high school seniors who realized the dangers of using cocaine even experimentally jumped from 34 in 1980 to 48 percent in 1987. Because adolescence is a time of great concern over the integrity of one's body, the ability to promote effectively the physical hazards associated with the use of mood-altering drugs might well be accompanied by a decrease in drug use.

Not only must the information presented be consistent with the participant's own personal experience, but it must be in concert with the mores of both the community and society. Many examples of inconsistencies exist: advocating total abstinence from alcohol while drinking is actively engaged in and widely advertised; decrying the hazards of marijuana use while minimizing the untoward effects of alcohol consumption; and, perhaps most important, declaring a total "war on drugs" in the presence of numerous articles in the press describing our support of governments known to tolerate or even profit from the drug trade. Such actions detract from the credibility of the message transmitted and must be altered.

Provide Appropriate Resources and Social Supports
to Change Behavior

Understanding factual information, however, is only one aspect of prevention and alone may not be an effective means of preventing use for some individuals.[13] Thorough and frank discussions as to why one may turn to the use of mood-altering drugs, the situations in which such use is facilitated or intensified, and the appropriate response of a person when found in such a situation are essential, yet often neglected, components of education and prevention whether dealing with adolescents or adults. Although this issue is regularly addressed in treatment programs for drug dependence, it has only recently become an integral part of prevention. Because, ultimately, an individual must take responsibility for his/her own actions, it is essential to provide support and guidance to allow development of skills to enable one to say "no" in a manner that will not result in alienation from the peer group. Group activities can be directed by relatively few members of the group who are regarded as leaders. If these individuals are those who have appropriate responses to situations where drug use is at risk of occurring, then the entire group will benefit. The use of adolescent role models in prevention programs is, therefore, quite important.

Incorporate Information on the Acquired Immunodeficiency Syndrome (AIDS)

Any prevention program must include information on the human immunodeficiency virus (HIV), and behaviors that can increase the risk of becoming infected with the HIV. It is estimated that as many as one million persons in the United States are infected with HIV, with an expected 50,000 to 80,000 cases of AIDS to be diagnosed in 1992. Of those with AIDS, 21 percent are heterosexual, intravenous drug users.[17] Although many teenagers are aware of the concept of safe sex being an important factor in diminishing the risk of HIV infection, the relationship with mood-altering drug use is often not stressed.

The proportion of HIV infections occurring in heterosexual/non-drug users, women, African Americans, and Hispanics has markedly increased, with the incidence of AIDS in African Americans and Hispanics three times greater than that seen in Caucasians. All groups should be instructed in the ability of mood-altering drugs to foster high-risk behavior through impaired judgment. The evidence that those who are high from alcohol or other drugs are more likely to engage in unprotected sex is impressive, although the findings have varied depending on groups studied. If prevention efforts are targeted toward groups known to engage in IVDU, then specific instructions should be provided concerning risks of needle sharing, ways to disinfect used needles, and advantages to participating in needle exchange programs, if available.

Deglamorize the Use of Mood-Altering Drugs

Promotion of alcohol and tobacco use by those who are viewed as role models is all too frequent, as are commercials touting the advantage of over-the-counter medications to relieve anxiety or permit restful nights. It is in this area that private sector initiative is essential. Advertisements for alcohol should include risks associated with excessive consumption, drinking and driving, and drinking when pregnant. Most important is the message that drinking by the young is neither desirable nor healthy.

Individuals who are role models, such as athletes and movie stars, should ask themselves if the money is "worth the sale." Although the hesitancy on the part of the private sector to voluntarily take on this role is obvious, it is always preferable to be active rather than reactive, a response that may well be necessary in the near future.

With respect to illicit drugs, those who deal in drugs should be portrayed as they are, not as how they appear—surrounded by money and glamour. The greatest risk a dealer faces is not apprehension by law enforcement agencies, but death from competitors. The anxiety, fears, and eventual outcome from such activity should be presented.

Provide Viable Alternatives to Drug Use

For those who have little, drugs and alcohol may be the only realistic options for enjoyment to relieve the stress of living. In the inner cities where recreational resources are almost nonexistent, unemployment is high, and, due to the existence of single-parent family units or the need for both parents to work, supervision is minimal, the family unit becomes severely compromised. Drugs and alcohol are readily available and crime abounds. Violence becomes a way of life in order to survive. It is sobering to consider that homicide is the leading cause of death among young black men aged 15 to

19, occurring three times more frequently than among white men. This excess mortality is almost entirely associated with poverty and unemployment as compared to race.[18] Effective law enforcement and mandatory sentences, albeit immediately effective, are not the ultimate answers. The causes of criminal behavior cannot be reached by the police, only their effects can be contained. In New York, approximately 70 percent of state prisoners come from only eight neighborhoods in New York City.[14] Not surprisingly, these areas are "home" to the indigent and suffer from the lack of even minimal resources that can promote self-respect. Because violent crime has been observed to vary directly with the size of the teenage population, the time to develop these programs is upon us. It is estimated that the number of Americans under 18, now approximately 60 million, will reach 70 million by the year 2000.[19] Alternatives must be provided, including affordable day care, child development programs, well-staffed and well-supervised recreational centers, youth employment centers, and secure living environments, where one can venture outside without fear. This is admittedly expensive—yet, so is the current cost of alcohol and drug use in this country. Furthermore, if one were to decriminalize the use of illicit substances, the money saved by diminished arrests, prosecution, and incarceration would in all probability equal the funds currently allocated toward the war on drugs. This has been addressed to some extent by the 1994 Violent Crime Control and the Law Enforcement Act which has allocated almost $1.5 billion to crime prevention and development of substance abuse programs.[20] Unfortunately this represents less than 5.1 percent of the total funds authorized.

CONCLUSION

Diminishing the use of mood-altering substances is both complex and difficult but not insurmountable. It is an effort that cannot succeed by funding alone, although without sufficient and appropriate allocation of resources it is doomed to failure. Equally important is the commitment of government, the private and public sectors, and most especially, the individual who ultimately makes the final decision concerning the drug use. All of us have roles to play in diminishing use of mood-altering drugs. Until we realize this and

adjust our actions accordingly, we will remain less than effective in our endeavors.

REFERENCE NOTES

1. Eighth special report to U.S. Congress on alcohol and health from the Secretary of Health and Human Services. Rockville, MD: The Institute, 1993.
2. Sweanor DT. Canada's tobacco tax policies: Successes and challenges. Ontario, Canada, Non-Smokers Rights Association, 1991.
3. Skolnick AA. Anti-tobacco advocates fight "illegal" diversion of tobacco control money. *JAMA,* 1994. 271:1387-1390.
4. Warner KE. Profits of doom. *Am J Public Health*, 1993, 83:1211-1213.
5. Jones L. Scathing words for tobacco, but limited tax hike. *Am Med News,* September 5, 1994, 3, 12.
6. Chaloupka FJ. Effects of price on alcohol-related problems. *Alcohol Health and Research World*, 1993, 17:46-53.
7. Kondro W. Cuts in Canadian tobacco taxes. *Lancet,* 1994, 343:470.
8. Shapiro E. Cigarette burn: Price cut on Marlboro upsets rosy notions about tobacco products. *The Wall Street Journal*, April 5, 1993, Sec. A:1.
9. Greenfield T, Graves KL, Kasutas LA. Alcohol warning labels for prevention: National Survey Findings, *Alcohol Health and Research World*, 17:67-75.
10. Drug abuse in the United States: Strategies for prevention. *JAMA*, 1991, 265:2102-2107.
11. Hansen WB. School-based alcohol prevention programs. *Alcohol Health and Research World*, 1993, 17:54-60.
12. Chen K, Kandel DB. The natural history of drug use from adolescence to the mid-thirties in a general population sample. *Am J Public Health*, 1995, 85:41-47.
13. Elders M, Perry CL, Eriksen MP, Giosuo GA. The report of the Surgeon General: Preventing tobacco use among young people. *Am J Public Health*, 1994, 84:543-549.
14. Botvin GJ. Prevention of adolescent substance abuse through the development of personal and social competence. In Glynn TJ, Leukefeld CG, Lodford JP, (Eds.). NIDA Research Monograph 47, 115-140.
15. Ennett ST, Tobler NS, Ringwalt CL, Flewelling RL. How effective is drug abuse resistance education? A meta-analysis of Project DARE outcome evaluations. *Am J Public Health*, 1994, 84:1394-1401.
16. Johnston L, O'Malley PM, Bachman J. *Drug use among American high school seniors, college students, and young adults, 1975-1990.* Vol. 1. U.S. Department of Health and Human Services; Alcohol, Drug Abuse, and Mental Health Administration, Rockville, MD.
17. Rubin RH. Acquired immunodeficiency syndrome. In *Scientific American Mecidine.* Infect Diseases, 1993, 1-23.

18. DuRant RH, Cadenhead C, Pendergast RA, Slavens G, Linder CW. Factors associated with the use of violence among urban black adolescents. *Am J Public Health*, 1994, 84:612-617.

19. Krauss C. The nation: No crystal ball needed on crime. *The New York Times*, November 13, 1994, Sec. 4:4.

20. Johnston D, Holmes SA. Experts doubt effectiveness of the newly enacted crime bill. *The New York Times*, September 14, 1994, Sec. A:16.

Chapter 10

An Agenda for Action III:
Treatment, Evaluation, and Research

Despite effective primary and secondary prevention efforts, there will always be those who continue to use mood-altering substances and suffer the consequences of their use. Adverse effects are many, including the social dysfunction unrelated to a substance's legality. Thus, as noted earlier, adverse effects of alcohol and nicotine use exceed those of all illicit substances combined. Despite the need for expanding treatment, the proportion of funds directed toward treatment efforts has actually decreased over the last 15 years. The current ratio of federal spending–65 percent to reduce supply and 35 percent to diminish demand–is not only wrong, but is also extremely cost-inefficient. The insufficient amount of funds devoted to the treatment of the addiction is particularly galling. Although it is believed that 15 percent of health care dollars goes to treating the complications of alcohol and drug abuse, only 1 to 4 percent is used to actually address the dependency. This can be compared to psychiatric illnesses where up to 41 percent of the cost is directed to treatment activities.[1]

The effects of illicit drug use and excessive alcohol consumption in the workplace have been previously discussed. Approximately 15 percent of the workforce use these drugs with an associated 335 percent increase in absenteeism, 235 percent increase in disciplinary actions, and 120 percent increase in sick benefit claims as compared to nondrug users. These indications can be reduced by over 50 percent through initiating treatment.[1,2] Treatment of those convicted of criminal activity has also been shown to be effective even when such treatment is mandated by the courts rather than requested. It has been estimated that every dollar invested in treatment ultimately saves $11 in societal costs.[3] A study by the Rand Corporation demonstrated that doubling current treatment funding and reducing federal law enforcement by 25 percent would produce the same results at a savings of $5.3 billion annually.[4] Individual studies have shown treatment to significantly reduce costs incurred not only by the persons using these drugs, but by family members as well by as much as 50 percent.[5] The Center on Addiction and Substance Abuse has projected that an integrated program of treatment for chemical dependency could become part of an overall system of managed health care for an additional annual cost of $80 per participant.[6,7] This is far from an unreasonable investment considering the potential returns. On the other side, failure to diagnose and treat appropriately is associated with impressive costs. Alcoholism and use of other drugs are believed to be responsible for 15 cents of every American health dollar as well as up to 50 percent of all hospital admissions. Medicaid costs for hospitalization due to alcohol, tobacco, and illicit drugs have been estimated at $8 billion annually.[4] Prior to a crisis, costs increase by 350 percent, and baseline levels rise to tenfold just before the crisis develops.[4]

HARM REDUCTION

Licit Drugs

Because many people will not only continue to use mood-altering substances, but, in addition, may not be at all amenable to therapy, over the years the concept of harm reduction has become increasingly acceptable as a way of decreasing both individual and societal risk associated with drug use. Harm reduction is based on several basic premises.[8] (Table 10.1). With respect to licit substances, harm reduction addressed toward alcohol would include educating a person who consumes excessive alcohol as to the hazards of doing this on the job or when engaging in activities requiring concentration, such as driving or sports. The importance of having a "designated driver" has already been emphasized in public interest announcements as well as by concerned groups, and is believed to have been effective in diminishing the number of alcohol-related traffic fatalities.

With the smoker, because the risk of cancer is directly related to one's "pack history," harm reduction would involve convincing the smoker to markedly diminish the number of cigarettes smoked per day, or regulate the nicotine content of cigarettes, with the ultimate goal of discontinuing smoking completely. This would be accompanied by emphasizing the hazards of environmental smoke, and discouraging smoking in public areas and especially in the home when young children are about. Harm reduction efforts have begun to have results as has the successful creation of smoke-free environments.

In an attempt to diminish harm to the smoker, without affecting the need to continue to obtain nicotine, cigarette companies have gone to unusual lengths to "improve" their product. Nicotine delivery systems devoid of cool tar contaminants continue to be developed. These range from such products as "Premier," a smokeless cigarette that cost $300 million to develop before being abandoned as nonmarketable to other more ingenious devices.[9] Examples of the latter include electric battery-powered cigarettes and pipes. These devices certainly diminish having to convince the nonsmoker that smoking is really a way of delivering a dependency-producing drug and as such should be regulated by the Food and Drug Administration.

The concept of harm reduction applied to inappropriate use of prescription drugs consists of educating the public to not only the dependency-producing potential of these drugs but also the dangers of combining mood-altering drugs, including alcohol, to enhance a high. As an example, the combination of alcohol and tranquilizers

TABLE 10.1. Underlying Premises of Harm Reduction

1. Existing drug policy should not cause more harm to society and drug user than the drug.

2. To some extent, drug use is inevitable, therefore, one must at the least try to diminish the harm done to the individual who uses these drugs.

3. Drug users form a part of the community at large. Diminishing the harm to them ultimately benefits the entire community.

4. Policies developed should focus on harm caused by individual drugs rather than means to restrict all drug use.

5. Regardless of legality of a specific substance or the sanctions associated with its use, pragmatically one should attempt to diminish the harm associated with its use.

can result in marked impairment and even fatal central nervous system depression.

Illicit Drugs

Although the concept of harm reduction with alcohol and tobacco has few opponents, when applied to illicit drug use its acceptance greatly diminishes. This is due to our inability to clearly define the "degree of harm" that is acceptable to be reduced compared with the "harm" that may result from the particular measure harm reduction institutes. Irreconcilable opponents of harm reduction feel that any measure, other than "preventive" education implies, at the least, there can be responsible illicit drug use and, at the worst, is the first step to legalization. Those advocates who remain opposed to legalization feel that, appropriately applied, harm reduction allows health promotion, increases safety of the individual and society, and provides care to those who are in most need of it.[8] Each side can cite convincing data supporting their views, making it difficult for the uncommitted to decide. Several examples of harm reduction currently in use are presented below.

Harm reduction techniques applied to illicit drug use, especially when drugs are taken by injection, include instruction in the use of bleach to sterilize needles, institution of needle exchange programs, education concerning safe sex practices, free distribution of condoms, and institution of practices for injecting drugs that would diminish the risks of secondary infection. Treatment on demand with respect to detoxification is yet another means of reducing harm to society associated with a person with the need for a drug but without the financial means for its purchase.

Harm reduction through needle exchange programs remains most controversial, being believed by some to have the potential to actually increase needle sharing. There remains considerable opposition to needle exchange despite evidence that programs have not been associated with increased levels of drug injection and have often enabled parenteral drug users to enter a medical setting for counseling and treatment. Equally important, increasing evidence exists that needle exchange may reduce the transmission of HIV to other intravenous drug users, their sexual partners, and their children by as much as 33 percent. Even if one forgets the public health value of such a program, the cost-benefit analysis with respect to preventing HIV infection is remarkable. Whereas the lifetime cost of caring for a person with HIV is estimated at $120,000, that of averting HIV transmission is $4,500.[7,10,11]

Another controversial example of harm reduction is the distribution of free condoms in the public schools. Although the appropriate use of a condom virtually eliminates the transmission of many (although by no means all) sexually transmitted diseases, prevents unwanted pregnancies, and deters HIV infection, nonetheless this practice has been strongly contested by many parents' groups and was, in part, responsible for the removal of a Chancellor of the New York City Public School System.

Harm reduction remains an important concept in addressing drug use; however, it needs to be more fully developed, explained to those who are opposed, and, equally important, fully evaluated so that those methods that are successful can be widely applied while those that are not effective can be discarded.

TREATMENT AND REHABILITATION

Sufficient facilities for treatment must exist to allow everyone desiring assistance to obtain it expeditiously. This includes providing adequate resources for evaluation and referral as well as a variety of treatment modalities. As of October 1993 there were 11,496 alcohol or drug treatment units treating 944,208 clients;[12] nonetheless, treatment is still not available on demand, nor have many modalities been adequately evaluated. It has been estimated that of the 3 to 6 million persons in need of treatment, our capacity for treatment is less than 2 million.[6] Financially, many forms of treatment are beyond the means of most of those who use drugs, and insurance for the few who have it is focused on short-term therapies for "long-term" problems. Many programs are "telescopic," addressing only one particular substance or even one particular treatment modality. Internecine conflicts among rehabilitation centers often abound in the scramble for the federal dollar, with those who use drugs being the ultimate losers. In the recent move to more cost-efficient care promoted by managed care advocates, conditions that can best be treated by establishing long-term therapeutic relationships are in danger of receiving scant attention.

Principles of Treatment

As with primary and secondary prevention efforts, it becomes essential to define the problem at hand. Is the person a sporadic drug user and not really dependent? Is a serious psychological problem also present with the drug use a symptom or even an often unconscious attempt to cope with this disturbance? Is drug use only recreational in the absence of viable alternatives? Equally important is the recognition of poly drug use. The use of multiple mood-altering substances has become the rule rather than the exception and is inadequately addressed in "single-substance" treatment facilities.

These questions are far from academic, and when not raised result not only in ineffective treatment but even needless suffering. A glaring example of the latter case has been the allegations against a treatment facility that hospitalized adolescents against their will for nonexistent drug dependence until insurance coverage for inpatient therapy expired, and then, abruptly discharged them from treatment.

At the other extreme, frequently the power of the dependency, if established, is often denied. The person dependent on narcotics or alcohol is often considered weak-willed and just not willing to stop. Perhaps the description of an actual physical dependence was best captured by William S. Burroughs when he described his 15 years of drug addition:

> I have seen the exact manner in which the junk virus operates through fifteen years of addiction. The pyramid of junk, one level eating the level below . . . there are many pyramids feeding on peoples of the world and built on basic principles of monopoly. . . . Junk is the ideal product . . . the ultimate merchandise. No sales talk necessary. The client will crawl through a sewer and buy the drug. The junk merchant does not sell his product to the consumer, he sells the consumer to his product. He does not improve and simplify his merchandise. He degrades and simplifies the client. He pays his staff in junk. You would lie, cheat, inform on your friends, steal, do any-

thing to satisfy total need because you are in a state of total sickness, total possession and not in a position to act in any other way. Dope fiends are sick people who cannot act other than they do. A rabid dog "cannot help but bite."[13]

The Laboratory Model

The reasons for this compulsive activity are complex but relate in most part to the conditioning effects associated with narcotic use.[14] This is not just "psychological." In the laboratory animal, heroin will be chosen over food and water. When an animal is given cocaine it will self-inject the drug until it dies. Animals dependent on narcotics and made to undergo withdrawal with a narcotic antagonist will, although drug-free for a year when given an opiate antagonist, undergo the same process of withdrawal. Furthermore, if a narcotic antagonist is administered to a dependent animal and, at the same time that withdrawal occurs, a red light is flashed, much later when the animal is drug-free a flashing red light will produce withdrawal. Clinically, this helps to explain why even prisoners who have been incarcerated and drug-free for years feel they have to "get a fix" when they return to their old neighborhood.

Detoxification is, therefore, a minimum but not a sufficient requirement to successful abstinence. Much more is needed. This point is often forgotten in the rush to cut costs and produce dramatic but short-lived results. It also is important to remember that the craving described by Burroughs for opium is really no worse than that seen with other addictions. It is equally difficult to remain drug-free if the drugs are cigarettes, alcohol, or even "food," for those who are compulsive eaters.

Developing a Treatment Plan

In attempting to provide appropriate treatment one must, therefore, address several existing biological, psychological, social, and environmental issues if the chances for success are to be maximized (Table 10.2). The first question is why the person initially began drug use. Unless this is carefully addressed, either relapse will occur or the use of another mood-altering drug will begin once the

TABLE 10.2. Issues to be Addressed in Treatment

- Why was drug use initiated?
- Is dependency actually present?
- What are realistic goals and objectives?
- What are the conditioning effects surrounding the drug use?
- Is there an underlying psychologic disorder?
- What are the existing environmental resources available?

initial drug use has ceased. Second, the physiologic effects of the drug on the body must be defined and appropriately managed to relieve the anxiety that frequently appears when the drug is discontinued. This issue is often ignored, especially by those who rely solely on psychotherapeutic modalities. Third, the patient's ultimate goals must be assessed and the rehabilitative process tailored toward these objectives. If a drug user can make three times as much money in criminal as compared to legal activities, then he/she may continue to do so, especially when the risk of apprehension is slight. Fourth, to minimize relapse, the conditioning effects surrounding drug use must be addressed. A person with no skills returning to the environment where drug use started will almost always relapse. Fifth, is there an underlying psychologic disorder that has been missed due to the emphasis placed on the use of the specific drug? If so, this must be addressed with equal concern.

Sixth, and last, what are the resources available to provide the needed support? This is most important in predicting the success of the intervention. A person without home or family cannot possibly benefit from outpatient care and would be most successfully treated in a residence facility. Similarly, some individuals with a severe physical dependency or with medical complications may well benefit from inpatient rather than outpatient care. On the other hand, the presence of a severe dependency to heroin might well be managed on an outpatient basis by administering methadone or another long-acting narcotic to keep the person comfortable while rehabilitation is ongoing. The advantages of being able to maintain a person in the "real world," rather than a closed facility are considerable if able to be accomplished successfully. All too often, as soon as drug use is identified, the person is "plugged" into the nearest treatment facility without sufficient consideration given to the issues surrounding the drug use. Such actions are almost guaranteed to result in a return to drug use and poorly serve those in need of assistance.

AVAILABLE TREATMENT MODALITIES

The existing modalities currently available for management of drug use are quite varied. Not infrequently, a facility or modality will, in fact, use more than one therapeutic alternative. A brief description of currently available treatment follows. This description is meant to be neither comprehensive nor evaluative of the particular modality.

Acupuncture

Acupuncture has been used for a number of years, primarily in the treatment of narcotic addiction. Although its proponents claim a good success rate as well as the ability to remain drug-free, it remains to be objectively evaluated.

Behavioral Therapies

The foundation of behavioral therapies is the belief that dependence upon a mood-altering drug is a learned behavior maintained and reinforced by conditioning due to the specific effect of drugs as reinforcers independent of other psychosocial conditions. Treatment includes developing new behavior incompatible with drug use, and learning to avoid situations associated with a high risk of recidivism. At times, techniques to relieve the anxiety accompanying the need or craving for the drug such as biofeedback, relaxation techniques, and meditation are also used. Types of behavior therapies can vary from contingency contracting–the setting up of a contract between patient and therapist resulting in rewards and/or punishments–to aversive conditioning, whereby the urge to use a drug or its actual use is coupled with an unpleasant reaction, to the actual extinction of the conditioning effect. Antabuse in alcoholism is an example of well-accepted averse conditioning. By causing nausea, vomiting, and cramps when alcohol is taken by a person on antabuse, the desire to drink is diminished. An example of extinction without adverse effects in narcotic dependency is the use of naltrexone (Trexan), a pure narcotic antagonist that prevents the heroin user from getting high. Unlike the classic psychotherapeutic approach, behavioral therapy is usually a time-limited process.

More recently, cognitive-behavioral therapy has been developed to address alcoholism. This modality views alcoholism as learned behavior that can be changed through conditioning and modifying one's actions but also by knowing and better understanding one's thoughts and feelings.

Civil Commitment

It may seem oxymoronic to consider civil commitment a form of treatment for illicit drug use. Indeed, initially the civil commitment facilities established by the U.S. Public Health Service in Lexington, Kentucky and Fort Worth, Texas in 1938 and supervised by the Federal Bureau of Narcotics and the Justice Department resembled prisons rather than treatment facilities.

Over the past two decades a number of states have experimented with civil commitment programs with varying degrees of success, the most recent attempts being the establishment of boot camps. These facilities operating in approximately 236 states have a total capacity of 8,880 offenders. Such programs, when appropriately staffed to truly provide rehabilitation as well as the ability to develop a sense of one's self-worth, can serve a worthwhile function. When offered as an alternative to prison for non-violent, petty, drug-related offenses, civil commitment programs can also help to decongest our prison system. The implementation of sanctions against those who have selected this as an alternative but who leave prematurely should enhance the chances of successful completion. In an ideal setting, such programs would be made available to all in need and would be able to provide training as well as psychological support. Although not inexpensive, when one considers the costs of prosecution and imprisonment, the balance is clearly in favor of a commitment effort.

Comprehensive Outpatient Treatment

There are a variety of outpatient programs that offer many different services ranging from drop-in centers to more formal counseling programs and free clinics that provide educational, medical, and psychological and rehabilitative services pertaining to substance abuse as well as other medical needs of the community. These programs, responsible for almost 50 percent of persons in treatment, provide easy access to those who do not wish to make a greater time commitment to therapy. As such, they may serve to provide the second step after detoxification.

Counseling and Employee Assistance Programs

Counseling usually is conducted by either those with degrees in counseling, social work, or psychology or those without formal degrees who, by personal experience and subsequent training, are able to provide assistance. By itself, counseling represents the most basic form of therapy. It is a philosophy that deals with practical problems of both the client and the family members in an attempt to provide support as well as appropriate referrals. A subject of counseling is Motivational Enhancement Therapy (MET). MET enhances motivation for drug rehabilitation by presenting change as possibility due to an internal force rather than externally learned behavior.

In the workplace, counseling is located within Employee Assistance Programs (EAPs). EAPs have been increasingly popular in many large businesses and optimally should serve as resources to help supervisors learn and recognize drug use in the workplace; identify those employees with the potential to develop a problem as well as those who are impaired; and provide appropriate resources in referral. All of this must be accomplished with a great concern for employee confidentiality. Limited studies have suggested that well-run EAPs can be quite effective for both employer and employee with a cost-benefit ratio of reform on investment estimated as high as 4:1. In the private sector employers have formed the National Drugs Don't Work Partnership to promote assisting smaller companies in starting EAPs. The effort of the public sector, however, is minimal and there is much room for the Administration to provide support and guidance.[4]

Detoxification

Detoxification is a first step common to initiating therapy for those drugs associated with a high degree of physical dependence. It allows a physically dependent individual to be gradually withdrawn while experiencing minimal, if any, discomfort. Detoxification may be accomplished with decreasing doses of methadone over a week to ten days or with the use of clonidine. Clonidine, a drug used to treat hypertension, has been found to decrease withdrawal symptoms; however, its use can be associated with marked drops in blood pressure as well as dysphoria. As a result, it is rarely used. Loflexidine, a clonidine analogue not associated with lowering the blood pressure, is being increasingly used where available. Most recently a rapid form of detoxification for opiate use has been described where the user is placed under deep sedation for six hours to eliminate any physical discomfort and naltrexone is administered to displace the opiate from the receptor sites in the brain. After this detoxification procedure, the person is maintained on naltrexone or enters another therapy for the addiction.[15] This treatment also remains to be adequately evaluated.

Detoxification by itself is really not rehabilitative but merely sets the stage for an individual to enter a therapeutic relationship or allows one with sufficient internal strengths to attempt to maintain abstinence on his/her own.

Detoxification centers available on a "walk-in" basis have been often criticized as a "revolving door approach" to addiction, as the recidivism rate is extremely high. Detoxification, however, does have several benefits to both the user and to the public. It can provide relief to a person dependent on illicit drugs without exposing either the individual or the public to the antisocial behavior needed to obtain money to support a habit. If even a superficial therapeutic relationship during detoxification can be established, it may allow one to become more amenable to consider a more long-lasting and productive relationship. During detoxification, existing medical problems can be identified and appropriately addressed. By allowing the individual to attempt to go it on his/her own and fail, it may emphasize the need for additional assistance.

Family Therapy

This therapy focuses on the family unit as a prime and motivating factor in working toward and achieving abstinence. The focus is to facilitate the development of a healthy interrelationship between family members.

Pharmacologic Therapies

In addition to the use of drugs in the detoxification process, there are a number of pharmacologic methods to assist those wishing to remain abstinent.

Antabuse

Alcohol-sensitizing agents have long been used to prevent drinking. Antabuse (disulfiram) is one of the oldest forms of "modern" pharmacotherapy. Through causing an unpleasant and at times frightening reaction when alcohol is consumed by increasing the level of a noxious substance in the blood (acetaldehyde), the negative effect of the Antabuse/alcohol interaction prevents one from drinking. This requires that a person be sufficiently motivated to take Antabuse each day and sufficiently frightened by the intensity of the reaction to refrain from drinking. This is the reason why a large multicenter study found Antabuse to be ineffective in maintaining sobriety over a extended period; however, for those in the study who continued to take Antabuse, alcohol consumption significantly decreased. Calcium carbamide has also been promoted as an adversive agent. Its effectiveness, however, remains to be proven.

Maintenance Therapy

This therapy is provided for those dependent on narcotics who, despite repeated attempts at detoxification or other forms of treatment, are unable to refrain from using narcotics. The rationale behind maintenance is to enable a person to remain comfortable on an oral long-acting narcotic at a dose sufficiently high to prevent an injection of heroin from resulting in a mood-altering effect. This eliminates the craving many dependent persons have for heroin and at the same time stabilizes their tolerance of the drug to allow them to function normally. Once the desire to obtain the drug is gone, medical and rehabilitative services are provided to allow the person to eventually become drug-free.

Although any narcotic can be used in maintenance, at present methadone is the drug used in virtually all programs. This is due to its effectiveness when taken by mouth and its long duration of action. Many studies have demonstrated both the social and economic effectiveness of methadone in allowing successful rehabilitation from heroin addiction. It is currently the largest of treatment modalities for narcotic dependency with over 100,000 persons enrolled in programs across the country. Recently, Levo-Alpha-Acetyl-Methadol (LAAM) has been approved for use in maintenance therapy. LAAM, a synthetic derivative of methadone, was originally developed in Germany as a long-acting analgesic. In contrast to methadone, the effects of LAAM do not begin until several hours after administration, and may last between 48 and 72 hours. The advantages of using LAAM rather than methadone in maintenance therapy consists of a longer duration of action, less of a chance of producing a "high" or sedation, and the ability to be taken on an every-other-day basis, obviating the need for daily clinic visits for medication or weekend take-home medication. For those persons who are not considered to be stabilized on methadone maintenance and are at risk for contributing to street diversion of methadone, LAAM is felt to be an appropriate substitute.

Buprenorphine is a narcotic with both agonistic and antagonistic properties. It is capable of producing mild dependence, yet can prevent the high produced by injection of heroin. It has a rather long duration of action of 29 hours, similar to methadone; however, unlike methadone it has a low potential for overdose when taken appropriately. Preliminary studies have found buprenorphine to be effective in maintenance therapy. Consideration is also being given to administer buprenorphine in combination with naloxone, a pure narcotic antagonist. However, it must be emphasized that due to its "agonist" properties buprenorphine can be misused. In fact it is a frequent drug of misuse in New Zealand and England where individuals dissolve tablets and inject the drug intravenously.

Nicotine Replacement Therapy

The first attempt to medically detoxify from nicotine addiction was with the use of a nicotine gum; however, similar to other short-acting preparations used to detoxify or to maintain, compliance problems frequently prevented the gum from being successful in allowing one to discontinue smoking. The approval by the FDA of a nicotine patch allowed the issue of compliance to be effectively addressed. Transdermal nicotine has been widely prescribed to help "detoxify" a person from narcotic dependence. Studies have shown the "patch" to be quite effective; however, the success rates vary completely with individual study.[16,17] Although many smokers who wish to quit request "the patch," in fact, there is a profile of smokers that is most often associated with its successful use. This profile includes a smoking history of over 20 cigarettes per day, the need to smoke within a half hour of awakening, development of withdrawal symptoms in the past when smoking was discontinued, the absence of any medical contraindications, and the inability to stop smoking prior to use of the patch. The evidence suggests that the chances for success can be maximized by remaining totally abstinent during the first two weeks of therapy and combining the patch with active physical intervention, counseling, and follow-up.

Narcotic Antagonists: In Opiate Addiction and Alcoholism

The rational of administering a narcotic antagonist to one dependent on narcotics is to prevent the effects of the narcotic from being experienced. This is accomplished by blocking the binding of the narcotic to the brain receptor. Injecting or snorting heroin no longer produces a "high for an individual," and thereby diminishes the incentive for that person to continue to be exposed to the risks of illicit heroin use or to spend money for its purchase. The drug currently approved for this is naltrexone (Trexan); however, in order to prevent withdrawal, naltrexone cannot be administered until two weeks after a person has last had heroin. In addition, in order to be effective it must be taken on a daily basis. As a result, many have not found this drug to be effective unless a person is highly motivated. Naltrexone (Revia) has also been used to decrease alcohol consumption and prevent relapse once drinking has ceased in conjunction with a comprehensive treatment program.[18] In this role, the naltrexone is believed to prevent the binding of the body's own opiates, the release of which is stimulated by alcohol, thereby preventing the "alcohol high." Although found to be quite helpful in two double-blind trials, the effectiveness of naltrexone in the general alcoholic population remains to be fully evaluated. Similar to the use of Antabuse in alcoholism, the drug must be taken on a regular basis in order to be effective.

Miscellaneous Therapies

There are a number of other drugs that are being studied for their effectiveness in allowing a person to remain free of illicit substances. These include appropriate psychotropic agents when an underlying psychologic disturbance exists regardless of the type of drug dependency. There are many drugs currently being tested for the ability to eliminate the cocaine craving. These include bromocriptine (Parlodel), amantadine (Symmetrel), and various antidepressants. Ibogaine, a hallucinogen extract from the African rain forest shrub Tabernathe iboga, has been promoted as a cure for heroin addicts, in that it eliminates craving and allows detoxification without withdrawal.[18] However, this drug has also been shown to be neurotoxic and in high doses can produce tremors, loss of muscle control, and hallucinations. Antidepressants that inhibit serotonin uptake, such as fluoxetine (Prozac), sertraline (Zoloft), and paroxetine (Paxil) have also been used to diminish alcohol consumption, as have dopamine agonists such as bromocryptine. Several antidepressants, especially fluoxetine, have also been suggested to be helpful in treatment of amphetamine and cocaine dependency. The effectiveness of any of these agents in well-controlled trials remains to be determined.

Psychotherapy

Psychotherapy may be provided by psychologists, social workers, rehabilitation counselors, and/or psychiatrists. It may be part of a comprehensive outpatient program or exist through an individual relationship developed with the therapist. It may vary in intensity depending upon one's needs as well as the particular training and beliefs of the therapist. Through allowing the client to understand his or her behavior, he or she can develop a rationale for change. Initially thought to be ineffective due to the severe personality disturbances accompanying addiction, it is now realized that many who abuse drugs can benefit from psychotherapy alone or in combination with other modalities.

Self-Help Groups

There are a number of well-organized self-help groups that have had a major impact on assisting alcoholics and others with chemical dependencies to maintain drug-free productive lives. The oldest and best known, Alcoholics Anonymous (AA), developed and run by "nonprofessionals," has chapters in every major city as well as in other countries. Other groups that address specific drugs of abuse are Narcotics Anonymous and Cocaine Anonymous, as well as codependent groups for families of those who live with the person who is on mood-altering medications. The only qualification for admission is the recognition of a drug-dependency problem and a desire to be helped. For many they have been provided a tremendous resource in dealing with alcoholism and substance abuse. Evaluation of the effectiveness of these groups is not easy. AA, being the oldest, has come under considerable scrutiny without clearly definitive findings. However, there is no question that many have been, and continue to be, greatly helped by these groups. In no small part this success is related to the individual commitment of participants.

Therapeutic (Residential) Communities

Therapeutic communities are targeted toward changing those parts of the personality of the drug abuser responsible for allowing the initiation and maintenance of drug-taking behavior. Since the foundation of Synanon in the 1950s, a large number of programs have developed throughout the country. Many therapeutic communities, unlike other treatment facilities, are amenable to admitting individuals with multiple drug problems, including alcoholism. Commitment to the process, however, must be total. Initial enrollment is, therefore, often accompanied by a high dropout rate. The therapeutic experience may result in an individual living in the community for one to two years, during which time the person will pass through successive stages of increasing responsibility prior to attempting reentry to the community at large.

EVALUATION

Defining the Issue

Many have felt that most treatment is ineffective in "curing" drug dependency with the evaluation of any modality fraught with too many confounding variables to allow for consistent results. These views reflect our inherent biases of those who use mood-altering substances. As discussed earlier, detoxification or "cleansing" the body of drugs is only the beginning of the rehabilitative process, which in fact can begin and be effective in the absence of early detoxification. It must be realized that addiction is a chronic disorder. Not only are physiologic changes produced in the body which persist after the drug has been discontinued but, in addition, the social or environmental forces which play such a great role in initiating the addiction must be addressed for rehabilitation to be successful. These concepts form the basis for both residence drug-free treatment as well as maintenance therapy for heroin dependency.

It has been amply demonstrated that persons who comply with their treatment regimens fare quite well, not only when in treatment but also in their ability to maintain abstinence once the full course of treatment has been completed. It is also true that persons who use mood-altering substances have a very low rate of compliance regardless of the treatment regimen. However, this is no different from the compliance seen in others with chronic diseases such as hypertension, diabetes, and asthma.[19] Studies in these conditions have demonstrated that although compliance is the most significant predictor of favorable outcome, it occurs in less than 50 percent of persons with these disorders. The reasons for noncompliance differ little from those seen in persons using mood-altering drugs. Contributors for lack of compliance with treatment regimens for diabetes, hypertension, and substance abuse include: lack of family support, low socioeconomic status, and comorbid psychiatric conditions–exactly the same factors that one associates with failure to treat dependency.[24] Yet, there is little public debate as to whether treatment for hypertension, diabetes, or asthma should receive continued health care coverage, while controversy abounds as to the need for providing adequate insurance to treat chemical dependence.

The technology to evaluate treatment modalities also clearly exists, although it is not frequently utilized. Parameters for evaluation include individual and societal assessments. On an individual level, the most objective assessment is documented decrease in alcohol and/or other drug use; however, other parameters, such as the ability to improve one's health as well as increase productive activity, can also be measured. From a public health perspective, parameters of effectiveness such as incidence of HIV infection, tuberculosis, hepatitis, and sexually transmitted diseases, arrests, and reported crimes can also be measured.

From this perspective success rates in treatment of the addictions have been found to vary from 40 to 80 percent for alcoholism, opioid dependence, and cocaine dependence.[24] Nicotine dependence, however, has a much lower level of success with only 20 to 30 percent of persons initially abstinent not returning to smoking within a year. As demonstrated by O'Brien and McLellan, however, "failure" rates defined by retreatment by physicians in emergency rooms for insulin dependent diabetes mellitus range from 30 to 50 percent, for hypertension 50 to 60 percent, and for asthma 60 to 80 percent.[24] Dependency on mood-altering drugs, for many, requires long-term attention and care similar to that of other chronic medical disorders. Unless this is realized, treatment for the dependencies will never achieve its full potential.

Cost-Effectiveness

At present, the evaluation of treatment modalities are viewed by the public on an economic or an "outcome" basis; however, even in this realm, political and psychological fears seem to take hold over reality. From a strictly cost-benefit analysis, even if treatment were effective in preventing future substance abuse, the costs of the most commonly accepted and widely used treatment modalities are still less than those generated by the untreated drug user. A study by the Rand Corporation in 1994 found treatment much more effective than law enforcement efforts to reduce cocaine use, with a $34 million investment in treatment equivalent to an expenditure of $366 million for interdiction or $246 million for enforcement.[4] Reduction of law enforcement by 25 percent and doubling treatment dollars was estimated to save $5.3 billion a year with a 15-year savings in social costs of over $150 billion.

In New York, an untreated drug abuser has been estimated to cost society $43,000 a year. If incarcerated, the cost is comparable to $40,000. This can be compared to residential drug-free treatment costs of $16,500, methadone treatment at $3,500, and outpatient treatment at $3,280.[20] The National Institute on Drug Abuse has estimated that for every dollar spent on treatment $4 to $7 are saved in reduced public costs and $3 are gained in increased productivity. Treatment has been consistently shown to have a number of salutary effects including reduced future health care costs, increased productivity, and diminished criminal acts.[21,22,23]

Current Evaluative Efforts

Despite the variety of facilities devoted to treatment of alcohol and substance abuse, which are very great in cost to both the public and the patient, nonetheless, effective evaluation of these modalities has been far from satisfactory, with published studies remaining open to serious criticism. This is not surprising, as it is quite difficult to obtain adequately matched groups of patients being treated and compare them to those who are not given a specific therapy. In many instances, incentives exist to enter treatment that are unrelated to the desire to eliminate drug use, such as to keep a family unit together, to maintain a job, or to remain out of prison.

As discussed above, frequently success is measured by those who complete the program and are able to remain abstinent rather than those who enter but subsequently leave prematurely. Successful outcome, with respect to remaining abstinent from a particular drug, may be marred by a person turning to a different mood-altering drug to relieve anxiety. Often follow-up studies are short in duration and dependent on self-reporting. The existence of underlying psychological disturbances also serves to confound the evaluation effort. In addition, some treatment modalities may not be considered socially acceptable and, therefore, are unable to receive adequate funding. This latter group includes programs involving controlled drinking, acupuncture, and needle exchange.

Finally, many professionals in the field have such strong feelings concerning specific therapeutic techniques or anxieties over the limited availability of funding that lobbying overtly or covertly occurs to prevent opposing modalities from being given appropriate attention. The importance, however, in adequately evaluating existing or newly designed therapeutic modalities cannot be overemphasized. There is no single, effective approach to addressing alcohol or substance abuse. Those treatments shown to be effective should be supported, and those hypothesized as being effective, adequately evaluated. Most important, at the onset of the evaluative process before treatment begins, a system must be established to allow a person to be diverted to a specific treatment modality that will maximize the chances of success for the individual.

FOSTERING AND EXPANDING EXISTING RESEARCH

Although support for research does exist, when compared to the total cost of drug use to society at large, the proportion of funds allocated for both evaluation and research is quite small and speaks to our true level of commitment. Over the years, the annual increases that have been allocated to research in substance abuse have been less than that of the cost of living. Research in 1994 received less than 4 percent of the federal drug budget. Kleber has suggested that research should account for 5 percent of the federal budget for drug control. Even this conservative request would raise the amount of available funds to 30 percent, from $425 million to $650 million.[5] The areas amenable to study are considerable, including basic psychological, biomedical, and neurobiological research, socioeconomic issues, means to effectively prevent drug abuse, AIDS research, and innovative treatment techniques. Each undertaking should be effectively evaluated, and no reasonable approach should be excluded.

It is unfortunate, but true, that our lack of research intensity is often driven by moral rather than scientific forces. A prime example is the effectiveness of smoking marijuana to prevent the nausea of chemotherapy, alleviate glaucoma, or promote comfort in the muscle-wasting syndrome associated with AIDS. To prevent smoking this drug we have developed synthetic THC and more potent antinausea agents. Many of those who have smoked marijuana and obtained relief have not been able to do so with the alternative drug. Physicians still remain unable to prescribe marijuana for specific medical indications, and persons who smoke it do so illegally. Yet, a well-designed study to evaluate its therapeutic effectiveness remains to be funded. Only through rigorous investigation and evaluation can we maximize the potential for success, as well as better direct the use of limited resources.

REFERENCE NOTES

1. Socioeconomic evaluations of addictions treatment: Executive summary. Washington, DC: President's Commission on Model State Drug Laws, Rutgers Center of Alcohol Studies, 1993.

2. Brick J, Langenbucher J. Facts on: Health care costs of addiction clearing house. Fact Sheet No. 29, Center for Alcohol Studies, Rutgers, NJ, 1994.

3. Confronting the drug problem: Debate persists on enforcement and alternative approaches. A report to the Chairman, Committe on Government Operations, House of Representatives, Washington, DC: U.S. General Accounting Office, 1993.

4. Keeping score: What we are getting for federal drug control dollars. *Drug Strategies*, 1995, Carnegie Commission, New York.

5. Langenbucher J. Rx for health care costs: Resolving addictions in the general medical setting. Alcohol: *Clin Exp Res*, 1994, 18:1033-1036.

6. Kleber HD. Our current approach to drug abuse–progress, problems, proposals. *New Engl J Med*, 1994, 330:361-364.

7. Moran C. Support growing for needle exchange programs. *Amer Med News*, December 13, 1993, p. 15.

8. DesJarlais DC. Harm reduction–a framework for incorporating science into drug policy. *Am J Public Health*, 1995, 85:10-12.

9. Hwang SL. Library search hints of electrifying news from big tobacco. *The Wall Street Journal*, February 6, 1995, Sec. A:1.

10. Frankel DH. Support for needle exchange programs. *The Lancet*, 1995, 346:895.

11. Needle exchange programs: Research suggests promise as an AIDS prevention strategy. General Accounting Office, U.S. Government Printing Office, 1993.

12. Source Book of Criminal Justice Statistics. In Macguire K and Pastore L (Eds.). U.S. Department of Justice, 1994. U.S. Government Printing Office. NCJ 154591. Washington, DC.

13. Burroughs, WS. *Naked Lunch*. Weidenfield, NY: Grove, 1959, pp. xxxviii–xxxix.

14. Stimmel BD, Glick SD. Animal-human correlates of narcotic dependence: A brief review. *Am J Psychiat*, 1978, 135:821-825.

15. UROD: Ultra Rapid Opiate Detoxification. Center for Research and Treatment of Addiction, 1995, Israel.

16. Hurt RD, Dale LC, Fredrickson PA, Caldwell CC, Lee GA, Offord KP. Nicotene patch therapy for smoking cessation combined with physician advice and nurse followup. *JAMA*, 1994, 271:595-600.

17. Kenford SL, Fiore MC, Jorenby DE, Smith SS, Wetter D, Baker TB. Predicting smoking cessation: Who will quit with and without the nicotene patch? *JAMA*, 1994, 271:589-594.

18. Anton RF. Medications for treating alcoholism. *Alcohol Health Research World*, 1994, 18(4):265-272.

19. McLellan AT, Metzger DS, Alterman AI, Woody GE, Durell J, Weisner CM, O'Brien CP. Is treatment for substance abuse worth it? Public health expectations, policy-based comparisons. In Lewis DL (Ed.), *Training About Alcohol and Substance Abuse for All Primary Care Physicians*. New York: Josiah Macy Jr. Foundation, 1995, pp. 165-212.

20. Communique. The center for substance abuse treatment. Spring 1992, p. 2, U.S. Department of Health and Human Resources.

21. Hubbard RL, Marsden ME, Rachal JV, Harwood, HJ, Cavanaugh ER, Ginzburg HM. *Drug Abuse Treatment: A National Study of Effectiveness*. Chapel Hill: University of North Carolina Press, 1989.

22. Yandrick RM. Taking inventory. *EAPA Exchange*, July 1992, pp. 22-29.

23. Holder HD, Blose JO. The reduction of health care costs associated with alcoholism treatment: A 14-year longitudinal study. *J Studies Alcohol*, 1992, 53:293-302.

24. O'Brien CP, McLellan AT. Myths about the treatment of addiction. *The Lancet*, 1996, 347:237-240.

Chapter 11

An Agenda for Action IV: Protection of Those Who Do Not Use Mood-Altering Drugs

The need to protect those who choose not to use drugs from the actions of those who do so is clear, yet often neglected in any discussion of illicit drug use. The most effective means of accomplishing this, however, remains uncertain. With respect to licit drugs, protecting the nonuser without abrogating the rights of those who use these substances is also of concern. A reasoned approach to addressing this problem beginning with a clear definition of whom we are trying to protect will ultimately allow for a greater chance of success.

THE FETUS AND NEWBORN

It is believed that up to 11 percent of all infants in utero are exposed every year to alcohol or mood-altering drugs.[1] Protecting the fetus from maternal drug use by means other than increasing attempts to educate women more effectively as to the harmful effects of drug use during pregnancy has not been successful. A preliminary study to incarcerate pregnant heroin users in order to enforce abstinence was, as might be imagined, less than effective. Recent attempts to prosecute women who inject heroin while pregnant for a "drug delivery felony" have not been sustained by the courts and may ultimately serve to frighten drug-dependent pregnant women from seeking help. If, however, a pregnant woman is arrested for a crime unrelated to drug use, appropriate social service and treatment should be offered as an alternative to prison. Large-scale educational efforts to inform women about the hazards of continuing to smoke or drink excessively while pregnant have been ongoing for a number of years with variable success. Most important is increasing the availability of treatment programs specifically designed to provide prenatal care and rehabilitation. Although several states have legislated the establishment of comprehensive treatment services for pregnant women, nonetheless this type of treatment is available for only a small proportion of women in need of these services.[4]

With respect to nicotine, even passive exposure to cigarette smoke may be harmful. A recent study of mothers with passive smoke exposure found their infants to have significantly higher nicotine and conicotine concentrates in their hair than those not exposed.[2] More important are the recent findings concerning the sudden infant death syndrome (SIDS) believed to occur in one of every 700 live births, being the most common cause of death in infants between one month and one year of age. A relation between SIDS and maternal smoking during pregnancy has been demonstrated as well as the effects of maternal and paternal passive smoking in the same room as an infant.[3]

Regardless of whether maternal drug use is licit or illicit, the importance of assessing the home environment when maternal drug use is known is essential to provide protection to the newborn. All too frequently, this is not able to be performed due to inadequate funding of agencies charged with this responsibility. This results in many children being exposed to neglect or even abuse for long periods; however, merely preventing the newborn from being placed in such an environment is not always the optimal solution as long-term hospitalization while waiting for foster care, which may also be inadequate, is, in itself, deprivation.

Education is probably the best way to prevent unwanted pregnancy. Such education, if effective, can prevent a lifetime of misery not only for the young mother and the unwanted child, but for society as well. Once pregnancy has occurred, the development of support groups to enhance maternal self-esteem is one of the best solutions, but, as of yet, has not been able to be adequately realized. Equally important is the availability of special programs to provide comprehensive medical services should the woman wish to complete the pregnancy. Although such services exist, their availability, especially outside of urban areas, is quite variable.

CHILDREN AND ADOLESCENTS

It belabors the obvious to observe that one of the best ways to help children exposed to parental drug use is to help the parents. This includes provision of adequate mental health services as well as vocational guidance. The existence of child abuse and neglect is not only associated with parental drug use but also with subsequent use of mood-altering substances by the child. Yet, Bureaus of Child Welfare throughout the country are woefully underfunded and understaffed, often employing those with insufficient training. Physicians are, quite appropriately, being required to take training to enable them to identify child abuse, yet, once abuse is identified, most often, the response of social service agencies is too little, too late. Funding of the agencies should be increased considerably. Similarly, courts should place a much greater priority on expeditiously assessing and addressing cases of domestic violence and child abuse.

Protection of children from violence associated with drug gangs has also been far from easy. In addition to the fear of bodily harm from not participating, equally important is the inspiration that gangs offer many children devoid of appropriate parental support, alternatives to become involved and "cared for." The false image of the freewheeling drug dealer and the easy money become important "lures" to the drug culture. There is clearly a need to provide viable alternatives for youths to fill their time and to relieve those in the inner cities from injuries or death from drug-related shootings.

The Centers for Disease Control and Prevention have predicted that by the year 2003, firearm-related deaths may become the leading cause of injury-related deaths.[5] Twenty-five percent of students in central cities report gang activity in their schools. In these schools, 78 percent of students report easy accessibility to drugs. Victims of violent crimes are three times as likely as nonvictims to report fear of attack at school and are more than twice as likely to avoid certain places at school out of fear.

Violence-prevention programs including conflict-resolution techniques should be established as an integral part of a school's programs. Better police efforts to establish safe havens, drug-free zones around schools, rapid suspension of students found to be carrying weapons, passage and enforcement of gun control legislation, and incarceration for the length of the sentence when violent crimes are committed will all serve to enhance the safety of high-risk areas.

Finally, because violence often breeds violence or at least an indifference to it, pressure should be placed on television studios to monitor both the type of programs produced as well as the times those programs are shown. It has been estimated that preteens and teenage children may watch as much as 23 to 28 hours of television a week and are able to see as many as 20 to 25 violent acts per hour on weekend viewing, including children's programs.[4] Frequently drug use is presented in these shows as a glamorous and exciting lifestyle. Although viewing violence and committing it does not follow a one-to-one relationship, a significant relationship between exposure to television violence as a preteen and antisocial behavior more than two decades later has been observed.[6] Station managers must assume responsibility for what is produced as well as when it is shown.

SAVING THE COMMUNITIES

Perhaps societally, the most ravaging effects of the illicit drug trade have not been on those who use these substances but on the fabric of community life where these drugs are sold. In 1992, more than 1.9 million Americans were victims of violent crime, with homicide being the second leading cause of death among persons 15 to 25 years of age. In the face of this increase in homicides is the not surprising observation that violence committed by teenagers using guns has increased by 70 percent over the last ten years. With respect to the increasing homicide rates, alcohol and other drugs are felt to be responsible for 61 percent of all violent crimes, 49 percent of homicides, 50 percent of spouse abuse, 52 percent of rapes, and 38 percent of child abuse cases.[7,8] Communities at particular risk are virtually always part of the inner cities and comprise many individuals who just manage to survive economically, especially the elderly, without adequate resources, all of whom are held hostage to the local drug trade.

Statistics from the Bureau of Justice regarding violent crimes are staggering. Sixty-one percent of offenders were reported to be obviously under the influence of drugs or alcohol.[8] In such communities, no one feels safe either on the streets or in the schools.

The police response to "saving the streets" has often been less than satisfactory. At times, the concentration on the high-level drug dealer has resulted in a low priority to street sales. This has resulted not only in an emboldened group of street dealers who terrorize communities, but, in addition, due to the competition for turf, when gunfire breaks out, the death of innocent bystanders. One need only to speak to members of these communities or physicians working in their emergency rooms to appreciate the magnitude of the problem. In fact, the request of the mayor of Washington, DC for activation of the National Guard to patrol the streets underscores that, at the most basic level, we are failing in our responsibility to many citizens.

The resources that are being ineffectively spent to curtail production of illicit drugs in other countries should be directed to local police and community efforts. Not all of this should be spent on law enforcement. Providing viable alternatives as described below is equally important; however, the streets must be made safe. Those who have engaged in violent activity should be treated accordingly and not plea-bargained. By focusing on violence and not possession or small-time sales, the courts can be decongested sufficiently enough to improve their function. Sentences given for violent crimes should be fully served. One need not be a mathematician to realize that if one serves only one-third of a sentence prior to being eligible for parole and, if more than half of those arrested are repeat offenders, then merely serving one's sentence would go a long way toward decreasing violence in the community.

Corroboration by witnesses to obtain convictions is often difficult to obtain due to fear of reprisal and a loss of faith in the police as protectors. Drug dealers often take over apartments in housing projects and are unable to be evicted, and terrorize the entire community. Informing the police of this activity is not only personally dangerous, but, at times, may be associated with civil liability. Once released, dealers frequently return to their "old neighborhoods" to resume sales as well as exact retribution on those responsible for their arrests. This must change. The presence of the police in a community should be a welcome, not a fearful, presence. Resources should be provided to increase constructive community police work as well as establish a truly confidential system for reporting violence and drug sales. Community mobilization should be supported both financially and legally. The President's Commission on Model State Drug Laws has recommended a series of steps to accomplish this, which should be implemented on a local level.[9]

Community coalitions, however, should also receive federal support not only with funds but with expertise in training and educating community leaders. State and local agencies, especially law enforcement and mental health agencies, should work closely with community groups to establish programs individually tailored to specific community needs. Such support should include funds for making these communities more attractive places to live. Although described as "pork" by critics of the most recent federal crime legislation, these funds are essential in diminishing crime and illicit drug use. The "broken-window theory" of anticrime efforts is far from theoretical. When a community is allowed to deteriorate, it becomes an invitation for those who are engaged in illicit activities to move in. This, in turn, intimidates those who live in the community, keeping them off the street which, in turn, foments more crime with less chance of detection. Police efforts represent only one aspect of combating illegal drug use. Consequently, mobilization and involvement is no less important.

DIMINISHING INJURIES
ASSOCIATED WITH DRUG USE

Alcohol and Violence

Surveys of homicides, robberies, sexual assault, and domestic violence have all shown alcohol consumption to be present in a significant proportion of these behaviors.[10] Drinking not only is often seen among the perpetrators but among the victims as well; however, the association of alcohol with such behavior does not necessarily imply that it is the primary cause. Because many people in this country drink, and the ability of alcohol to cause a loosening of inhibitions is well known, the association is not surprising. In determining public policy, however, it does become important to assess whether restricting the availability of alcohol will actually result in a decrease in violence.

Several observations support this hypothesis.[11,12] One "natural" experiment occurred in Norway when there was a nine-week group strike by employees of the state-owned and -operated liquor monopoly. During the strike, there was a 22 percent reduction in domestic disturbances and a 15 percent reduction in interpersonal violence as compared to a similar period the preceding year. In contrast, there were no changes from the preceding year in these parameters both prior and subsequent to dates of the strike. Effects of beer excise taxes on violence have demonstrated that increases in taxes are associated with a decrease in all types of violent crime;[12] however, these changes are quite modest, and, to date, the evidence that alcohol plays a primary etiological role in violent behavior remains less than convincing.

Assuring safety of others by decreasing the injuries associated with excessive use of alcohol or other drugs is essential and more easily able to be achieved than many other goals. Although virtually all states have raised the minimum drinking age to 21 years, in many, minors can still purchase alcohol in stores. This should be changed. Enforcing driving-while-intoxicated laws, prohibiting plea bargaining, mandating felony charges for leaving the scene of an accident, revoking licenses immediately, and intensifying drivers' education for those driving while intoxicated (DWI) have been promoted by a variety of public interest groups, with a fair degree of success. Equally important is publicizing the risks of consuming alcohol at any blood level when driving. Public interest groups, such as Mothers Against Drunk Driving (MADD) and Remove Intoxicated Drivers (RID) have been exceptionally helpful in educating the public as to the effects of driving while intoxicated, as well as removing such drivers from the road.

Such activities have been effective. The rate of alcohol-related traffic fatalities has been diminished from 57 percent of all fatalities in 1982 to 25 percent in 1994.[13] However, this proportion differed considerably by age group with 44 percent of all fatal crashes of persons 18 to 20 years of age being alcohol-related in 1994. Two out of five people in the United States will be involved in an alcohol-related auto accident at some time during their lives.[14] Many states have not addressed the importance of setting appropriate blood-alcohol concentration (BAC) levels considered indicative of impairment in minors. Of those states that have lowered legal BAC levels, the proportion of teenage nighttime fatal crashes diminished by 30 percent when compared to states that maintained a single BAC level.[15]

Unambiguous legislation condemning DWI and thus requiring the mandatory loss of license has been found to be a more effective deterrent than rehabilitative measures such as mandatory alcoholism treatment. However, enforcement of existing DWI laws is not always successful. It is estimated that for every 300 to 1,000 trips by an impaired driver, only one arrest will occur. Use of increased police checkpoints can be quite effective in diminishing the number of impaired drivers on the road. Penalties should also be appropriate to the offense. It is ironic that DWI, which is responsible for more deaths than all illicit drugs combined, is associated with far less severe punishment. Arrests for simple possession or sales of small amounts of illicit drugs can result in mandatory minimum prison sentences of many years, whereas DWI, even when associated with a fatality, may result in probation or minimal incarceration.

It is also important to emphasize that DWI should not refer only to alcohol. All mood-altering substances can affect coordination and are far more difficult to address legally as safe levels have not been defined and, indeed, probably do not exist. The contribution of illicit drug use to automobile accidents is considerable yet often undetected as urine testing is not routinely performed on drivers who appear impaired. One study, where urine testing was routinely administered to reckless drivers, found 59 percent to test positive for cocaine or marijuana.[16] Another study found one-third to one-half of those arrested for traffic offenses tested positive for illicit drugs.[4]

Not often realized is the role illicit drugs may play in other acciden-tal deaths and injuries. A recent study in New York City documents cocaine to be present in 27 percent of all residents receiving fatal injuries from a variety of causes.[17] In this study, if fatal injuries after cocaine use were considered as a separate cause of death, cocaine would rank among the five leading causes of fatalities among young men between 15 and 44 years of age in New York.

Nicotine and the Nonsmoker

The increasing evidence of the many adverse effects of environmen-tal tobacco smoke on nonsmokers has resulted in a growing commit-ment to curtail areas where smoking is permitted. Cigarette smoking has been banned from air flights occurring solely within the United States. Laws restricting smoking in private-sector workplaces exist in 17 states. Institutions devoted to health care, such as hospitals and clinics, are increasingly instituting a "smoke-free" workplace, and the responsibilities of private employers and municipalities to protect workers and the public in public spaces from environmental tobacco exposure is becoming increasingly recognized.

Such activities have not been uniformly favorably reviewed. Not unexpectedly, those who do smoke complain of an increasing in-fringement on what they regard as their own personal freedom. Yet, the public clearly feels that limits to this freedom must occur when the health and discomfort of others are at stake. In spite of legal challenges, it is entirely likely that the move to restrict the space occupied by smokers will continue.

Not unexpectedly, in response to the increasing attacks on pas-sive smoking, the tobacco industry has responded with gusto. It has questioned the validity of critical studies, sponsored scientific sym-posia to emphasize the relative innocuous nature of secondhand smoke and, as always, has contributed heavily to political cam-paigns. However, realizing that such efforts will have only transient success, the industry has devoted much more attention to diminish-ing the toxicity of secondhand smoke. The R. J. Reynolds Company has announced its plans to market a cigarette with the same nicotine content as its current products, but that when smoked produces little odor or smoke.[18] A charcoal filter extracts coal tars, and this new product is said to deliver five- to tenfold fewer toxic substances to the system and the environment. It is promoted as maintaining the flavor of smoking, without burning tobacco. Although diminishing the criticism of "passive" smokers if effective, it clearly defines cigarettes as a drug-delivery system that could place the product under the auspices of the Food and Drug Administration, thus seriously limiting its use.

CONCLUSION

Decreasing the use of mood-altering substances is both complex and difficult, but not insurmountable. It is an effort that cannot succeed by funding alone, although without sufficient and appropriate allocation of resources, it is also doomed to failure. Equally important is the commitment of government, the private and public sectors, and most especially, each of us who as individuals have appropriate roles to play. Until we realize this and adjust our actions accordingly, addressing the problem of mood-altering drugs will be a tale "full of sound and fury, signifying nothing."[19]

REFERENCE NOTES

1. Improving treatment for drug-exposed infants. U.S. Department of Health and Center for Substance Abuse Treatment, 1993, DHHS Pub. No. (SMA) 93-2011.
2. Eliopoulos C, Klein J, Phan MK, Knie B, Greenwald M, Chitayat D, Koren A. Hair concentrations of nicotine and conicotine in women and their newborn infants. *JAMA,* 1994, 271:621-623.
3. Klonoff-Cohen JS, Edelstein SL, Lefkowitz ES, Srinivasan IP, Kaegi D, Chang JC, Wiley KJ. The effect of passive smoking and tobacco exposure through breast milk on sudden infant death syndrome. *JAMA*, 1995, 273:795-798.
4. Keeping score. What we are getting for our federal drug control dollars. *Drug Strategies*, 1995, The Carnegie Commission, New York, 1995.
5. Deaths resulting from firearm and motor vehicle-related injuries–United States 1968-1991. *MMWR*, 1994, 43:37-42.
6. Violence and youth: Psychology's response. Washington, DC: American Psychological Association, 1993.
7. New directions for national substance abuse policy. Washington, DC: American Bar Association, 1994.
8. Zawitz MW, Klaus PA, Bachman R, Bastian LD (Eds.). Highlights from 20 years of surveying crime victims. The National Crime Victimization Survey, 1973-92: U.S. Department of Justice, Office of Justice Programs, Bureau of Justice Statistics, 1993.

9. President's Commission on Model State Drug Laws. Volume II: Community mobilization. Washington, DC: The Commission, 1993.

10. Collins JJ, Messerschmidt PM. Epidemiology of alcohol-related violence. *Alcohol Health Research World*, 1993, 17:93-100.

11. Room R. Alcohol and crime: Behavioral aspects. In Kadish SH (Ed.). *Encyclopedia of Crime and Justice*, Vol. I. New York: Free Press, 1983, pp. 35-44.

12. Cook PS, Moore MJ. Violence reduction through restrictions on alcohol availability. *Alcohol Health Research World*, 1993, 17:151-156.

13. Update: Alcohol-related traffic crashes and fatalities among youth and young adults–United States, 1982-1994. *MMWR*, December 1, 1995, 44(47):869-874.

14. Fell JC, Nash CE. The nature of the alcohol problem in U.S. fatal crashes. *Health Ed Quart,* 1989, 16:335-343.

15. Hingson R. Prevention of alcohol impaired driving. *Alcohol Health Research World*, 1993, 17:28-34.

16. Brookoff D, Cook CS, Williams C, Mann CS. Testing reckless drivers for cocaine and marijuana. *New Engl J Med,* 1994, 331:518-522.

17. Marzuk PM, Tardiff K, Leon AC, Hirsch CS, Stajic M, Potera L, Hartwell N, Igbal MI. Fatal injuries after cocaine use as a leading cause of death among young adults in New York City. *New Engl J Med*, 1995, 332:1753-1754.

18. Hilts P. Little smoke, little tar, but full dose of nicotine. *The New York Times*, November 27, 1994, Sec. 1:1.

19. Shakespeare W. *Macbeth* Act V, Scene V, line ii.

Index

Page numbers followed by the letter "t" indicate tables.

Detoxification, 90,177,182-183,188
   antabuse, 183
   maintenance therapy, 183-184
Developing a treatment plan,
   177-179
   issues to address, 178t
Diminishing drug use, plan for,
   127-129,130t
Distribution of drugs, 16
Diversion, of licit drugs, 51-52
Drinking and driving, 10,153,202
   groups against, 201
Drug abuse, 1
   educating the public about,
      163-164
   and the family, 20
   "hard-core" users, 5
   and hidden costs resulting
      from, 12
   image of, 63-64
   by inmates, 11,14
   law enforcement efforts
      to prevent, 105-106
   rehabilitation programs for, 90-91
   in the workplace, 11
   by youths, 2-3
Drug Abuse and Mental Health
      Administration, 12
Drug cartels, 109,119
Drug czar. *See* William Bennett
Drug dealers
   profits of, 106
   risks of, 108
Drug Enforcement Agency, 50,128
   and foreign countries, 100,101
   and prescription of controlled
      substances, 66
   seizing drugs, 105,109
Drug Free Workplace Act, 87,88
Drug laws, future of, 136-138
Drug prevention programs, 159-161
   designing of, 162t
Drug trade
   and automatic weapons, 25-26

Drug use
   as a cause of death, 16t
   cost for providing alternatives,
      129
   and crime, 13-16
   deterrence of, 110-112,155
   diminishing injuries associated
      with, 200-203
   distribution of drugs, 16
   economic costs of, 12-13
   and the fetus, 19-20,195-197
   and the "get tough approach," 22
   glamorized by entertainers, 42-43
   individual responsibility
      of, 117-119
   lack of time and money
      to address, 71-72
   and the physician, 61-63
   plan for diminishing,
      127-129,130t
   rehabilitation of drug users, 90
   and suicide, 21
   surveys, 3
DTA. *See* Chemical Diversion and
      Traffic Act
DWI. *See* Drinking and driving

EAP. *See* Employee Assistance
      Program
Ecstasy (hallucinogen), 6
Educating the public, on drug abuse,
      161-164
Elderly, and cost of drug use, 12
Eliminating the supply of illicit
      drugs, 94-97
Employee Assistance Program,
      88,181-182
Entertainers, and glamorizing drug
      use, 42-43

Family
   and drug abuse, 20
   physician. *See* Physician
   protecting from drug use, 198